SOUTH SUDAN'S CIVIL WAR

T0353255

ABOUT THE AUTHOR

John Young has a PhD in Political Science from Simon Fraser University in Vancouver. He has worked in the Horn of Africa since 1986 as a teacher of technical English in Sudan, journalist at *The Sudan Times*, lecturer in Political Science at Addis Ababa University, consultant for the Canadian government on federalism in Ethiopia and the Sudan peace process, advisor to IGAD, a monitor of the conflict in South Sudan, and political advisor to the Carter Center for the 2010 national elections in Sudan, the referendum on South Sudan's secession in 2011 and various security matters. He has authored two books, *Peasant Revolution in Ethiopia: Tigray People's Liberation Front, 1975–1991* (1998), *The Fate of Sudan: Origins and Consequences of a Flawed Peace Process* (Zed 2012), and more than 30 peer reviewed articles and chapters on conflict in the Horn of Africa, armed groups, and peace processes. He works primarily as a consultant with various international agencies.

SOUTH SUDAN'S CIVIL WAR

VIOLENCE, INSURGENCY AND FAILED PEACEMAKING

John Young

ZED

South Sudan's Civil War: Violence, Insurgency and Failed Peacemaking was first published in 2019 by Zed Books Ltd, The Foundry, 17 Oval Way, London SE11 5RR, UK.

www.zedbooks.net

Typeset in Plantin and Kievit by Swales & Willis Ltd, Exeter, Devon
Index by Rohan Bolton
Cover design by Keith Dodds

Cover photo © Guy Martin/Panos

A catalogue record for this book is available from the British Library

ISBN 978-1-78699-375-5 hb
ISBN 978-1-78699-374-8 pb
ISBN 978-1-78699-376-2 pdf
ISBN 978-1-78699-377-9 epub
ISBN 978-1-78699-378-6 mobi

CONTENTS

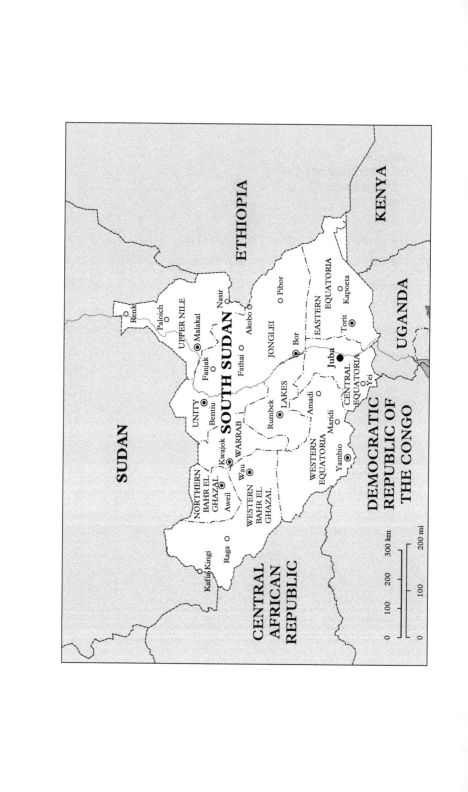

ABBREVIATIONS

ANC	African National Congress
ARCSS	Agreement for the Resolution of Conflict in South Sudan
AU	African Union
CCM	Chama Cha Mapinduzi
CIA	Central Intelligence Agency
CPA	Comprehensive Peace Agreement
CTSAMM	Ceasefire Transitional and Security Arrangements Monitoring Mechanism
DDR	Disarmament, Demobilization and Reintegration
DRC	Democratic Republic of Congo
DUP	Democratic Unionist Party
EPLF	Eritrean People's Liberation Front
EPRDF	Ethiopian People's Revolutionary Democratic Front
FD	Former Detainees
GNU	Government of National Unity
GOS	Government of Sudan
GRSS	Government of the Republic of South Sudan
GUN	Greater Upper Nile
GWOT	Global War on Terror
ICC	International Criminal Court
ICG	International Crisis Group
IDP	Internally Displaced Person
IGAD	Inter-Governmental Authority on Development
J1	Presidential Palace in Juba
JEM	Justice and Equality Movement
JMEC	Joint Monitoring and Evaluation Commission
LRA	Lord's Resistance Army
NCP	National Congress Party
NDA	National Democratic Alliance
NEPAD	New Partnership for African Development
NGO	Non-Governmental Organization
NIF	National Islamic Front
NLC	National Liberation Council
NRM	National Resistance Movement (Uganda)
OLS	Operation Lifeline Sudan
POC	Protection of Civilian (camps)
R2P	Responsibility to Protect

RPF	Regional Protection Force
SAF	Sudan Armed Forces
SLA-Abdalwahid	Sudan Liberation Army – Abdalwahid
SLA-Manawi	Sudan Liberation Army – Manawi
SPLA	Sudan People's Liberation Army
SPLM	Sudan People's Liberation Movement
SPLM/A-N	Sudan People's Liberation Movement/Army – North
SPLM-DC	Sudan People's Liberation Movement – Democratic Change
SPLM-IO	South Sudan People's Liberation Movement – In Opposition (sometimes abbreviated as simply IO)
SSDF	South Sudan Defence Forces
SSLA	South Sudan Liberation Army
TGoNU	Transitional Government of National Unity
TPLF	Tigray People's Liberation Front
UNMISS	United Nations Mission in South Sudan
USAID	United States Agency for International Development

ACKNOWLEDGEMENTS

This book draws on many years of research and experience in Sudan and South Sudan, but of specific relevance were studies carried out immediately before the outbreak of war in December 2013 to the end of 2017. In the lead up to the war I carried out research in Greater Upper Nile and Juba with the assistance of Riak 'Franco' Pouk Nyab, who had been my translator and fixer during research that provided the background for *The Fate of Sudan: Origins and Consequences of a Flawed Peace Process* (Zed Books: 2012). For the rest of the work I was accompanied to the field by Bol Gatkouth Chuol, a man whose life has been so diverse as to constitute the subject for a book. Bol is good-humoured, has a wide number of contacts in South Sudan and the region, and has a keen political mind. This study could not have been completed without his assistance and it would also not have been so enjoyable. Another person that needs to be thanked is Dr Lam Akol, who is not only a very astute politician, but has a keen academic mind and a penchant for details, and that proved useful in his perusal of a draft of this book and in my many meetings with him. I want to thank Dr Riek Machar who has always made himself available and welcoming, despite my criticisms of his leadership in this book, most of which were first made in person. Thanks, are also due to others who would prefer that their names not be mentioned. And beyond them I have had the cooperation of literally hundreds of South Sudanese. Lastly, I want to thank my wife, Dorothea Geddert, who has encouraged my interest in South Sudan and corrected my faulty English.

PREFACE

At 10:00 PM on 15 December 2013 shooting broke out in the barracks of the Sudan People's Liberation Army (SPLA) Presidential Guard in Juba, capital of the fledgling state of South Sudan, after Nuer soldiers resisted being disarmed by their Dinka colleagues. Dozens of soldiers were killed before the Nuer soldiers retreated, after which *Mathiang Anyoor*, a militia loyal to President Salva Kiir made up entirely of Dinka from his home area, began systematically slaughtering unarmed Nuer civilians in the capital. The number of people killed is unknown because Hilde Johnson, the head of the United Nations Mission in South Sudan (UNMISS), the only organization in the country capable of gathering such figures, made an executive decision not to count the dead, although she subsequently said they numbered in the 'thousands'. The same forces also attacked the house of the country's Nuer vice president, Dr Riek Machar, who was accused of attempting to carry out a coup and for being responsible for the ensuing killing spree. This was not only belied by the fact that he and his wife, Angelina, were forced to flee the assault in their pyjamas and eight members of their household were killed, but also by an African Union Commission of Inquiry which subsequently concluded that 'the evidence does not point to a coup'. Instead, the evidence suggested that Riek was the target of an assassination attempt by forces loyal to the president.

Through cell phones and social media knowledge of the Juba killings quickly spread to the global Nuer community and to Greater Upper Nile, where most of the Nuer lived. Thousands of Nuer youth self-organized as a *white army* mobilized and were joined by Nuer soldiers who had defected from the SPLA. On 18 December – only three days after the Juba killings commenced – they captured the Jonglei state capital of Bor and began marching on Juba. Fearing a humanitarian disaster when the ill-disciplined and revenge-seeking Nuer youth reached Juba, the US and other Western states warned Riek to stop the attack or face charges before the International Criminal Court. The US also endorsed Ugandan President Yoweri Museveni's decision to send his army to Juba to protect the inhabitants and the government. Later, these forces were deployed to government towns across Greater Upper Nile where they fought the rebels. In fact, Museveni was more concerned with ensuring that, given its influence over the Salva-led government, the Islamist government in Sudan did not take advantage of the rapidly deteriorating situation to exert control over the government and pose a threat to Uganda. But Museveni's fears were overcome when Riek convinced the regular forces under General Peter Gadet to temporarily stop their attack and that of the white army. Museveni's role in the defence of the Juba regime, the politics surrounding the peace process, and the advance of Uganda's interests while supposedly playing the cat's paw for his US sponsors, show a man adept at political manoeuvres in the region.

Based on the mistaken assumption that Riek was in full control of the various forces that launched the largely spontaneous attacks against government positions across Great Upper Nile, the Western sponsored regional security organization, the Inter-Governmental Authority on Development (IGAD), invited him and Salva to participate in a peace process which focused on re-dividing state power among the SPLM elites that caused the war. Instead, the appeal of the common Nuer, which neither IGAD nor its Western backers ever responded to, was the answer to the question of why their people were attacked in Juba. As a result, those who fought the insurgency were never represented in the negotiations and the reason they took up arms against the government – the Juba massacre – was never considered.

For the US, which Secretary of State John Kerry said had 'midwifed' the independence of South Sudan only two years previously, after supporting a long peace process and spending enormous amounts of money in the country, the war was both shocking and humiliating. The US had claimed the peace agreement that ended the war in Sudan and granted independence to South Sudan in 2011 was a major foreign policy success at a time when its various political and military involvements in the Greater Middle East had been failures.

Over the next five years almost half of the country's 11 million people were displaced or made refugees in neighbouring countries, tens of thousands were killed, the towns of Greater Upper Nile were destroyed as they repeatedly changed hands, and the largely oil-based economy all but collapsed. The first IGAD initiative failed in March 2015, but a second expanded initiative produced an agreement in August 2015 between Riek, who again became the First Vice President, and Salva, who retained his position as president. However, Salva made clear he had only accepted the agreement under duress and threw up numerous obstacles to its implementation which the international peace-makers did nothing to overcome. A resumption of the war was entirely predictable and on 8 July 2016 fighting broke out between government soldiers and the handful of Sudan Peoples Liberation Movement – In Opposition (SPLM-IO) fighters in Juba, after which the SPLA attempted to kill Riek, slaughtered many more Nuer civilians in the capital, and forced thousands into UN camps.

Riek and his soldiers were forced to evacuate the capital and began what became a 30-day march to the Congo and safety. Meanwhile, Salva appointed the SPLM-IO's defecting Taban Deng Gai first vice-president in breach of the peace agreement. And with US support it attempted to isolate Riek in the region and achieve an internal peace. Instead the war intensified and spread from Nuer-inhabited Greater Upper Nile to Western Bahr al Ghazel and the Equatorial states where it increasingly took the form of genocidal attacks by government forces against civilians who in turn launched similar attacks on Dinka civilians.

But behind a tale that could be understood as another African tribal conflict and failed efforts by the US government to stop the killing was a tragedy that was the result of long US support for the SPLM and the Juba government. This despite overwhelming evidence of its administrative incompetence, massive corruption, and systemic abuse of human rights. The US government and various academics and researchers also perpetuated the false narrative that Riek Machar was a militarist and the primary cause of the conflict. The negative US role in the conflict reached its peak after it gave up on a peace agreement that it had devoted two years to reaching and another year to implementing in favour of giving tacit support to the Juba SPLM government's campaign to defeat the rebels militarily, which resulted in the killing of thousands of innocent civilians and the displacement of hundreds of thousands more.

But US hopes that the Salva government could militarily defeat its enemies proved misplaced, the war continued and spread, and Riek remained the leader of the largest opposition faction. As well as attempting to understand the causes of the war, its dynamics, and the reason the peace processes failed, this study will also endeavour to answer the question of why the Clinton, Bush, and Obama administrations devoted so much political and financial capital to bringing about South Sudan's independence and ending the civil war.

For the US government the descent of the SPLM regime into war was both an embarrassment and a refutation of the analyses and assumptions upon which three presidents based their policies on Sudan and South Sudan. It also represented the collapse of an illusion perpetuated by a host of largely American lobbyists as to the character of the SPLM, the state it dominated, and the conviction that Western liberalism could develop roots in South Sudan.

Organization of the Book

Chapter 1 provides the political background, including a potted history of Sudan's first and second civil war, which officially ended with the signing of the Comprehensive Peace Agreement (CPA) in 2005. This set the stage for the 2010 national elections and the 2011 referendum on secession. In the subsequent transitional period up to the outbreak of the December 2013 civil war, the SPLM failed to bring peace to the war-weary peoples or establish a viable and democratic administration. The transitional period was followed by two years of independence which were characterized by deepening insecurity, mal-administration, and endemic corruption. Tribes fought tribes in the absence of effective local administration, disaffected generals launched insurgencies, and the capital was afflicted by deepening power struggles which made clear how ill-prepared the country's leaders were for independence and how poorly the US-led international community which turned power over to the SPLM misunderstood conditions. The country was able to survive because of enormous international support and high oil prices, but when the oil market collapsed the patronage system which held the fractious leadership together disintegrated.

Chapter 2 examines US policy on southern and then South Sudan under the Clinton, Bush, and Obama presidencies. While US engagement derived in the first instance from a desire to maintain global hegemony in the post-Cold War era, lobby groups played an important role in shaping public opinion, demonizing the Islamist Government of Sudan, and making the murderous SPLA out to be liberators. This helps explain the extent of US engagement in a country of little strategic or economic interest.

Chapter 3 considers the outbreak of the war and makes clear that the international community misunderstood its causes, failed to identify the key actors, and organized a peace process which could not bring sustainable peace to South Sudan. The South Sudan civil war had its roots in the failures of the Comprehensive Peace Agreement (CPA), and is thus one of the 'consequences of a flawed peace process', the sub-title of my 2012 book on Sudan's civil war and the international-led peace process.¹ But the immediate stimulus for the insurgency was an attack by the SPLA and a Dinka militia loyal to President Salva Kiir on Nuer civilians in Juba.

Chapter 4 focuses on the origins, developments, controversies, and splits of the rebel SPLM-IO. Although Riek Machar's claim to be leader of the insurgency was accepted by the Western-backed regional Inter-Governmental Authority on Development (IGAD), initially he had no control over it, fleeing as he had from Juba like other hapless Nuer. Moreover, the party over which he claimed leadership was bitterly divided over the goals of the insurgency, conduct of the war, and how to advance the peace process. Failing to understand the character of the insurgency and devoted to elite accommodation the approach of the peace-makers could not succeed.

Chapter 5 is concerned with the regional IGAD peace process which, after making a token attempt to engage civil society and consider the root causes of the conflict, concentrated on finding a power-sharing formula agreeable to the SPLM factions which had brought South Sudan to the verge of collapse. Despite a narrowed focus, a welter of threats, and the imposition of sanctions against SPLM and rebel generals, the peace process collapsed. IGAD and its backers concluded that the failure of negotiations was due to insufficient international pressure to bring the parties to accept an agreement and thus its membership was vastly expanded. The second effort led to a 'forced agreement' in August 2015, but the government continued to place its hopes in a military victory over the SPLM-IO.

Chapter 6 considers developments between the signing of the peace agreement and its collapse 11 months later because of the failure of the peace-makers to ensure its implementation in the face of multiple government breaches. The US government pressed Riek to return to Juba, thus setting the stage for the predicted conflagration which took place on 8 July 2016. The SPLA attempted to kill Riek and launched another attack on the Nuer civilians of Juba, after which the SPLM-IO forces in the capital retreated to the Congo. Having lost faith in its own peace agreement, the US concluded that marginalizing Riek and supporting a government of President Salva Kiir and the SPLM-IO renegade Taban Deng, who was appointed First Vice President, offered the best prospects of peace.

Chapter 7 summarizes developments in the year since the collapse of the peace agreement and makes clear that instead of ending or even reducing the conflict, US policy and its tacit support of the Salva–Taban government failed. Moreover, the peace agreement between the Dinka and Nuer elites helped stimulate the spread and fragmentation of the conflict into other areas of the country. US leadership had driven the peace process, but even before the coming to power of Donald Trump that leadership had dissipated and a political vacuum ensued in which none of the belligerents was capable of militarily defeating the other.

The concluding chapter returns to a consideration of the reasons for the US intervention in South Sudan and why it not only failed but made it more difficult to resolve. Although some American lobby groups continue to call for deepening US engagement in South Sudan, under the Trump administration that is unlikely. Against that background, two alternative approaches to dealing with the conflict will be considered – giving war a chance and the imposition of an international trusteeship. The book ends with an appeal for attempting to resolve this conflict by addressing the concerns of the indigenous people at war and not with Western notions of statehood and power-sharing that have little meaning for most South Sudanese.

1 | THE DEEP ROOTS AND TWISTED PATH TO CIVIL WAR

Introduction

This chapter begins with a potted history of southern Sudan up to the signing of the peace agreements in 2005 and 2006 which makes clear the incomplete incorporation of the territory under three different regimes and the many political and developmental handicaps it faced in the lead up to independence. These obstacles should have precluded consideration of South Sudan's independence, particularly under the Sudan People's Liberation Movement (SPLM), which had not militarily defeated the Sudanese army, nor demonstrated any competence in administering its liberated territories.

The chapter will then turn to a more detailed consideration of the transitional period when the SPLM attempted and failed to bring peace to the war-weary people of South Sudan, establish a viable and democratic administration as per the Comprehensive Peace Agreement (CPA) of 2005, overcome its internal conflicts, and generate development in one of the poorest countries on the planet. Lacking a viable ideology and with a leadership more dependent upon the international community than its own people, the SPLM stumbled from one political and military crisis to the next. Coming to power at a time of high oil prices, the SPLM was able to temporarily buy off discontented and ambitious politicians and generals, but this approach was not sustainable, encouraged more demands on the state and ruling party and could not continue when oil prices crashed. For a movement built on militarism and with limited political skills it could only respond to crises by resorting to violence and this paved the way for the outbreak of the entirely predictable civil war.

Beginnings to the First Civil War

The problem of southern Sudan can be dated to the British campaign to free General Charles Gordon, who in the service of the Ottoman

Empire to end slavery in southern Sudan found himself besieged in Khartoum by the army of the Mahdi, a would-be Islamic reformer. But in a classic tragedy the rescuing force arrived only days after he had been killed and the city captured. While the British government played on the sentiments of the public to rescue Gordon, the real intention was to gain control of the upper reaches of the Nile to ensure the security of the Suez Canal and the route to India. Having captured this vast territory and its polyglot of people, however, the British had to administer it. In the economically viable and strategically more significant lands along the northern stretches of the Nile the British constructed one of its most developed colonies in Africa. At its core was the Gezira Scheme, which harvested the waters of the Blue and While Niles to produce the largest agricultural project in Africa. But the counterpoint to the developed northern riverine core were the largely ignored lands of the Moslem east and west, and the pagan south.

Southern Sudan was brought into the global economy by trade in ivory and slaves and the encroachment of the Mahdists in the second half of the nineteenth century. However, British policy to end slavery and control the ivory trade largely ended the only formal economy in southern Sudan. With the disparate peoples of the south too divided by tribe to pose a threat to the British, the new colonial power did little to develop the economy, operated through existing structures, and the result was an administration of benign neglect.

Southern Sudan hosted a diverse population of pastoralists, the biggest tribes being the Dinka and Nuer, and many small tribes of subsistence farmers in the better watered tropical lands of Equatoria in the far south. Social organization ranged from the kingships of the Zande, Shilluk, and Anuak, to the largely stateless Nuer. While the Dinka and Nuer are best considered nations in their own right with their often warring clans and sections, the harsh environment and lack of development ensured the survival of a host of smaller tribes. What these people shared was the lands of the Nile basin and a common struggle for scarce resources, principally grazing lands and water. In the north the pastoralists also shared their lands with Arabized Islamic nomads, who moved their herds to the better-watered lands to the south on a yearly cycle that frequently produced conflict.

In time, the plight of the southern Sudanese gained the interest of British humanitarians and Christians who feared that Islam spread by itinerant northern Sudanese traders – *jalabas* – would convert the indigenous people. Although not welcomed by the non-Moslem British colonial administration, missionaries from various denominations set up Christian schools and churches that catered to a minuscule number of students drawn from the traditional elite. To further 'protect' the southern peoples and those on the northern border lands from Moslem conversion, the British administration established 'closed districts' which stopped the trade of the *jalabas*, and even precluded the use of the Arabic language and wearing of Arab clothing. In time this led to the formation of an elite closely linked to the colonial state, English speaking, Christian, anti-Moslem, and anti-Arab.

These developments served to isolate southern Sudan from its natural links to the north and place it on a path of unity with the non-Moslem British colonies in eastern Africa. Late in the day, however, the colonial authorities changed their mind and decided that north-ern and southern Sudan should be united in preparation for eventual independence. Appreciating the enormous discrepancy in develop-ment between the north and south, the British began to develop the south, but during the Second World War it had few resources and after the war it was near bankrupt. Nonetheless and to the surprise of the colonial authorities by the 1950s they faced demands for inde-pendence from a politically conscious riverine north that they were ill-placed to resist.

First Civil War

The traditional southern Sudanese elite knew they were an une-qual match for unity with their northern counterparts and only agreed because of British pressure and the commitment of northerners to a federal system to ensure British colonialism would not be replaced by northern Sudanese colonialism. In the event, successive northern governments failed to keep that commitment and instead attempted to construct a Western-modelled nation-state with one national reli-gion, Islam, and one culture, Arabism.[1] In response, armed resistance to northern incorporation began even before Sudan gained inde-pendence on 1 January 1956, but became more sustained during the 1960s when the various rebel forces united to form the South Sudan Liberation Army (SSLA), or *Anyanya*, and demanded secession of the south. With the assistance of the region and Israel (always anxious to undermine an Arab state) the SSLA was increasingly able to challenge the Khartoum government.

In 1969 General Jafar Nimeiri came to power through a coup, but after failing to suppress the southern rebellion he decided to opt for peace. This took the form of the Addis Ababa Agreement of 1972, brokered by Emperor Haile-Selassie, under which the SSLA reluctantly accepted a federal system of government. When compared to the experience of the independent SPLM government, the post-Addis Ababa Agreement southern governments performed reasonably well – the leaders came from both senior military and civilian backgrounds, accepted parliamentary democracy, and had some administrative skills. In contrast, the post-2005 SPLM government was almost exclusively military, lacked administrative experience, suffered from endemic tribalism, and had little of the tolerance of its predecessor. Both regimes, however, suffered from the perennial problem, caused by the efforts of the cattle-raising Dinka, to dominate the country. This problem came to the fore when the more developed and largely farming Equatorians appealed to Nimeiri to break the Addis Ababa Agreement and divide the south into regions. Nimeiri agreed, much to the anger of the Dinka elite, and this set the territory on course to Sudan's second major civil war.

Second Civil War

The second civil war began with the desertion of southern soldiers based in the south who refused orders to be transferred to the north and fled to the western Ethiopian territory of Gambella. Dr John Garang, a Dinka and colonel in the national army who acquired his PhD at Iowa State University, was ordered by his superiors to suppress the growing rebellion. Instead he defected to Gambella and after defeating his opponents appointed himself chairman of the Sudan People's Liberation Army. With the Ethiopian military regime or Derg combatting a number of insurgencies, including that in Eritrea for independence, its support for the SPLA and Garang as its leader was premised upon an armed struggle for a united and reformed 'New Sudan', and not the secession probably supported by most educated southern Sudanese at the time. Garang's approach followed from his commitment to leftist and pan-African politics. But it also served the practical need of acquiring military assistance, winning support in northern Sudan, and avoiding the enmity of powerful Arab and Moslem countries in the region that would come to Sudan's rescue if they concluded the Arab world was under threat.

While mainstream history contends that the second southern Sudanese rebellion began under the SPLA in 1983, in fact Nuer calling themselves Anyanya 2 launched a minor insurgency along the Ethiopian border six years earlier demanding secession. In the ensuing struggle between Anyanya 2 and the SPLA the Dinka-dominated SPLA with the support of the Derg was victorious. But in the contest to assume the dominant position in the war against Khartoum, Garang noted, 'The first bullets in the southern war were fought against separatists'. He might also have said that the first people killed by the SPLA were Nuer, including their leader, Samuel Gai Tut, and those events are still a source of grievance for Nuer.

Despite enormous support from the Derg, the Eastern Bloc, cash hand-outs from Libya, and assistance from Zimbabwe and other African states, SPLA successes were limited. Its efforts were undermined by the growing internal opposition it fostered among southern Sudanese angered at the SPLA's brutality, arrogance, and the Dinka's practice of bringing their crop-destroying cattle into the farming lands of Equatoria. Frequently, these communities formed local self-defence militias that were supported by Khartoum, which considered them a means of counter-insurgency on the cheap. The foremost internal armed resistance movement to the SPLA that emerged was the South Sudan Defense Force (SSDF), a Nuer-dominated organization, but which included components from virtually every community in southern Sudan. Like Anyanya 2, which it largely absorbed, the SSDF called for secession from the north.

With its national agenda, the SPLA also carried out military operations in the north of the country and while not successful in the riverine core or Darfur, with the assistance of the Derg and its successors, the Ethiopian People's Revolutionary Democratic Front (EPRDF) and the Eritrean People's Liberation Front (EPLF), it captured the border territory of Blue Nile state and a swath of territory in eastern Sudan. Lands along the Ugandan border in southern Sudan were also captured by Eritrean, Ethiopian, and Ugandan forces and turned over to the SPLA. The biggest success of the SPLA, however, was in the Nuba Mountains in the centre of Sudan, and its peoples soon formed a major component of the SPLA. These same Nuba Mountain rebels would later be disillusioned with the SPLA when the territory did not gain the right of self-determination or affiliation with an independent South Sudan.

In 1989, the National Islamic Front (NIF) came to power in Khartoum as a result of a coup against the democratically elected government of Sadig al Mahdi. The in-coming Islamist regime not only set out to subvert neighbouring states, but also declared the war in the south to be a *jihad* and devoted enormous resources to defeating the SPLA. Making matters worse for the SPLA, Drs Riek Machar, a Nuer, and Lam Akol, a Shilluk, broke with the party in 1991 over the lack of internal democracy and Garang's opposition to southern self-determination, and took many thousands into opposition with them. While Riek and Lam probably had the support of most southern Sudanese over these demands, Garang had international credibility and could gain assistance far beyond their reach. As a result, Riek and Lam were increasingly forced to turn to Khartoum for support and this soon took the form of an alliance.

At the core of this alliance was the 1997 Khartoum Peace Agreement under which the national government agreed to a generous sharing of oil revenues and committed to holding a vote on southern self-determination. However, the NIF was divided on implementing the Khartoum Peace Agreement and some of Riek's followers, including his first lieutenant, Taban Deng, returned in frustration to the SPLA. Riek too left Khartoum and first took up residence in Nairobi, attempting to establish a rival organization before reconciling with Garang in 2002 and assuming the number three position in the SPLM behind Salva. Lam followed a similar trajectory and returned to the SPLA.

NIF subversion of neighbouring states led to not only direct push back from the states involved, but also increasing cooperation and support for the SPLA. Fear that the NIF would undermine its regional allies led to the US introducing increasingly severe sanctions against Sudan and providing military support to countries in the region facing NIF subversion. Some of these supplies were turned over to the SPLA. Regional opposition to the NIF and support for the SPLA developed to the point that it appeared the regime might be overthrown, but such hopes were dashed when Eritrea and Ethiopia fought a brutal border war between 1998 and 2000. This led them to reconcile with Khartoum, giving the regime a new lease on life.

Despite this new-found unity, the SPLA was never able to defeat the Sudanese army, win the support of the people of southern Sudan, much less provide an adequate administration in its liberated territories. By the early 2000s a south–south conflict had overtaken the north–south conflict between a similar sized Dinka-dominated SPLA and a Nuer-dominated SSDF. The inability to end the war either militarily or through internal negotiations, the increasing threat it posed to regional security, and the growing humanitarian crisis provided the stimulus for a number of external peace initiatives. In the end, however, the initiative by the regional IGAD became the accepted process. IGAD was created and funded by Western states to meet its development needs in the Horn of Africa and later its members were pressed to establish a peace committee, which was likewise funded by the West, and it was this body that assumed the task of peace-making in Sudan.

Crucial to realizing this task was gaining the support of the US, and this was only accomplished after its close regional ally, Kenya, assumed the primary role in the mediation. Actual negotiations were conducted by General Lazrus Sumbeiywo, who was trusted because he had devoted his military career to keeping the country's aging dictator, Daniel arap Moi, in power and had a record of closely cooperating on security matters with the CIA. To further ensure Western interests were kept at the fore, the IGAD mediation was supported by a Troika made up of the US, UK, and Norway, and they in turn were financially assisted by the Friends of IGAD, a group of Western donor states.

These efforts in turn could not have succeeded without the ideological shift that Garang's SPLA underwent to distance itself from its Communist past and endorse the new US-led post-Cold War world order. The ideological shift was made possible for three reasons: first, the SPLA's commitment to Marxism was skin-deep and shaped by the opportunistic need for largely Derg and Eastern Bloc support; second – and this will be considered in the next chapter – the skills of its American supporters in repackaging Garang as a liberal democrat and the subsequent narrative of American evangelical Christians that the SPLA was leading a war of persecuted Christian Africans against an Arab Islamic expansionist government in Khartoum; and lastly, the SPLA could no longer send its cadres to Eastern Europe for training. Instead, increasing numbers of them began joining the movement via Kenya and the US where they had supped deeply on the prevailing anti-socialist doctrines of those states. Western democratic rhetoric became the order of the day, even though that could not have contrasted more with the tightly controlled strictures of the SPLM or the feudal-tribal realities of rural South Sudan.

The pieces were falling into place for the success of the IGAD/ Troika negotiations. What remained was the interest of the NCP in pursuing the peace process. First, although the NCP had a responsibility to protect the national integrity of the Sudanese state, it had a partisan interest in pursuing an Islamist agenda and in that light southern Sudan was a drag and even a threat. Better to let the territory go, in the view of many Islamists, in order that a fully Arab and Islamic society could be constructed. Second, the war was financially debilitating, with further costs being borne as a result of US-led efforts to economically marginalize the country. Pursuing peace with the SPLA offered the prospect that the sanctions would be lifted, while opposing the peace process meant facing the threat that yet more sanctions would be applied.

While there were many demands that armed groups – particularly those in Darfur – other opposition parties in the north and south, as well as civil society, participate in the negotiations, the mediators limited the process to only two parties – the NCP and SPLM. This assumed, mistakenly it turned out, that they alone represented the sentiments of the people in their respective territories. It was also erroneously concluded that a successful resolution of the north–south conflict would provide a model to end the country's other conflicts. Despite the SSDF's size, considerable support base, and the crucial role it played in defending the oil fields which were rapidly becoming the major source of income for the government and the focus of the north–south conflict, it was likewise refused participation in the negotiations because it was supported by Khartoum. Although the peace process was elitist, secretive and there would be no referendum on the results, IGAD and the Troika contended that there would be popular accountability because the people would be permitted to express their views through an election. In the event, parties that did not endorse the agreement were not permitted to participate in the 2010 national elections.

The peace-making process proceeded at a snail's pace and only made progress when Garang and Sudan Vice President Ali Osman

Taha met behind closed doors and made the big decisions that were endorsed by their respective parties. The result was the Comprehensive Peace Agreement of 2005, which committed the parties to end the conflict, national unity, democratic transformation, formation of a national unity government for the six-year interim period, the holding of a 'popular consensus' for the 'Two Areas' in the north (Southern Kordofan and Blue Nile) where the SPLA held territory, and the conduct of a referendum on southern secession in 2011.

Garang, however, did not live to assume his positions of president of the government of South Sudan and vice president of the Government of National Unity, dying in a still unexplained helicopter crash on 30 July 2005. After fears that the SPLM would break up over succession struggles, the party leadership reluctantly accepted the chairmanship of Salva Kiir, a military officer not noted for his intelligence or political experience, but who was second in the party hierarchy. Salva was described by William Richardson, Bush's Special Envoy on Sudan as, 'shrewd, clever, and deeply committed to a better future for his people. I've seen him take courageous steps, putting his own political interests at risk to do what he believed was right for his people'.[2] But that was not the common conception of Salva, who was viewed as little more than Garang's errand boy, and kept in the dark about many issues. Although chief of staff, he acknowledged that Garang frequently exerted direct control over particular officers, such as Peter Gadet.[3] Moreover, Salva was a separatist and while that position was favoured – as the 2011 referendum would demonstrate – by the majority of southern Sudanese, it was not initially the position of the close followers of Garang, and was completely at odds with the party's programme dating back to 1983.

Southern Secession or Democratic Transformation

Supporters of the original SPLA vision contended that the primary contradiction in Sudan was between a privileged Arabized and Islamic minority inhabiting the country's riverine core and the marginalized communities inhabiting the periphery. According to Garang, and endorsed in repeated party statements, the best means to deal with this problem was not to carve up the country, but to democratically restructure the state and address the problems of centre–periphery relations and unequal development. This analysis not only suggested a more complicated rendering of the problem than secession, it also necessitated a marked change in the economic order of the country, a position that had a strong following during the Cold War but was not viewed so sympathetically by the West after the defeat of socialism and the Eastern Bloc.

The SPLM was a founding member of the National Democratic Alliance (NDA), which was based in Asmara and whose representatives came from virtually all corners of Sudan. Although reflecting widely different political views and interests, all were united in their opposition to the NCP, support for a united Sudan, and – at least in theory – a commitment to democratic transformation. Moreover, with the legalization of the SPLM in the context of the peace process, most of its members came from the north. All of which makes it hard to argue for reducing the understanding of conflict in Sudan to a struggle between a supposedly homogeneous Arab Moslem north and an African non-Moslem south.

This more complicated understanding of the war was not popular in US circles, which preferred wars where the good and bad parties could be readily distinguished. There was a need for a peace process which would undermine the Islamist government in Sudan, and with Garang's death there was no commanding figure in the south calling for a united New Sudan. Nor was the call for a Sudan-wide democratic transformation supported by America's East African regional allies, which were not well informed about political conditions in Sudan, typically had an aversion to Arabs and Moslems, and were anxious to pull southern Sudan into their orbit. The best means possible to do this was through a peace process constructed around the principle of self-determination. Authoritarian governments themselves, they could not be expected to favour appeals for a peace process focused on democratization. Lastly, the NCP was more disposed to a peace process premised on southern self-determination than democratic transformation, given that in the last democratic election in Sudan in 1986 it had gained a mere 15 per cent of the vote.

Tomes have been written on self-determination and the pre-requisites for achieving it, but the reality has been that the US will not support any secessionist movements against its allies – witness the struggles of the Palestinians against Israel, the Polisario against Morocco, the Kurds against Turkey, or the Kashmiris against India. But Sudan under the

Islamist NCP was a different matter. The early NCP destabilized US allies in the region and abroad and – within its capability – attempted to undermine US foreign policy globally.

Moreover, as well as dispensing with the commitment to a united New Sudan, the SPLM increasingly moved away from a commitment to democratic transformation, as evidenced by its performance in the CPA-created Government of National Unity, in which it supported NCP measures to tighten security and restrict human rights to ensure that the transitional process moved forward and the referendum on secession took place.[4] As a result, one of the SPLM's biggest supporters in the north, the Sudan Communist Party, subsequently acknowledged that its support was a mistake.[5] While American lobbyists demonized the NCP and regularly predicted that it would abort the peace process, the authoritarian NCP and SPLM were able to achieve a surprising level of cooperation.

Crucial to ensuring the implementation of the CPA was the need to reconcile the SPLA and the SSDF, which was opposed by Garang, who understood that integration would seriously dilute the domination of the Dinka in the army and by extension his own power. But the Dinka who dominated the SPLA came from Garang's home area of Bor in Upper Nile, and they also posed a threat to Salva, who along with his supporters came from Gorgrial in the north. Moreover, Salva's support for secession meant that his thinking was in line with the leaders of the SSDF, thus removing another barrier to integration. Salva was thus able to reach an agreement in January 2006 with Paulino Matiep, leader of the SSDF, on the integration of the SSDF forces into the SPLA. It was this agreement, and not the CPA, that brought the war to an end in much of the country. Moreover, the Juba Declaration was reached without the support of the international peace brigade. Integration, however, meant that while the leadership of the army continued to be dominated by the Dinka increasingly from Salva's home area, the majority of the common soldiers were Nuer, and this would prove to be an untenable arrangement.

Next on the CPA political calendar was the 2010 national elections, which neither the Khartoum government nor the SPLM favoured, but were pressed to accept by the international community. Salva, however, refused to run as the SPLM candidate for the national presidency, fearing that his colleagues wanted to marginalize him in a contest with Bashir that he was likely to lose. Furthermore, it made little sense given his aspiration to achieve an independent South Sudan. A northern SPLM member, Yasir Arman, was thus selected to carry the party banner, but when it appeared that against the odds he might possibly win (on a second ballot) he dropped out of the campaign to ensure the victory of the Islamist candidate, Omar al-Bashir. This again made clear that secession and not democracy was the primary concern of the SPLM.

In the event, the elections were less than fair, even though the international observer missions gave them a qualified pass. While NCP rigging concentrated on voter registration and candidate buying that could largely be carried out beyond the purview of election monitors, the less sophisticated SPLM resorted to blatant brutality to gain their ends.[6] In the south the result was so skewed that only Joseph Bakosoro, who ran as an independent candidate for the governorship in Western Equatoria, could be said to have conclusively won. This widespread rigging was largely ignored by the international community to keep the peace process on track and by most southern Sudanese to ensure that the path to secession was not derailed. But it also made clear that Western rhetoric about democracy and the CPA commitment to democratic transformation was insincere. The end result of the election was a divided Sudan, with an authoritarian NCP controlling the north with a new legitimacy, and an authoritarian SPLM controlling the south.

The Manufacture of Southern Unity

Crucial to gaining a strong vote for secession in the 2011 referendum was for the south to be united. However, the SPLA's brutal conduct of the war had divided the people and was made worse by the high-handed manner in which the SPLM conducted the 2010 elections. After achieving a measure of security as a result of the Juba Declaration, Salva now focused on winning the support of the disaffected opposition political parties. To achieve that he needed to share power, or at least be seen to share power. Salva's close ally, Bona Malwal, together with the main parliamentary leader, Dr Lam Akol, formed the Political Parties Leadership Forum in October 2010, made up of 24 southern political parties. According to the conference's final communiqué, after the announcement of the referendum results (and there was little doubt the result would be a vote for secession) a National Constitutional Review Commission would be convened and adopt the 2005 Interim Constitution for Southern Sudan as a transitional constitution. This was to be followed by an all-party constitutional conference that would consider a permanent constitution and form a broad-based transitional government led by Salva that would govern for the duration of the transitional period. This transitional government would oversee the holding of a census and elections for a constituent assembly that would promulgate a permanent constitution. It was also agreed that one week after the official announcement of the results of the referendum that the parties would re-convene in Juba and begin planning for the transition.

This agreement gave every appearance that despite the 2010 election, the Salva SPLM government was committed to the country's democratic transformation, and certainly the formation of the Party Leadership Forum achieved its immediate aims of gaining the support of the political parties and a measure of good will. The 2011 referendum on secession was thus predictable. The national government made a token effort to campaign for unity, but clearly was not committed to the process, while the SPLM refused to hold a convention on the matter because with northern Sudanese now the majority in the party they would oppose secession. Instead, the southern leadership of the SPLM made their own decision to support secession and their northern comrades fell in line, some believing that this would be a first step toward the eventual overthrow of the Islamist Khartoum government and the achievement of Garang's vision of a New Sudan. Such notions were fanciful, however, and the SPLM South devoted all its energies to achieving a massive vote for secession and in the event southern Sudanese voted 99 per cent for this option. Sudan was fatally fractured, and the independent state of South Sudan was born. Although SPLM supporters in the US had long predicted that the NCP would refuse to accept the outcome of the referendum, Sudan was the first country to recognize South Sudan's independence. Bashir even went to Juba to participate in the celebrations.

It quickly became apparent, though, that having gained the necessary unity to successfully conduct the 2011 referendum the SPLM leadership saw little use for the Political Parties Leadership Forum. They now argued that it had no legal basis and instead established a technical committee made up overwhelmingly of SPLM members to prepare for the transitional constitution. The government further decreed that the Forum would not be given authority to amend the draft constitution, and nor would there be an opportunity to fully discuss matters of concern such as power-sharing and the length of the transition. The SPLM had driven another blow to the hopes of democratic transformation.

Transitional Period

During the six-year transitional period provided by the CPA and the two plus years before South Sudan's civil war began, the SPLM proved unable to govern while its private army, the SPLA, together with assorted militias caused or exacerbated insecurity in the country. The lack of development in spite of a vast oil wealth and international goodwill produced a growing sense throughout South Sudan that the great promise of independence was being squandered. During the long war with the north the party-army leadership was only able to create a semblance of national unity by focusing on the hated Arab government in Khartoum. But with the conclusive vote for secession that fragile unity broke down and the barely contained contradictions and power struggles came to the fore, typically finding expression in the form of tribal based conflicts.

Unable to either militarily or politically overcome these conflicts, the SPLM used the growing oil revenues to buy off discontented politicians with newly created positions in the expanding government while rebellious generals were granted promotions in an increasingly top-heavy officered army. Kleptocracy became the dominant form of government, but this approach produced further disaffection and demands, at the same time limiting the capacity of the state to provide services and development to its poverty-stricken and increasingly alienated citizens. It also created an environment where power-hungry urban-based politicians could make common cause with disaffected cattle herders and peasants. The government's mercenary approach to discontent could never be sustainable and was only successful in the short-term when there was a steady flow of oil revenues. When the government cut off oil production in a failed attempt to pressure Khartoum to reduce the oil transit fees to the Red Sea, and then suffered a budget shortfall due to the global collapse in petroleum prices, its conflict reduction strategy quickly broke down.

The largely Nuer-inhabited states of Greater Upper Nile suffered a disproportionate amount of violence in the transitional and independence period because of the break-down of law and order, lack of development, and the people became increasingly resentful of a government they viewed as predatory and a failure. Crucially, it was a Dinka-led government of the SPLA which many had opposed under first Anyanya 2 and then the SSDF. On the east bank of the Nile this opposition was largely led by the white army – a Nuer youth resistance group formed to defend their local communities, but which could be mobilized to fight the SPLA when it attempted to disarm the fighters. These battles radicalized the Nuer civilian population and prepared them for the eventual full-scale war against the government.

Regional Revolts

In response to the fraudulent 2010 elections a series of revolts broke out, the most serious of which was in Unity state on the border of Sudan. The background lay in Salva's appointment of Taban Deng to the governorship of Unity state in 2005, although the president made the appointment conditional on him gaining the acceptance of Paulino Matiep, the strong man of the state, leader of the now dissolved SSDF, and deputy leader of the SPLA under the Juba Declaration. Once he had gained the approved of Paulino, Taban turned on him and together with the SPLA Chief of Staff, James Hoth, arranged for the SPLA to attack the house of Paulino, killing 12 of his body-guards and forcing a UN evacuation of the rest of the guards to Juba. With Paulino marginalized, Taban constructed an administration which was little more than a crime ring, with most of the state finances handled by his personal representatives in Khartoum and Doha. Taban also played a key role as a conduit of military supplies from Juba and Uganda to the various rebel groups fighting in the north. Never popular, prior to the 2010 elections Taban lost the leadership of the state SPLM to former governor Dr Joseph Manytuil which should have precluded him contesting the governorship. With support from Salva, however, he ran and was opposed by the wife of Riek Machar, Angelina Teny. There is reason to believe that the election was seriously flawed,[7] but the National Election Commission, with the tacit support of the international observers, accepted the victory of Taban.

Anger with the election results in Unity state led to an insurgency, but it did not take off until Peter Gadet defected from the SPLA and assumed command. The insurgents who would take the name of South Sudan Liberation Army (SSLA) from the earlier rebellion, issued one of the defining opposition statements – the Mayom Declaration – in April 2011. It followed a common script of condemning the corruption and lack of democracy under the SPLM, the bloated, ineffective, and unaccountable security organs, and a politicized judiciary. But its authors also emphasized that South Sudan's ills could not all be blamed – as the regime was doing – on Khartoum. The Declaration went on to complain about traditional leaders being deprived of their authority, commissioners turning their counties into fiefdoms, the SPLM refusing to allow other southern political parties the right to propagate their ideas and present their political programme to the people, and using the SPLA high command to intimidate other leaders. The Declaration called for the formation of a broad-based government and agreement on a two-year transitional period 'to prepare the newly born state for independence'.

Although an accurate summation of the problems of South Sudan, the SSLA and Gadet were not able to convince enough Nuer to defect from the SPLA to overthrow the state government of Taban Deng. As a result, Gadet negotiated his way back into the SPLA, but the rebellion he unleashed continued with the support of the Khartoum government.

After a skirmish with the Sudanese army on the Unity state–Southern Kordofan border on 26 March 2012, forces of the SPLA and Justice and Equality Movement (JEM) from Darfur followed the retreating force and ended up occupying the oil fields of Heglig. After being roundly condemned by the international community and pressed by the US government angered at this threat to the peace process, on 20 April Salva responded to UN Secretary-General Ban Ki-moon's demand that his forces leave by saying, 'I am not under your command'. He then organized demonstrations against the UN,[8] before announcing a withdrawal of the SPLA and JEM. This public condemnation by the US represented virtually the first time the US treated South Sudan on a par with Sudan, rather than only condemning the latter.[9]

The shock was all the greater because the Salva government assumed that Washington would always side with it, particularly in a dispute with the NCP.

In 2013 the wheel turned again and after serving as a crucial ally against Riek, Salva feared that Taban was again making common cause with Riek and wanted him replaced by Dr Joseph Manytuil. Given Taban's influence over the SPLA, though, he could not be readily removed unless Salva was assisted by an armed force. This set the stage for an agreement between Salva and Bashir (who was also happy to see Taban removed because of his support of northern rebels) that involved the SSLA under Bapine Manytuil (Joseph's brother) return to Unity state. Salva's fear that Taban would again become Riek's first lieutenant was proven correct when the insurgency broke out in mid-December 2013.

Civilian Disarmament: Another Step on the Road to Civil War

Another security problem that was to provide a key link to the civil war was the repeated attempts by the SPLA to disarm a host of nominally civilian forces in the country, the most important being the various sections of the Nuer white army. Organized at the local level to protect community cattle these armed youth groups played a significant role in the second civil war and were the main fighting force in Riek's attack on Garang's homeland of Bor in 1991 in which 3,000 civilians were killed and thousands of cattle stolen.

As interested in looting as any political objectives, the fighters of the white army were nonetheless brave, tough, highly mobile, and distrustful of the SPLA, which they viewed as an army of occupation and a threat to their cattle herds. The government and the SPLA meanwhile refused to accept armed groups which posed a threat to their claimed monopoly on the instruments of violence. With the SSDF being integrated into the SPLA under the 2006 Juba Declaration the government concluded that the time was ripe to disarm them. The youth, however, were often not prepared to give up their weapons in an environment of continuing insecurity, particularly to the SPLA.[10] Despite the supposed national character of South Sudan, which served as the basis for the claim to the right of self-determination, the tribes of the territory often viewed one another as their most bitter enemies. To disarm was to risk annihilation from their fellow South Sudanese, not a foreign power.

As vice president and their leader in the 1991 Bor attack, Riek was commissioned by the government to convince the white army to turn over their weapons. He failed, after which the SPLA began to forcefully disarm the youth, mostly by killing them, and punishing the resident civilian population by living off their cattle.[11] The white army was eventually defeated, but the SPLA success was transitory. In the lawless environment of South Sudan to be without a weapon was suicidal and with a ready supply of weapons in the region in exchange for cattle the youth were soon re-armed.

Deadly as these campaigns against the Nuer white armies were, the fighting that took place in Jonglei state after 2009 and until the eve of the civil war was even more violent. Although raiding by Lou Nuer and the Murle of one another's cattle had been endemic for years this fighting was on an altogether different scale. The spread of modern weapons because of the war, the dependence of both communities on cattle in the absence of other resources, the lack of jobs, insecurity, the politicization of the conflict, widespread poverty, and some of the lowest levels of development and infrastructure in South Sudan, meant that what was considered a tribal conflict took the form of a mini-war. Hundreds of people were killed in each battle, women and children systematically butchered, villages burned down, and tens of thousands of cattle stolen. The government's response was to announce yet another civilian disarmament campaign – Operation Restore Peace – which began in March 2012.

In 2008 General Peter Bul Kong, a Lou Nuer who led the SPLA disarmament campaigns against his own clan, told me he had never conducted a campaign against the Murle because they were so hated in the region that if disarmed they would be subject to genocide by their neighbours. However, when 30,000 SPLA soldiers were mobilized under Peter Gadet, Commander of Division 8, to disarm the Murle, it was the SPLA that was defeated. While the SPLA suffered from a weak and divided leadership, poor logistics which involved placing highly trained and equipped soldiers in the field alongside recent conscripts without shoes,[12] the Murle youth had high morale and were joined by personnel from the wildlife forces, prison services, and police, all of whom were fighting in their homeland and viewed the SPLA as enemies and occupiers. They were also so skilled that Gadet said 'each shot took out a soldier'. With the army forced to flee the battlefield 'the hunter became the hunted', according to Gadet, who withdrew from the field after three months of almost continuous action.

The Murle victory gave the tribe leverage to demand their own separate state and a few months later when the civil war broke out they found themselves in the position of king-makers between the government and the Nuer led SPLM-IO. Another incentive for the government to accept Murle demands was fear of Lou and Murle reconciliation that would threaten their shared enemy, the Bor Dinka, and even worse that these arrangements might be engineered by Riek. Since the government had more to offer than the rebels, the Murle aligned with the government and accepted their ethnic-based state and were temporarily neutralized.

SPLA Fighting Itself

From its inception, the SPLA was designed to meet the needs of John Garang, ensuring his Bor section dominated decision-making, and maintaining his personal power over the army. Indeed, defence authorities in Eritrea and Ethiopia which trained many units of the SPLA during the war told the author they were shocked that the structures they created were destroyed by Garang to ensure his personal control. Other examples of the SPLA being its own worst enemy was its unwillingness to integrate southern officers after independence who had served in the Sudanese army because of a lack of trust.[13] Lt.-General retired Joseph Lagu, former leader of Anyanya, said that these officers were far superior to their counterparts in the SPLA and should have been welcomed and used to train the far less skilled SPLA soldiers. Instead they were marginalized, embittered, and if Nuer, many would join the insurgency.

The SPLA never had a national character and what little it did have was diluted by the integration of the Nuer under the Juba Declaration. In addition, a major weakness of the SPLA is the absence of a centralized command, with many soldiers falling under the leadership of generals from their own tribe. Even the Presidential Guard was divided between Salva's largely Dinka component, Riek's Nuer section, and – until his death – Paulino Matiep's largely Bul Nuer soldiers. Another source of instability was that approximately 60 per cent of SPLA soldiers on the eve of the civil war were Nuer in a country where they numbered less than 25 per cent of the population and most were opposed to the SPLA leadership.

An additional problem was that the SPLA was far too big, with estimates running as high as 250,000, although the number of active soldiers is likely to have been about half that number. The large numbers were due to a government which looked to military means to solve political problems, field commanders who inflated their numbers so they could collect the salaries of 'ghost' soldiers, and the 'big tent approach', whereby rebelling factions were bought off by bringing them into the SPLA but were never fully integrated. As a result, the SPLA, together with the other security agencies and assorted militias, consumed at least 40 per cent of the budget in South Sudan according to government figures.[14] This was a severe drain on government finances even when the government was flush with oil revenues, but when it stopped oil production to pressure Khartoum to reduce the transit fees and in 2012 international oil prices dramatically dropped these expenses were no longer sustainable. This led to increasingly violent struggles over declining finances and 'corruption in South Sudan … shifted from being an integrated and self-sustaining system during the country's brief economic boom period to being a disintegrative and self-destructing system'.[15]

Finally, from the time of independence through to the present both the SPLA have fought and the party has ruled under the label of Sudan, the only serious objections being raised by Sudan's President Bashir. Moreover, no serious efforts have been made to break the link between the SPLA and SPLM, and leaders from each component move freely between them, usually keeping their titles and often double-dipping on their salaries. The SPLA is viewed by the leadership as the only functioning element of the government and its generals have dominated the country's governorships and commissionerships. Likewise, the police, prison guards, wildlife forces, etc. are militarized and often staffed with former members of the SPLA. The militarization of governance and society at large did not increase security and instead fostered insecurity and brutality. Although the government and SPLA leadership claimed to support Disarmament, Demobilization and Reintegration (DDR), in the face of enormous opposition, bureaucratic inertia, and corruption in both the army and the UN, almost no progress had been made on the eve of the civil war.

Officially the SPLA has gone to great lengths to break down the tribal character of the army by dispersing members of the various militias it has integrated and ensuring that units and senior officers in the field come from different ethnic communities. While at the staff level there remained a preponderance of Bor Dinka officers, in the field the SPLA looked as if it was tribally integrated. Looks, though, were deceiving. Soldiers routinely went to their tribal cohorts to deal with issues and army divisions frequently had four or more generals from different tribes. Instead of soldiers living in barracks where they would mix with counterparts from other tribes, typically they resided in their own homes or settlements and identified with their family and hosts. Even in barracks the Nuer and Dinka usually kept apart. Despite the security services consuming much of the national budget, soldiers' wages were frequently in arrears, while weapons and munitions were sometimes in short supply. It was not uncommon for soldiers to go into battle without shoes, and there are even reports of soldiers suffering from malnutrition.

Morale in the SPLA was undermined by continuing bitterness over the integration of the SSDF into the SPLA. While Nuer officers considered the signing of the Juba Declaration to be Salva's greatest achievement and more important than the CPA in ending conflict in large areas of South Sudan, the way the agreement was implemented undermined this goodwill. The SSDF's leader, Paulino Matiep, was tolerated by the army brass as deputy leader of the SPLA because he was infirm, expected to die soon, and without speaking English or fluent Arabic could not readily exert his authority over the army. Moreover, despite retaining a large group of guards in Juba the forces loyal to him were dispersed throughout the country. The attack on the Bentiu house of Paulino and the attempts by James Hoth to marginalize the man who was his superior caused lasting anger among the former SSDF officers.

An even greater source of anger was caused by many former SSDF officers being placed on the inactive or reserve list, effectively retaining their link to the SPLA, but not granting them pensions they could live on. By keeping them nominally in the SPLA it was hoped they would not consider rebellion, a misplaced hope as it turned out, with former SSDF officers placed on the inactive list among the first to rebel in December 2013. Arguments of professionalization were raised to justify the dismissal of the former SSDF officers, and while some of them did suffer from a lack of education and training, there were also many cases of highly educated former SSDF officers being placed on the inactive list. Thus, Salva's greatest achievement was undermined during the implementation of the Juba Declaration. A process that began by providing him with a large block of Nuer supporters to limit the power of the Garangist officers turned full circle and the Nuer were ripe to join the December 2013 rebellion.

SPLM Power Struggles

The SPLM power struggle came to the fore at the 2008 SPLM Convention when Salva proposed that James Wani Igga serve as his vice president and running mate in the 2010 elections instead of Riek, and that Taban Deng replace Pagan Amum as secretary-general of the party. In the ensuing uproar there was fear that these divisions could take the country back to war, and indeed, Paulino Matiep was dispatched to Unity state to mobilize his forces. Fearing the worst, Roger Winter from the Friends of South Sudan (see next chapter) made two proposals: first that the party focus on the referendum, and second, preservation of the status quo which meant ending the challenges to the presidency of Salva Kiir, and Riek and Pagan retaining their existing positions as vice president and secretary-general of the party respectively. These proposals were accepted but had the effect of merely temporarily freezing the conflict. Postponing rather than addressing fundamental contradictions was a time-honoured tradition in the SPLM. It also did not improve relations between the president and vice president and numerous witnesses reported they had almost no personal contacts and largely operated within their own ethnic communities, thus following the government pattern whereby most ministries were largely staffed by members of the minister's tribe.

Responding to fears that Riek was using the committee on national reconciliation – which he chaired – to pursue his political ambitions, Salva abruptly removed him in April 2013. This was followed by another postponement of the SPLM general conference which reflected both the growing divisions within the leadership and Salva's desire to avoid a leadership contest.

In a further effort to limit opposition the government placed a bill regarding NGOs before the Assembly on the eve of the civil war, modelled after similar legislation in Khartoum, but even more severe because it required representatives from the security agencies to serve as members of the agencies' board of directors and that the NGOs only provide services, thus denying them any role in monitoring or advocacy. On 7 November 2013 Information Minister Michael Makuei contended on national television that the president was the symbol of the government and of the people and it was therefore unacceptable for journalists to criticize him. The minister further said that all journalists in South Sudan must have the requisite credentials as determined by him before they could practise their trade.[16] This created a climate in which journalists felt under government siege, were regularly arrested, and some would be killed under circumstances which suggested the involvement of the security forces. Meanwhile, the National Electoral Commission barely functioned and the National Constitutional Commission had stopped operating.

As well as the tensions produced by the government's increasingly authoritarian bent there were also problems related to the hang-over of the Garangist commitment to a New Sudan, which caused problems in Juba's relations with Khartoum. Based on the belief that South Sudan could never be free of insecurity as long as the NCP ruled Sudan, the government supported rebels in the north and the closure of the oil pipeline to Port Sudan as a means to stimulate internal struggles in Sudan. The US position was not entirely clear, but during this period and throughout the subsequent civil war it was strongly influenced by the Ugandan government of Yoweri Museveni, who feared the regime in Khartoum. Despite assurances of SPLM-North leaders that Bashir could be overthrown through insurgencies in Blue Nile and the Nuba Mountains and a parallel civilian uprising in Khartoum, these plans have not been realized. While the people of these two areas had been among the most committed SPLA fighters for New Sudan, increasingly after the independence of South Sudan they were used as cannon fodder by the SPLA-N to achieve militarily what the party could not achieve politically.[17] The Juba government mistakenly believed that stopping the transit of oil through Sudan would help stimulate a popular uprising. While it clearly hurt the Bashir regime it did not crumble, and instead would have brought about the collapse of South Sudan were it not for loans and the support of the international community.

Countdown to War

South Sudan's growing political tensions, endemic conflict, mismanagement, and systemic corruption led long-time SPLM supporter and American citizen, Ted Dagne, to leave his position with the Congressional Research Service, and with the support of the US's UN Envoy Susan Rice, the head of the UN Mission in South Sudan, Hilde Johnson, and his friends in the SPLM become a special advisor to President Salva Kiir. In this role Dagne wrote a letter signed by Salva Kiir which accused 75 present and former leaders of the government of looting $4 billion of oil revenues that constituted South Sudan's virtually only source of revenue.[18] Leaked to the media, the letter naively asked the thieves to return their ill-gotten gains to an anonymous bank account in Nairobi. The letter did not have the desired effect and instead of money being returned it caused a firestorm which forced Dagne to flee the country in fear of his life.

Although not representative, visits to party offices at a number of locations in Greater Upper Nile (GUN) by the author on the eve of the civil war (i.e. October to December 2013) underlined the problems of the SPLM in terms of declining memberships and the view, as one party official put it, that 'the community is facing us and we have no response or direction'. In Upper Nile, the Renk county SPLM had completely shut down, while in Wadakona and Melut party officials said that the party had largely ceased to function. The terms of officials elected in 2008 had expired and they were frustrated that meetings of party organs and a convention had not been held or even planned. Local party officials in Upper Nile and Jonglei said there had been no progress in renaming the party and national army, separating them, and agreeing on a genuine national flag, rather than simply adopting the SPLA flag. Others contended that these issues should not be taken up at this time and the Melut County Commissioner said that the SPLM and SPLA are 'brothers and if one is killed the other will die'. The SPLM in Upper Nile was further afflicted by a power struggle between Dok Jok Dok, the party chairman, and John Kor Dieu, the secretary-general with Governor Simon Kun, whom they accused of corruption and mismanagement. There was also a conflict between the party leadership and many officials of the counties who wanted to move quickly to a state convention, considered the present party leadership as care-takers, and made clear their lack of confidence in them.

As was the case in Juba, one regularly heard complaints that party officials were devoting their energies to self-aggrandizement and not spending sufficient time with party affairs, despite the fact that the county chairpersons and secretaries are paid positions. These officials may have been following the practice of former Secretary-General Pagan Amum, who was widely accused of failing the party because of his pursuit of private interests, or Riek who told me that party officials should only devote half the day to private business and the other half to party business, presumably because that is what he did.

Opposition parties existed in the state capitals, but beyond them even SPLM officials admitted that these parties were not free to operate, and their supporters might be arrested by the SPLA should they meet with researchers. Indeed, even though the SPLM-Democratic Change party of Dr Lam Akol served as the official parliamentary opposition and people in Upper Nile heard on the media that Salva accepted its right to freely participate in political activities, in practice it was acknowledged that this was not the case.

In response to the growing dissent in the party Salva repeatedly urged Riek and his supporters to establish their own party. As was evident in the 2010 elections, though, only parties with money and an army behind them have the capacity to successfully run and there is little reason to think that any election in the near future would be any different. Indeed, the few opposition parties that won seats typically went into the government, lost their identity, and dispensed with their programmes so they could share in the benefits of the state and ensure their security. Moreover, under the one-party SPLM state bequeathed by the peace process, elections were a mere formality to gain international legitimacy while the real contest took place within the SPLM organs. Crucially the chairman of the party becomes the de facto president of the country after show elections. To be outside the SPLM was thus to be in the political wilderness.

Unlike Riek's first attempt to take power in 1991, which led to a party schism and the loss of many lives, this time he played by the rules, bided his time, and nominally supported the president. With Salva and Riek held to be the sole credible candidates for the 2015 elections, they began assuming different positions on the issues of the day. While the Dinka Salva distanced himself from the conflict over the border territory of Abyei, Riek began supporting the Ngok Dinka of the territory who demanded a referendum to decide whether they would be affiliated with Sudan or South Sudan, as stipulated in the CPA. While Salva tried to isolate and marginalize the Garang supporters, Riek courted them and, although only a short time before they had reviled Riek, they began to view him as the best means to challenge Salva. Such an association could only be tactical, based on the premise that the 'enemy of my enemy is my friend'.

Peaceful competition could not last long in a militarist party like the SPLM, however, and the problem came to a head in late 2012 when party leaders pressed Riek to decide whether he would contest the presidency in 2015. Riek's response was to ask the president whether he would run and after initially suggesting he would not, Salva referred them to his advisor on decentralization, Tor Deng, who said that the president would stay in office until 2020. Riek then announced that he would run for the SPLM presidential nomination because in his view Salva had failed as a leader. He went on to issue a statement criticizing the performance of the government.

Against that background Salva appointed a committee to investigate the matter, which ascertained that Riek intended to run against Salva in the next convention for the party leadership. However, its members also accepted his criticisms of the president, much to Salva's shock. These criticisms took the form of a seven-point statement which included corruption, institutionalized tribalism, rampant insecurity, lack of development despite oil revenues, poor international relations, loss of vision, and instituting dictatorship by concentrating power in the hands of the President.[19] As well as Pagan, James Wani Igga indicated his interest in running for president, although James made clear that his candidacy depended on Salva not running. Efforts were made at reconciliation, but they broke down.

Added to Salva's concerns that a Riek-led opposition to his presidency was developing, was the growing upset nationally at the poor performance of the government as conveyed in a survey carried out by the SPLM in 2013. Meanwhile, a senior SPLM official, Deng Alor, attempted to overcome the differences between the two main contesting factions. As a result, in May–June Deng reported to Thabo Mbeki, Chair of the African Union High-Level Panel on Sudan, that his efforts had failed and urged the Panel to intervene.[20] Deng and unnamed generals in the SPLA reported that the failure to overcome these problems could lead to civil war. Despite Mbeki's intervention and similar efforts by the Church and a handful of senior SPLA military officers there was no break-through – this despite the fact that there was little ideologically that divided the belligerents.

To add to Salva's concerns, in early June 2013 Bashir threatened to close the oil pipeline because of Juba's continuing support for rebels in Sudan. The pipeline had only been re-opened in April after the SPLM government had shut it down for almost a year – thus depriving itself of 95 per cent of the country's revenue – to extract a better deal on transit costs to the Red Sea, an action described by one critic as setting off 'an economic doomsday machine'.[21] While the South Sudanese cabinet were the first to try to stop oil production to achieve financial and political objectives, they belatedly realized that it was a double-edged sword. After almost bringing about the collapse of the country, Salva went into panic mode and to emphasize Juba's commitment to stop supporting the northern rebels dispatched Riek to Khartoum, where on 30 June he met Vice President Ali Osman Taha to implement the previously agreed Cooperation Agreement. Tensions quickly eased and Riek told the author that this meeting was critical to the subsequent improving relations between the two countries.

But stable relations with Khartoum could not be sustained with a cohort of Garangists committed to New Sudan in the South Sudanese government and security services that continued to support their SPLM allies in Sudan. Together with Salva's desire to be rid of Riek and shift the blame from himself for the failures of his government, the pieces were in place for a major shake-up. On 23 July 2013 Salva dismissed his entire cabinet of 29 ministers and their deputies along with 17 police brigadiers, Vice President Riek Machar, and removed the governors of Unity, Jonglei, and Lakes states on the spurious grounds of insecurity. SPLM General-Secretary Pagan Amum was suspended and ordered not to speak publicly or leave the country, while James Wani Igga launched an investigation of allegations of corruption in the party under his watch. Meanwhile, two other cabinet ministers – Kosti Manibe and Deng Alor – who had earlier been charged with fraud and suspended pending an investigation were also dismissed.

The biggest victims of the shake-up were the Garangists. Foreign supporters of the SPLM cannot have been happy to see them shunted aside and learn how little popular support they had in the country, while the US government found itself without its main interlocutors. Also surprising was to find the Garangists and Riek in the same camp. The Garangists, however, were only prepared to use Riek to undermine Salva, not to support his leadership ambitions or join him in the subsequent armed rebellion. Indeed, fear of the influence of the Garangists in the US was likely a factor in Salva's decision to remove them from the government.

Immediately after dismissing Riek, Salva left for his heavily defended ranch outside Juba at Luri, where his private militia sometimes conducted training exercises and he would be safe if his opponents rebelled. Although accusing the president of moving towards dictatorship, Riek urged his supporters to accept his dismissal peacefully and understand that it was within the rights of the president. In the event, there was barely a ripple of protest among the Nuer, although whether that was because of Riek's exhortations or because party squabbles were not of major concern is not clear. Indeed, the argument most heard by Nuer for their apparent lack of action was that they were not prepared to fight for Riek to retain his position as vice president when they thought that a Nuer, and not necessarily Riek, should now have his turn as president after the failures of the Dinka government.

Salva's new government was largely made up of unknown political figures and people who were formerly members of the NCP or close to the regime in Khartoum. As one Garangist minister dismissed in the July shuffle said, 'It is one thing to be dismissed, but quite another to be replaced by someone from the NCP!' and he was of the view – shared by the other Garangist ex-ministers – that there was a master plan to oust them and infiltrate NCP operatives and their allies.

The closest to a mastermind of the replacement of the Garangists and Riek with NCP supporters was the powerful Sudanese ambassador, Dr Mutrif Siddig. Mutrif helped reconcile Bashir and Salva, arranged regular visits of Sudanese security officials to Juba, including National Intelligence and Security Service chief, Mohammed Atta, where they provided evidence to Salva that elements within his intelligence services and the SPLA supported northern rebels. Mutrif and the NCP had reached the conclusion that the most effective means to end the security threat posed by the Garangists and their continuing commitment to 'New Sudan' was to have them removed from the government. Mutrif also told me that stability was most likely in South Sudan if the ruler came from the largest tribe, i.e. the Dinka, which also had ties to the military, and thus they supported Salva in the upcoming elections. But stability also involves a government's actions being predictable and issues ranging from cutting off oil, occupation of Heglig, dismissal of state governments, reversal on currency devaluation, and endemic instability, set the country on a downward spiral that did not inspire confidence, long before the outbreak of civil war.

Others who were suspected of being involved in the conspiracy – Bona Malwal, Lam Akol, Telar Deng, Alieu Ayieny Alieu, and Riek Gai – participated in the Kenana Conference in April 2009, which was attended by 65 prominent South Sudanese political leaders who laid the ground for an anti-SPLM – or, given the way events unfolded, an anti-Garangist – alliance that was to be reflected in Salva's new government. Indeed, Telar, Alieu, and Riek Gai were all given senior portfolios in the newly formed government, while Lam Akol joined the government in November. Telar had been dismissed from his position as Deputy Minister in the Government of National Unity because of allegations by the Garangists that he was too close to the NCP. Lam was likewise accused for his performance in the same government as Minister of Foreign Affairs, and there was no doubt as to Riek Gai's links to the NCP since he had been the deputy leader of the national party. Salva's new government also included Abdullah Deng Nhial as Minister of the Environment, who had run as Turabi's Popular Congress Party candidate for the national presidency in the 2010 elections. Understood to be a sop to win support among South Sudan's largely ignored Moslem community Abdullah was only in the government for a few days before he was involved in a punch-up with an MP close to Salva, after which he was dismissed.

Bona, however, never wanted to be in the Juba government, in part because even with Salva as its leader and a composition much more to his liking it was still a government of the SPLM, which he abhorred. But as a leading southern critic of the Garang-led SPLM he played a key role in, if not forming the new government, then convincing Salva of the need for a radical re-ordering of his ministers. Bona has long had close ties with Salva, previously urged Salva to overthrow Garang, and had his own representative in the government, Martin Elia, who was then and at the time of writing the Minister of Cabinet Affairs and leader of the South Sudan Democratic Forum, a party formed by Bona. He is also an intimate of most of Sudan's political elite after living in Khartoum much of his life, was a presidential advisor to Bashir, and a member of the National Commission for his campaign for the presidency in the 2010 elections where he called for a ten-year transitional period in line with NCP policy. In addition, he campaigned against charges laid against Bashir by the International Criminal Court. He urged the south to stop supporting Ngok Dinka aspirations in Abyei and refrain from providing assistance to the SPLA-N and Darfur rebels. Bona abhorred the Garangists and always held that South Sudan's independence, indeed survival, depended on having conciliatory relations with Sudan.

Salva's July appointments are best understood as being due to his desire to dominate the political landscape, respond to criticisms of the poor performance of his government by cleaning house, eliminate potential challengers to his presidency, as well as anyone perceived as being sympathetic to Riek Machar, and improve relations with Khartoum. Salva gave the vice-presidency to James Wani Igga, who was widely viewed as politically weak and not popular in his home area of Equatoria, but would not challenge Salva. The message to the Equatorians was that they, and not the Nuer, were closer to the ruling Dinka and they were also given the key cabinet positions of Finance and Cabinet Affairs. Salva and the Dinka in his government knew they were hated by the Equatorians and feared if the Nuer made common cause with them their days would be numbered. Meanwhile, soon after the dismissals Salva began giving speeches throughout the Dinka heartland of Bahr al Ghazal, claiming he had removed the enemies of South Sudan from the government, particularly Riek, who he reminded his audiences had rebelled against Garang and the SPLM in 1991.[22]

The count-down to the final phase of the leadership crisis began on 15 November 2013 when assuming that any meeting of the Politburo could undermine his position, Salva first postponed it and then announced that all party organs be dissolved except the Secretariat and the Chairmanship. He then called a meeting for 9 December.

On 6 December Riek, together with his Garangist allies and two non-Garangists, the sole Equatorian, Alfred Ladu Gore, and Dr Peter Adwok, held a press conference to condemn the president's actions and refute allegations of their corruption. Riek also criticized the influence of Khartoum in the latest government, a sentiment shared by the Garangists. Again, these critics urged Salva to convene the SPLM Politburo to set the agenda for a meeting of the National Leadership Council and announced they would hold a public rally at Garang's Mausoleum in Juba on the 14th. The campaign for reform and democracy in practical terms meant the displacement of Salva, but since the Garangists were held by South Sudanese to be among the most corrupt members of the government their dismissal was widely approved, and their claims rang false.

Those sentiments were shared in Riek's Nuer camp, who viewed his alliance with the Garangists with considerable discomfort. Equally contradictory was Riek's attempt to portray himself as a reformist while making common cause with the Garangists, who wanted to revert back to the old SPLM and reassert their increasingly challenged dominance in the army. Many of these critics would have preferred Riek to have resigned from the vice-presidency in April 2013 when Salva reduced his powers and go to the people with a genuine programme of change untainted by association with SPLM dinosaurs.

When the Salva-controlled SPLM General Secretariat scheduled the opening of the session of the National Leadership Council it was clear that the two SPLM groups were heading towards a clash. As a result, church leaders and Dinka elders appealed to the two leaders to postpone the rally and NLC meeting and reach agreement on their areas of contention. Riek agreed to postpone the rally, but the NLC meeting went ahead on 14 December with Salva accusing his opponents of challenging his decisions and threatening to take the country 'back to the days of the 1991 split'. Salva's allies defeated the efforts of his opponents to call a meeting of the Politburo and to have voting at the party's convention done by secret ballot instead of a public show of hands, where typically tame SPLM members could be expected to not publicly challenge Salva. Indeed, the resounding defeat of Riek and his allies at this meeting made clear that Salva dominated the party apparatus. In response Riek and his allies announced their boycott of the 15 December session. On the evening of the 15th the civil war began.

Conclusion

That the SPLM government would collapse into war should not have been a surprise to any discerning observer of the party, and indeed was in the first instance a 'consequence of a flawed peace process' that brought the party to power. There was more than enough evidence to conclude that the SPLM was neither up to the tasks of governance – since it had never acquired the relevant skills during its long war against Khartoum – nor that it had ever had the required internal democracy that could hope to resolve the inevitable problems of leadership faced by a movement transitioning from a liberation movement to a governing party. Moreover, the SPLM was always a Dinka-dominated party whose leaders were never prepared to genuinely share power with other communities or parties.

Unlike neighbouring liberation movements such as the National Resistance Movement (NRM) in Uganda, Tigray Peoples Liberation Front (TPLF) in Ethiopia, and Eritrean Peoples Liberation Front (EPLF) in Eritrea, which endeavoured to build links with their local populations, provide services, and win their allegiance, from its outset SPLA leaders and fighters had little sense of identity or empathy for communities other than their own, and even those they sometimes ravaged. In the wake of the signing of the CPA, the Ethiopian ambassador to Sudan told me that 'the SPLA never learned the fundamental rule of a liberation movement – serve the people'. As the recipients of enormous funds and supplies from Ethiopia, the Eastern Bloc, Libya, and other sources, it did not need the support of the South Sudanese in whose name it fought. Without a genuine support base, realistic programme, and commitment to a transformative vision, its actions were informed by militarism.[23] Although Garang voiced the appropriate Marxist rhetoric to keep the support of the SPLA's principal beneficiary, the Ethiopian Derg, it rarely rose above the level of slogans and crude anti-Arabism, and was never able to project a convincing post-war vision.

Under the influence of the international community and the auspices of the peace process, the SPLM accepted a democratic form of government and a liberal constitution under the CPA. But very soon the government assumed an increasingly authoritarian bent and ignored the constitution. Forcing the NCP and SPLM to accept the 2010 elections did not contribute to a fulfilment of the CPA's commitment to democratic transformation. Instead the ruling parties used the elections to assume hegemonic positions in the north and south. SPLM leaders in turn looked to the West and particularly the US, believing that by establishing Western institutions (even if they did not function), South Sudan would overcome its backwardness, achieve development, and assume a Western character. The Western backers of the peace process shared these sentiments. What is surprising is that in designing the governance system of South Sudan, the Troika and IGAD peace-makers learned little from the mistakes of the departing colonial powers a generation previously, namely that Western models of governance have a poor record of success in Africa. This suggests either woeful ignorance or more likely a blind faith in Western superiority and neo-liberal notions of governance and democracy.

Typically, revolutionary parties in Africa attempted to overcome sectional loyalties and tribal-based patrimonialism by fostering a national identity. But the SPLA never had a political party until very late in the day. New Sudan was more of a vision than an ideology – it never captured the minds of southern Sudanese and was jettisoned after Garang's death by leaders whose own loyalties were to their tribes over the nation and self-aggrandizement. Tribalism and patrimonial politics dominated the SPLM and its scope expanded when the party assumed a hegemonic position in the state after the referendum for secession. The regime only survived as a result of international support and even then it lurched from one crisis to the next. When the oil revenues which fed the patronage network dwindled tensions steadily grew, particularly between an insecure President Salva Kiir and his SPLM colleagues led by Riek Machar.

Against that background Salva's circumvention of the constitution and use of tribalism to maintain power cannot be a surprise. To survive politically in South Sudan, one must play the game as it exists, not based on Western precepts and values, and inevitably that meant ignoring the institutions only recently imposed by the peace process. It is easy to under-estimate Salva, who is not an intellectual, has a limited appreciation of the world beyond the region, lacks the easy charm of Riek Machar, and is notoriously indecisive. But in the turbulent politics of the SPLM he is cunning, slow, and careful in his decision-making, and although looked down upon by Riek and Garang's followers, has managed to win a measure of popular support. Crucially, he has survived in the turbulent world of SPLM politics and until the civil war served to unite the Nuer, Salva was more effective than Riek in gaining the support of his tribe.

Meanwhile, Riek alienated many among the Nuer elite who frequently drew attention to his failure to defeat Garang in the wake of the 1991 schism despite the popularity of his appeal for self-determination and democracy, his inability to end Dinka hegemony, his mismanagement of the Khartoum Peace Agreement, and his support for the disastrous decision to shut the oil pipeline to Sudan. Although the appointment of cabinets and other politically prominent positions were made exclusively by Salva and the Garangists without Riek's consultation, he cannot entirely dissociate himself from eight failed years in government. Riek is regularly accused by outsiders of being a tribalist, but what caused the most upset among the Nuer was his unwillingness to give his tribesmen a disproportionate share of state benefits as other South Sudanese leaders do, although this probably had less to do with equity than a desire to win popular support from other tribes. His biggest weakness may have been a naïve belief in Western notions of democracy and governance, albeit supplemented with pursuit of private business interests that few people in South Sudan would consider corruption or a conflict of interest.

In a one-party state – even a ramshackle one like that of South Sudan – any crisis in the ruling party threatens the viability of the state and that is what happened in South Sudan. The SPLM leadership failed over years of armed struggle to provide development, security, or construct a workable alliance with the many other aggrieved groups in Sudan to overthrow a hated regime in Khartoum. The SPLM only came to power through the efforts of the US government and its Western and regional allies, since it never came close to defeating the Sudanese army or later the SSDF. During six years of transitional government and two years of independence the SPLM was the beneficiary of enormous international good will and reaped the rewards of an oil boom, but it continued to fail the people of South Sudan in every sphere of endeavour. Ultimately, money and international support could not overcome the intrinsic weaknesses of the SPLM.

The only thing that held the country together was the provision of minimal services by international NGOs, support provided by foreign professionals to the government bureaucracies, and the fact that the long-suffering South Sudanese had grown accustomed to being pillaged by officials and soldiers – be they from the SPLA or the Sudanese army – and had learned the necessary survival skills. South Sudan's status as a legal entity increasingly depended on international recognition since it failed to meet the basic requirements of a nation-state, such as a monopoly on the use of violence or control over its territory.

2 | THE MISADVENTURES OF
AN AMERICAN MIDWIFE

Introduction

The SPLM claims that the independence of South Sudan was due to its armed struggle against the Sudan government, but the facts suggest that Secretary of State John Kerry was correct in concluding that the United States helped 'midwife the birth of the new nation'. US engagement in Sudan and later South Sudan proceeded from its role as the global hegemon, but was given its ideological underpinning in the post-Cold War era by notions such as the US as the exceptional nation or indispensable state, and the Responsibility to Protect (R2P) doctrine.[1] Influential lobbyists operating within that framework proved remarkably successful in pressing for US engagement in Sudan and South Sudan and providing a narrative that identified good and bad actors.

US leadership in the process to break up Sudan and create South Sudan was also possible because with the end of the Cold War Africans were no longer viewed as subjects in an international contest between the West and the Soviet-led bloc, but as helpless victims in senseless conflicts that could only be resolved by humanitarian-inspired Western interventions. Far from being politically disinterested, though, these engagements have been devoted to deepening Africa's integration into a US-dominated world order. The form of the peace process and the shape of the newly independent South Sudan were the product of neo-liberal ideas about democracy, governance, and the economy which have proven to be completely inappropriate for the country.

Since the onset of the Cold War, Western theorizing and policies have endeavoured to place responsibility for the lack of development on peripheral states and give short-shrift to international factors. This was epitomized by modernization theory which rejected imperialism, the global economy, and the international state system as causes of under-development and insisted that underdevelopment was entirely due to internal factors. Meanwhile, the Cold War victors insisted that the only road to development was that of the West and this involved acceptance of free markets and liberal democracy which were held to be universal values, a position that continued to follow modernization theory. The West's definition of democracy stressed individual human rights, rule of law, free and fair multi-party elections and rejected any notions of economic democracy. Under this rendering private enterprise was held to be the foundation of democracy. The growing inequalities within states and between states were legitimized and held to be a necessary product of development. Socialism, meanwhile, was viewed as antithetical to democracy and associated with a failed Soviet model.

Africa's underdevelopment and uneven development fostered conflicts that in the post-9/11 period were held to be threats to the security of the US. As a result the continent became an increasing focus in the Global War on Terror (GWOT).[2] As well as military engagements and the establishment of military bases, the US has looked to peace processes to ensure its interests are protected. These peace processes are sometimes led by the US or its allies, but more often are pursued through regional development-security organizations that are funded and dominated by the West, such as IGAD, which was the chosen vehicle of the US to pursue peace processes in Sudan and South Sudan.

Instead of serving to realize African solutions to African problems – as is claimed – these institutions deepen the role of the US and the West in the continent and undermine the sovereignty of weak states, and make them dependent on the West, and ensure that other potential powers do not assume a leading position. While the US and its human rights advocates contend that weak or predatory African states produce conditions that necessitate international interventions, it was precisely the failures of US-sponsored peace-making that was a cause of South Sudan's civil war. While international NGOs and humanitarian advocates and lobbyists present themselves as disinterested actors by framing the conflict and identifying the 'good' and 'bad' actors they provide the dominant narrative and in the case of South Sudan both called for and furnished the rationale for US engagement.

US Relations with Sudan: Rise of the National Islamic Front

It was only in the wake of the 9/11 attacks in the US that President George Bush made his now famous statement that countries are either with us or against us, but even before this the US never accepted non-alignment and always insisted on subordination. This proved a perennial source of tension between the US and successive Sudanese governments until 1972 when, in the wake of a failed coup attempt by a section of the Sudan Communist Party, the regime of Jafar Nimeiri broke relations with Moscow and ended the first war in southern Sudan. This opened the door to improved relations, but in 1973 the US Ambassador and the Deputy Chief of Mission were assassinated in Khartoum by members of the Palestinian Black September group. The killers were captured, tried, and sentenced to life imprisonment, but Nimeiri commuted their sentences, thus angering Washington. However, in the mid-1970s he provided almost solitary support in the Arab League to Anwar Sadat after the US-brokered Camp David peace agreement with Israel led to Egypt's expulsion from the organization. Nimeiri also facilitated the transit of Ethiopia's Falasha Jews to Israel,[3] which gained him the censure of the Moslem world, and in 1976 he helped arrange the release of ten Americans held by an Eritrean rebel group. Supporting President Reagan's opposition to Libyan President Muammar el-Qaddafi, Nimeiri permitted the transit of US weapons to the Chadian army of Hissene Habre which was fighting Libya-aligned forces, and allowed the CIA to establish a base in El Fashir in Sudan's western Darfur region.[4]

The coming to power of the Soviet aligned Derg in Ethiopia served to make Sudan a bastion of anti-Communism in the Horn of Africa and the country became the biggest recipient of US economic and military aid in sub-Saharan Africa – $160 million, of which $100 million was for military assistance.[5] Neither the resumption of the southern war as a result of Nimeiri breaking the Addis Ababa Agreement, the increasing dictatorial character of the regime, nor his introduction of *Sharia* law led the US to break relations with the regime. Nimeiri was in Washington on 5 April 1985 appealing for military support when his regime was overthrown by a popular insurrection.

Washington's close relationship with Nimeiri was not appreciated by the in-coming Transitional Military Council, which appealed to

Libya for weapons to fight the growing insurgency in the south and to stop supplying weapons to the SPLA and in return it stopped supporting groups opposed to el-Qaddafi. The election in 1986 of the Umma Party under Sadig Al-Mahdi proved to be another nail in Reagan's proxy war against Libya since the party had close relations with el-Qaddafi, even permitting him to use territory in Darfur to assist rebels opposed to the US-supported Chadian regime of Hissene Habre. The US was also angered at Sadig's non-aligned foreign policy, which included improving relations with the Soviet Union and Ethiopia and downgrading relations with the US and Egypt, as well as his failure to move forward in ending the war in the south, while the US Treasury was upset at his unwillingness to reach an agreement with the IMF. The US suspended concessionary food sales to Khartoum, and as one analyst noted should have been pilloried for 'playing politics with food' in the media, were it more professional.[6]

The US even quietly indicated it would not be opposed to a military coup, based on the assumption that a 'successor regime would steer a more pro-Western course'.[7] This provided a stimulus, but the timing of the NIF coup made clear it proceeded from opposition to the developing peace process. The NIF left the coalition government after the National Assembly endorsed the Koka Dam Agreement between the opposition Democratic Unionist Party and the SPLA as a result of negotiations in Ethiopia, and the Assembly further suspended the Islamic laws as demanded by the SPLA. Four days before Sadig was due to meet with John Garang, Omar al-Bashir carried out a coup.

The US initially pursued a policy of constructive engagement with the in-coming Bashir regime, in part because of assurances from ally Egypt that the new government was not Islamist, but nationalist in character, thus demonstrating the ignorance of that country's officials on matters concerning Sudan. However, it became clear that it was the NIF under the direction of Hassan al-Turabi which had overthrown the democratically elected Sadig government. Still not appreciating the character of the in-coming regime, former President Jimmy Carter attempted to organize a peace process between the new government and the SPLM at a time when the NIF had no interest in peace and its ideologues spoke of plans to take their Islamist programme to the far reaches of Africa and beyond. Soon, however, the NIF began attacking civil society, ending Sudan's system of parliamentary government, supporting Iraq in the 1990–91 Gulf War, developing relations with Iran, and supporting Islamic movements globally. As a result, the new regime found itself in an escalating conflict with the Clinton administration.

Claiming an impending terrorist attack because of anger in Sudan at the US invasion of Iraq, Washington ordered the closure of its embassy in Khartoum in February 1991, an action which angered the evacuated diplomats.[8] Relations with Sudan further deteriorated when the US alleged that the NIF supported groups it deemed to be terrorists and that the regime played a role – albeit never proven – in the 1993 bombing of the New York World Trade Center. The US was further upset at the leading role of Turabi in establishing the Pan-Arab Islamic Conference, which brought together Islamists from around the world. Meanwhile, Khartoum's growing relations with Tehran and its refusal to support the US-led invasion of Iraq not only angered Washington but lost the country important financial support from the Gulf. Although Washington was rife with stories of thousands of Iranian Guards in Sudan training Palestinian, Egyptian, Algerian and other radical Islamist terrorists, the US ambassador to Sudan said, 'the truth was far less alarming'.[9]

These developments led the Clinton administration to declare Sudan a rogue state and sponsor of terrorism on 12 August 1993, although the US ambassador acknowledged that placing the country on the list of state sponsors of terrorism was 'essentially symbolic' and had 'no significant economic impact'.[10] Despite regularly being instructed by Washington to make these allegations to the Sudan government, the US ambassador said that he was never presented with any hard evidence of official Sudanese involvement with terrorists.[11] The US also restricted exports and imports, with the notable exception of Gum Arabic, which the Clinton administration belatedly learned was a critical component in Coca-Cola and other industrial processes, and not readily replaceable. The US justified these actions by claiming that Sudan supported international terrorism, destabilized neighbouring states, abused human rights,[12] and claimed that 'the policies of Sudan constitute an extraordinary and unusual threat to the national security and foreign policy of the United States'.[13] Secretary of State

Madeleine Albright, then US Representative to the UN, called Sudan a 'viper's nest of terrorism'.[14]

National Security Council director for Eastern Africa and advisor to Susan Rice at the Department of State, John Prendergast, admitted that the US government was assisting the Eritrean-based opposition National Democratic Alliance, a coalition of northern Sudanese opposition groups and the SPLA committed to the violent overthrow of the NIF.[15] According to de Waal, the decision of the Clinton administration to support the SPLA amounted to 'a policy of regime change by proxy', with the effect of endorsing Garang's despotism and undermining those within the SPLA who were struggling to reform the movement.[16] Against a background of growing antagonism with Sudan the US provided $20 million in 'non-lethal' military aid to what it considered the 'front line states' of Eritrea, Ethiopia, and Uganda to defend themselves against Sudanese incursions. It was widely speculated at the time, and never denied by the administration, that most of this assistance would go directly to the SPLA.

The campaign against Khartoum went into high gear with widely reported allegations that Khartoum supported a slave-trade of southern Sudanese, a subject designed to gain the attention of Americans sensitive about their own historical involvement with slavery. At the instigation of Representative Donald Payne, an Afro-American Democrat, and Frank Wolf, a conservative evangelical Republican, who were influenced by Ted Dagne, an Ethio-American, head of the Congressional Research Service, and a Garang devotee, the US Senate passed a resolution condemning the 'tens of thousands' sold in Sudan's 'slave trade'.[17] However, it soon came to light that the 'slave trade' was a money-making scam of the SPLA who 'sold' supposed southern slaves to Western Christian agents, notably the Swiss-based Christian Solidarity International (CSI), which in turn raised the finances to free the 'slaves' from gullible supporters, including American school children.[18] An SPLM leader, the late Dr Samson Kwaje, admitted that SPLA commanders were behind the project and that the supposed slaves 'were coached in how to act and stories to tell'.[19] The slave-redemption programme nonetheless proved highly effective in not only bringing to the attention of the public the civil war in Sudan, but in identifying the good and bad parties in the conflict.

Eritrea sent its army deep into Sudan to assist rebel groups to help them gain territory along its border, while Ethiopia trained and worked with the SPLA to jointly capture territories in bordering South Blue Nile state. Uganda assumed a similar role in the south. Eritrea and Ethiopia also sent large mechanized detachments overland through Kenya to Uganda, and together with the Ugandan army captured a wide swath of territory in Equatoria and Bahr al Ghazal before handing it over to the SPLA. Much of this territory served as the heartland of the SPLA's 'liberated territories', although its supporters have been reluctant to acknowledge that these lands were captured by neighbouring states.

After Riek Machar split from Garang in 1991 he increasingly found himself in an alliance with the NIF and the principle outcome was the 1997 Khartoum Peace Agreement, which served to forever tarnish him in the eyes of foreign supporters of Garang and the SPLA. The Khartoum Peace Agreement was never implemented, but the regime was less than enthusiastic about implementing the CPA until pressured by the international community. The US refusal to endorse an agreement which met most of the demands of the SPLA and was more generous than the CPA on issues like the distribution of resource revenues was due to the Clinton administration's commitment to regime change. But overlooked by the Americans, who increasingly linked their interests to Garang and the SPLA, was the fact that throughout much of non-Dinka-inhabited southern Sudan, and even in some Dinka areas, the SPLA was viewed as an 'army of occupation', its leader, John Garang, a dictator, and its programme dictated by the Ethiopian Derg.

Expulsion of Osama bin Laden and Bombing Khartoum

The US went on to be caught short in its handling of Osama bin Laden, who had established a large construction firm in Sudan. When pressed by the US, the NIF forced bin Laden to leave Sudan and take up residence in Afghanistan, where he aligned with the US in their shared objective of bringing down the Soviet-backed regime in Kabul. The Sudan intelligence service repeatedly offered to provide vital information about bin Laden's *al-Qaeda* network and the group involved in the bombing of the US embassies in East Africa in 1998, but these offers were turned down by the Clinton administration at the instigation of National Security Advisor Susan Rice.[20] Mansoor Ijaz, a member of the US Council of Foreign Relations, reported that he opened unofficial channels between President Omar al-Bashir and the regime's intelligence chief, Dr Gutbi Mahdi, and US National Security Advisor, Samuel Berger, and Susan Rice in which Sudan offered to provide information on Hisbollah, Hamas, the World Trade Center bombers, and to arrest and turn over bin Laden to the US, but these efforts came to naught.[21] The hawks in the US government led by Rice were so committed to regime change and supporting the SPLM that they were not prepared to engage with Khartoum, even when US national security interests were threatened.

In August 1998, the US launched a cruise missile attack against the Al-Shifa pharmaceutical plant in Khartoum North, which was justified at the time because Sudan was held to have been involved in the recent bombings of US embassies in Nairobi and Dar Salam, a claim which former Ambassador to Ethiopia, David Shinn, described as a 'mistaken belief'.[22] The *New York Times* noted, 'within days of the attack, some of the administration's explanations for destroying the factory in Sudan proved inaccurate'.[23] When no evidence emerged to prove a Sudanese link to the East African bombings, the US alleged that the Al-Shifa plant was producing chemical weapons and that it possessed soil samples taken outside the plant of Empta, a key ingredient in the deadly VX nerve agent. But that was never proven and the further allegation that the plant was somehow linked to bin Laden also went nowhere. Nonetheless, the US Senate passed a resolution condemning Sudan's 'chemical weapons' factory and then went on to implicate Sudan in the 1993 bombing of New York's World Trade Center, another unproven claim.[24] Baroness Cox from Christian Solidarity International, who had played the lead role in the slave redemption scam, was also quick to claim that Khartoum was producing chemical weapons, but a study by the House of Lords refuted the allegation.[25]

When these allegations did not fly, it was claimed that the Al-Shifa plant was heavily guarded (there was only one night watchman at the time of the bombing and he was killed) and that Iraq was using the plant to develop chemical weapons. None of these allegations have been proven and attempts by the owners of the plant to take the US government to court over the matter in the US were stopped. In recent years, it has been widely acknowledged that the US bombing was based on false intelligence, that the Al-Shifa plant never produced chemical weapons and in fact had a contract with the UN to provide medicines. I was in Khartoum at the time of the Al-Shifa bombing and opponents of the regime were mystified by the US attack on a plant which they all said produced anti-malarial and other drugs.

Realizing that the Clinton administration had just handed them a golden opportunity, the NIF filled the streets of central Khartoum with demonstrators carrying placards claiming that the US action was designed to divert attention from the negative press Clinton was receiving at the time over his affair with Monica Lewinski. Western journalists suddenly found that long-standing requests for Sudanese visas were granted and they were given widespread access to government officials and to the bombing site. The regime also sent diplomatic teams throughout the Islamic world claiming to be a victim of US aggression and at both the propaganda and financial levels its campaign proved highly successful. In response, the US again moved its diplomatic staff from Khartoum to Nairobi, a city where more than 200 of its embassy personnel had been killed (mostly Kenyan) weeks before in a bombing, an action which one of the American diplomats at the time told me involved 'moving staff from one of the safest cities in Africa [Khartoum] to one of the most dangerous [Nairobi]'. I later witnessed some of the departing US diplomats at Khartoum airport crying because they did not want to leave.

The Clinton administration and the US Congress were not the only government sources of confusion and distortions on Sudan. Created by Congress in 1998 to win the support of Christian fundamentalists, the US Commission on International Religious Freedom named Sudan along with four other countries (China, Iran, Iraq, and Myanmar) as being of 'particular concern'.[26] This list is curiously made up of US enemies, while allies like Saudi Arabia which persecute even Moslems that do not ascribe to its Wahhabi faith were notably absent. Another government agency, the House Republican Task Force on Terrorism and Unconventional Warfare, claimed erroneously that during the Gulf War Iraq had transferred 400 Scud missiles and 1,200 vehicles to Sudan.[27]

SPLA and US Regime Change

On 29 November 1999 President Clinton signed a bill authorizing the US to directly supply the SPLA, thus contravening previous laws which forbade the funding of belligerents in combat and despite widespread allegations of the SPLA's brutality and lack of respect for human rights.[28] The Clinton administration never attempted to present this assistance as humanitarian but made clear that the supplies were meant to further SPLA military operations. This support was channelled through the 'front line states', the NDA, and selected USAID-assisted NGOs like Norwegian People's Aid, which a Norwegian government-appointed commission found was 'closely related to the political and military strategies of the rebel movement'.[29]

Former President Jimmy Carter had just managed to get President Omar al-Bashir and Ugandan President Yoweri Museveni to sign an agreement to stop supporting one another's rebels (the Lord's Resistance Army or LRA on the part of Sudan and the SPLA for Uganda) and that agreement was now in tatters. Carter's response was that assisting the SPLA was a 'tacit demonstration of support for the overthrow of the Khartoum government', which would undermine John Garang's willingness to negotiate because he could look to the neighbouring countries and the US to carry him to power.[30]

The *New York Times* concluded that, 'John Garang's S.P.L.A. has squandered a sympathetic cause ... they have behaved like an occupying army, killing, raping and pillaging'. While Secretary of State, Madeleine Albright described Garang as a 'dynamic leader', the *Times* said he was one of Sudan's 'pre-eminent war criminals'.[31] By the 1990s many human rights organizations were publishing studies that highlighted the role of the SPLA in abusing civilians, ethnic cleansing, mass rape, large-scale thefts, killing of aid workers, diversion and sale of humanitarian supplies, and the killing of prisoners of war.[32] To quote just one such NGO, Human Rights Watch, in a public letter to Albright,

> The SPLA has a history of gross abuses of human rights and has not
> made any effort to establish accountability ... This record makes
> any form of US support – food or otherwise – wholly inappropriate
> and wholly out of step with the values that you have tried to inject
> into US foreign policy ... This makes the provisions of any aid to the
> SPLA wrong, because it would support an abusive force and make
> the United States complicit in those abuses.[33]

'Sudan experts' and the pro-SPLA faction in the Clinton administration, like UN Envoy Susan Rice, John Prendergast in the National

Security Council (during Clinton's second term) and later deputy to Rice, and Ted Dagne, consistently ignored the SPLA's record of abuse. Harder to understand was Prendergast, who had field experience in southern Sudan and recorded at length in his 1997 book, *Crisis Response: Humanitarian Band-Aids in Sudan and Somalia* the same litany of abuses by the SPLA as those reported by the human rights organizations. When he became a member of the Clinton administration, however, he sang the praises of the SPLA and defended the US government providing food for its soldiers. Indeed, in his book Prendergast made a direct comparison of US policy in Nicaragua supporting the Contras and US policy in Sudan.

While the politicos in Washington could safely live with their contradictions, the international NGOs which operated in the movement's liberated territories could not. When in February 2000 the SPLA insisted that aid agencies carrying out programmes in areas under its control sign a memorandum which dictated SPLA control over their activities, aid distribution, employment of nationals, and the imposition of taxes, they refused. What is striking by way of comparison is that during the 1984–85 famine in Ethiopia/Eritrea many of these same agencies had no hesitation about cooperating closely with the TPLF and EPLF, an operation which many observers found remarkably effective.[34] The difference was that the international agencies understood that the TPLF and EPLF needed their civilian population to ensure their own survival and thus could be relied upon to – with some minor diversions to their own forces – efficiently distribute the relief.

That said, the Norwegian People's Aid was not alone, and it is striking how many people working for international NGOs in SPLA-controlled areas assumed anti-Arab and anti-Sudanese prejudices even when they had often never met a Sudanese 'Arab'. Genuine solidarity relations between the aid community and the SPLA were never realized because of the systemic abuse by the SPLA of its own citizens, but a climate of opinion developed among many aid workers that they were collectively involved in a struggle against the Arab regime in Khartoum. The most significant expression of this was Operation Lifeline Sudan (OLS), a large consortium of aid agencies which took form in 1989 and operated under UN auspices flying into SPLA territories from bases in Kenya and northern Sudan which became a crucial mechanism of support for the movement. The OLS practice of providing food to people in SPLA-controlled areas but refusing the same service for SSDF-captured territories because of its links to the Sudanese government is a case in point. Often this meant that a community which abhorred the SPLA nonetheless was forced to put up with it because the people could not long survive having its food source cut off even after local inhabitants had sometimes joined with the SSDF to be rid of the SPLA.

The 'Council' and the SPLA: The Role of US Lobbyists

Operating within an ideological environment which favoured US engagement on either humanitarian or *realpolitik* grounds were the most influential lobbyists, both in establishing a narrative about the southern Sudan conflict and in influencing US policy. Calling themselves 'the Council' and later the 'Friends of South Sudan' they included Brian D'Silva, Roger Winter, John Prendergast, Ted Dagne, and after 2001, Eric Reeves,[35] with Susan Rice playing a supportive role in the wings. The first devotee of John Garang and the SPLA was Brian D'Silva, who became a friend of the subsequent SPLA leader when both were studying for their doctorates at the University of Iowa and later worked with him at the University of Khartoum. Returning to the US in 1980, D'Silva began a long career with the US Department of Agriculture and USAID where he pressed the interests of his friend and the SPLA.

He was later joined at USAID by Roger Winter, who had visited Sudan in 1981 with an NGO, the US Committee for Refugees, and came back to the US a devotee of the SPLA cause. Winter became assistant administrator of USAID where he had only two concerns: advancing the interests of the Rwandan Patriotic Front of Paul Kagame and the SPLA of John Garang. Winter and D'Silva used their positions in government to organize trips for State Department officials to the war-affected areas of southern Sudan and later Darfur, but never to northern Sudan. In Congressional testimony in 2009 Winter claimed, 'the people of the SPLM are democrats. They respect the kind of approach to governance that is taken in the United States of America'.[36]

With the end of the Clinton administration Prendergast became the International Crisis Group (ICG) Africa Program Co-Director, and authored *God, Oil and Country: Changing the Logic of War in Sudan*, which complained about 'institutionalized slavery' in Sudan. After leaving ICG he established the Enough Project with Roger Winter and Gayle Smith, another SPLA sympathizer and future USAID director. Understood by the media to be a human rights or anti-genocide organization, the Enough Project expressed the same politically partisan positions as the Friends, including a call three weeks before South Sudan's independence for the US government to provide the SPLA with air defence systems to protect the country from Sudan subversion.[37]

Meanwhile, Prendergast became 'a media phenomenon, an activist whose specialty is recruiting celebrity-cum-activists',[38] including Angelina Jolie and especially George Clooney, with whom he has regularly appeared as an expert witness before Congressional hearings on the southern Sudan conflict.[39] Together the two formed the Satellite Sentinel Project on 29 December 2010, a partnership between the Enough Project and DigitalGlobe 'to detect, deter and document war crimes and crimes against humanity'.[40] It in turn was largely funded by the Not On Our Watch Organization, made up of Hollywood celebrities and human rights activists. In 2015 the Sentinel Project was folded into The Sentry, which is part of the Enough Project and in turn part of the Center for American Progress, which has the task of dismantling the financing of Africa's conflicts and whose membership again included Clooney and Prendergast. It is financed by a number of organizations, including Not On Our Watch and the Open Society Foundation of George Soros.[41]

Ted Dagne, an Ethio-American, became the director of the Congressional Research Service and was later seconded to the House of Representatives Subcommittee on Africa, all the while maintaining a close friendship with Garang. Although the work of these bodies was supposed to be neutral, Dagne has always been openly partisan. The former House Subcommittee Chair, Senator Harry Johnson said, 'Ted was very suspicious of the Sudan government, and so I became very suspicious'.[42] In 1993 Dagne drafted a non-binding congressional resolution that was passed unanimously, endorsing the right of southern Sudanese to self-determination. Dagne repeatedly urged policy-makers to consider regime change, covert action, unilateral military action, and providing air defence systems to the SPLA. With Garang's personal approval, the Council took up the cause of Darfur, where Prendergast was also active. Dagne was the de facto leader of the Council and was known as 'the Emperor'.

Eric Reeves, an English language and literature professor from Smith College, has never been in government, only briefly visited southern Sudan, and never the north, but through his prolific writings has been held – at least by the US Congress which has repeatedly invited him to provide briefings – the foremost authority in the country on Sudan and South Sudan. A recurring theme in Reeves's articles has been the condemnation of the US government for its perceived 'moral equivalency' in sometimes equating the faults of the leaders of South Sudan with those of Sudan. He argues that the former were simply defending their country while the latter should be viewed as criminals. This perspective became so deeply rooted that former US Envoy to Sudan and South Sudan, Princeton Lyman, complained that the US government found it very difficult to achieve a balanced position when dealing with Sudan and South Sudan.[43] This same argument was taken up in the South Sudan war where Reeves condemned any sign of the US Government equating the rebel leader, Dr Riek Machar, who would forever be condemned for his rebellion against Garang in 1991 and alliance with the NIF, with Salva Kiir, as president of South Sudan. Reeves also wrote at great length on Darfur and although his publication of widely inflated mortality rates in the territory were contested in 2006 by the US Government Accountability Office,[44] this failed to put the avid polemicist of the SPLA off his stride.

The work of the 'Council', and later the self-styled 'Friends of South Sudan', was never of a humanitarian nature, but always devoted to the independence of South Sudan and defence of the SPLA and its leader, John Garang. Its members knew little of the internal political dynamics of southern Sudan, had little interest in fact-based analysis, justified the most blatant misrepresentations in support of their principles and commitments, and never acknowledged that their hero was a life-long supporter of Sudan's unity, as well as a mass murderer. The SPLA for them was John Garang and some of those he had raised up (sometimes called the 'sons of Garang' and who dominated the party for many years), such as Pagan Amum, Deng Alor, Oyai Deng, Nihal Deng, Majak D'Agoot, and in later years his secretary, Cirino Hiteng. The Council had almost no association with Salva Kiir, who was number two in the hierarchy but did not have Garang's charm or education and rarely travelled abroad. Hence the shock and confusion among Council members and the US government generally when Garang died in a helicopter crash.

During the Clinton administration, this group led the pack among lobbyists, civil society activists, human rights groups, the Congressional Black Caucus, evangelical Christians, and assorted academics in influencing US foreign policy on Sudan and South Sudan. The Council's infatuation with the SPLA was, however, at odds with the dominant views in the region. Eritrean and Ethiopian government and army officials who had known the SPLA and their leaders closely from years in the field invariably viewed them with contempt for their fighting skills, lack of concern for the welfare of their fellow southern Sudanese, corruption, and failure to develop an effective political programme. The SPLA lobbyists and peace-makers also failed to listen to southern Sudanese who pointed to the deep cleavages within their society, the most violent and contentious being that between the Dinka and the Nuer. Indeed, while most southern Sudanese were opposed to the riverine clique that controlled Sudan, sharing common ground with other Sudanese, what the lobbyists considered a north–south, Arab-African war bore little resemblance to this configuration. Moreover, just as the mainstream SPLM aligned with the 'Arab' dominated NDA, the SSDF aligned with the 'Arab' NCP.

Like the Save Darfur Coalition that Mamdani wrote about in his *Saviors and Survivors* (2009), the Council and many other groups that took up the cause operated from moral principles which they held to be universal. The Save Darfur Coalition, however, never attempted to glorify any of the Darfur rebel groups or their leaders in the way the Council did with Garang. They did, however, degrade Sudanese 'Arabs' and Moslems, and that speaks to the importance of Christian and Jewish groups in the Coalition campaign. While the Save Darfur Coalition was more successful than the Council in influencing American public opinion, the Council had superior links to government, was better placed to directly influence policy, and paved the way for the groups that followed.

The SPLA and subsequently the government of South Sudan viewed many of the groups concerned with South Sudan, and particularly the self-styled Council, as important allies and were treated as heroes. Princeton Lyman wrote that the South Sudanese government repeatedly threatened to activate its American lobby groups when it disliked positions taken by the US administration,[45] which added to the distaste that many diplomats had for them. Supplementing their efforts, the South Sudan government has also used paid lobbyists to improve its image, keep US aid flowing, and stave off US-backed sanctions.[46] To be sure, the Friends of South Sudan were not the only groups involved in popularizing the SPLA. There were groups and individuals sympathetic to the SPLA throughout the West and there are numerous examples of international NGO officials crossing ethical lines in supporting the SPLA, but issues related to Sudan and South Sudan had a special resonance in the UK as the former colonial power.[47]

President Bush and the Evangelical Christians

While the influence of secular liberal interventionists in the US government declined with the election of George Bush, they were replaced by evangelical Christians, who were a significant component of the incoming president's political base. One quarter of Americans claim to be evangelical Christians and in the 1980s and 1990s increasing numbers were working abroad as missionaries and taking up issues like the persecution of Christians in Sudan and allegations of Arab slavery.[48] For them, 'Sudan's civil war was portrayed in simplistic terms as a "biblical conflict" between Arab Moslems of the North and African Christians of the South'.

George Bush would have become familiar with these issues through the Midland Ministerial Alliance, which was based in his hometown of Midland, Texas, and which he regularly attended. Another link to Sudan was through Reverend Franklin Graham, son of Billy Graham, who had given the inaugural address for nine incoming presidents and had a national following and his own NGO operating in Sudan, Samaritan's Purse. A few days before Bush's election Franklin Graham was widely quoted as making one request: 'Governor, if you become president I hope you will put Sudan on your radar'.[49] Soon to become Bush's 'spiritual advisor', Graham was also credited with helping to make the case among politicians and religious Americans for invading Iraq and engaging in a 'crusade' against terrorism.[50] Unlike the pro-SPLA secularists under the Clinton administration who tended to play down the religious element of the Sudanese conflict (although Eric

Reeves often worked with Samaritan's Purse), the evangelicals, and in particular Graham, regularly attacked Islam and in the wake of the 9/11 bombings Graham said, 'The god of Islam is not the same God of the Christian or the Judeo-Christian faith. It is a different god and I believe Islam is a very evil very wicked religion'.[51]

Despite such views, Samaritan's Purse was permitted to operate in government-controlled areas of northern Sudan and Graham frequently met Bashir – presumably because the regime wanted to maintain workable relations with a religious leader who had close contacts with President Bush. Khartoum's assessment was probably correct and in a *New York Times* op-ed Graham argued against the International Criminal Court (ICC) indictment of Bashir because it would threaten the peace process.[52] Graham's conciliatory relationship with Bashir is similar to that of another evangelical, Jimmy Carter, who had a workable relationship with the Islamist president.

The evangelicals' influence increased when they began to collaborate with non-evangelical groups, particularly the American Hebrew Congregations and the Anti-Defamation League, which also called for religious freedom in Sudan.[53] The departure due to illness of the black Moslem leader, Louis Farrakhan, who had defended the Islamic government of Sudan, permitted a rapprochement between African American groups like the National Black Leadership Committee and the National Association for the Advancement of Colored People with the evangelicals. Although divided on their desired US response to Sudan, some secular American NGOs were also brought into the alliance. Prominent NGOs like Care USA, Oxfam America, and Save the Children USA wanted a 'peace-first' policy toward Sudan, but a handful of smaller groups like the US Council of Refugees (headed at one time by Roger Winter) demanded that the US government provide the SPLA with anti-aircraft missiles.[54] The evangelical Christians also made common cause with academics under a loose grouping known as the Freedom House Coalition, which included various Washington think tanks calling for a peace agreement based on the notion of 'one country two systems'.[55]

What brought many of these disparate groups together was outrage at the Sudanese government bombing of UN and aid agency feeding stations in southern Sudan. Bush responded by making peace in Sudan a priority and appointing a former senator and Episcopalian minister,

John Danforth, as his envoy. The fact that this crucial appointment was made five days before 9/11 makes clear the importance of the lobbyists to Bush's Sudan policy. To his credit, Danforth brought the Sudanese Armed Forces (SAF) and the SPLA together and after lecturing them about international law regarding abusing civilians in time of war he called for measures to protect civilians. Together with a ceasefire in the Nuba Mountains, zones of tranquillity, and the establishment of the Civilian Protection Monitoring Team, these initiatives had some positive humanitarian impacts. Significantly, while acknowledging the genuine grievances of southern Sudanese, Danforth rejected secession and held that instead efforts should be made to ensure that the cultural and religious rights of the people be respected.[56]

In the wake of the 9/11 attacks, Washington, however, became increasingly conflicted between the demands of the powerful lobbyists and its security interests regarding the kind of intelligence Khartoum possessed after hosting various Islamist groups for many years. For its part, Khartoum saw in the new circumstances an opportunity to turn the page in relations with Washington, and according to US government sources Sudan provided concrete cooperation against international terrorism. The Bush administration also saw that a conciliatory approach to Khartoum could permit American oil companies to re-enter Sudan after being unceremoniously forced to leave two decades before. However, this put the US in the contradictory position of providing support to the Islamist government at a time when it was leading an international crusade against political Islam and calling for democratic transformation of the states in the Middle East. Improving relations with Khartoum was opposed by the evangelicals and the secular interventionists, and the thaw ended when Sudan's criticisms of American bombing of the Taliban in Afghanistan provided the rationale for keeping Sudan on the US terrorism list. President Bush's 'either you are with the US or with the terrorists' statement made clear that mere opposition to terrorism was not sufficient to be removed from the US terrorism list.

The same logic which encouraged the US to work through local power brokers like the NCP also facilitated relations with the SPLM. Thus, with the advance of the IGAD peace process the International Republican Institute, a non-profit organization that serves as a vehicle for the National Endowment for Democracy and the US Agency for

International Development, which was created by the Ronald Reagan administration in 1983, received US Government funding to train SPLM/A personnel in Nairobi and establish an office in Juba.[57] US involvement in the peace process also opened the door to DynCorp and later Blackwater, major American security companies, to gain contracts in southern and then South Sudan.[58]

The SPLM always relied on support from foreign benefactors, beginning with the Ethiopian Derg and the Eastern Bloc, and with the end of the Cold War it drifted into the embrace of the US. Under John Garang the SPLM had little trouble shifting from espousing state socialism when the Derg was its chief supporter, to claiming that it was fighting against expansionist political Islam when this would be favourably received in the US. And when the American GWOT went into high gear after 9/11 the US government appreciated the value of supporting a dynamic leader like Garang to hedge their bets and provide a check on Khartoum at a time when it was developing closer relations with its intelligence agencies.

On 13 June 2001, the House of Representatives passed the Sudan Peace Act, which was largely a stick with which to beat the Sudan government. The act forbade foreign oil companies with operations in Sudan from selling stock or other securities in the US, opposed loans, credits, and guarantees by international financial institutions to Sudan, denied Sudan access to oil revenues to ensure that the funds were not used for military purposes, downgraded or suspended diplomatic relations, and sought a UN Security Council resolution for an arms embargo on the Sudanese government.[59] This act did not achieve its objectives and much of it was never implemented, but the highhanded attempt to apply its laws to other countries was bitterly resented by the US's Western allies.

Although Congress remained very militant on Sudan, President Bush's Secretary of State, Colin Powell, promised to lift sanctions on Sudan, provide financial assistance, and remove the country from the list of state sponsors of terrorism if the government cooperated in advancing the southern peace process. Whether Khartoum was moved by these statements or proceeded on the basis of its own logic is not known, but in 2002 it signed the Machakos Protocol, a statement of principles upon which the CPA was premised. Despite Khartoum's cooperation in the peace process, though, and its culmination with the signing of the CPA in 2005, Powell's promise was not kept in the face of growing opposition in the US to the war in Darfur by the lobbyists and Congress. In the media, the *New York Times*' Nicholas Kristof kept up a steady drum beat of moral outrage, while the Save Darfur Coalition led the opposition to US government policy and demanded 'boots on the ground' in Darfur. Bush had hoped to reap the political rewards of overseeing the peace process and have Bashir and Garang attend his inauguration, but that plan was aborted and he declared that the government of Sudan was responsible for genocide in Darfur.

These allegations continued into the Obama administration, but Ambassador Shinn said the basis of these charges ended in 2004 and the former Assistant Secretary of State for African Affairs, Jendayi Frazer, said there was no genocide in Darfur when she assumed office in late 2005. This is consistent with the review of various mortality studies analysed by Professor Mahmood Mamdani, who found that Darfur deaths peaked in 2003 and were at less than emergency levels by 2004, even though the Save Darfur Coalition continued to claim high levels of deaths long after 2004.[60] According to Shinn, 'Neither the Bush, nor the Obama, administration was willing to acknowledge this fact in the face of intense pressure to the contrary from some members of Congress and domestic pressure groups such as the Save Darfur Coalition'.[61] In an apparent concession to the Darfur lobbyists, Roger Winter was appointed to the State Department with special responsibility for Sudan in July 2005.[62] The US and the African Union also took the leading role in the Darfur peace process, but the Darfur Peace Agreement signed on 5 May 2006 between the Sudan government and Mini Minawi's faction of the Sudan Liberation Movement (SLM-MM) collapsed and the war, although reduced in intensity, continued to the present.

Although the US made the requisite statements of outrage with the Sudan government, its Sudan presidential envoys, former USAID director Andrew Natsios and Richard Williamson, made clear the Bush administration's priority was with north–south peace and national security. Close relations developed between the Central Intelligence Agency (CIA) and Sudan's Mukhabarat, which detained al-Qaeda suspects for interrogation by US agents, turned over to the FBI evidence, including fake passports, recovered in raids on suspected terrorists' homes, expelled extremists, put them into the hands of Arab intelligence agencies working closely with the CIA, and is credited with foiling attacks against American targets by detaining foreign militants moving through Sudan on their way to join forces with Iraqi insurgents.[63]

At a time when the head of Sudan's Mukhabarat, Major-General Salah Abdallah Gosh, was accused of orchestrating attacks on civilians in Darfur, he was in regular consultation with the CIA. He was even flown to Washington and personally thanked for his assistance in the GWOT. By November 2001 the US had re-established a CIA station in Khartoum and was convinced that Sudan was no longer a state supporter of terrorism. But the negative publicity surrounding the war in Darfur and the activism of the anti-NCP and pro-SPLM lobbies made ending the sanctions politically difficult, and they remained in place until most of them were removed by President Trump in October 2017.

Despite the failure of the US to keep its promises on ending the sanctions, the intelligence cooperation limited pressure over Darfur and, according to Salah Gosh, served to end the threat that the US would bomb the country, which had been a major concern of the NIF after the US sent troops to Somalia. Gosh's public gloating about the relationship with the CIA, however, proved a mistake that US lobby groups used against their government, and Gosh's subsequent attempt to seek medical treatment in the US was denied. However, the security relationship between Khartoum and Washington was unaffected, and direct contacts with the Mukhabarat chief continued outside the US.

Obama, Sudan, and South Sudan

In 2007 and 2008, then Senator Barack Obama, along with his colleagues Joe Biden and Hillary Clinton, harshly criticized George W. Bush's administration for engaging with Khartoum. They advocated a no-fly zone for Darfur and called for using sticks against the government.[64] Susan Rice, who was to become Obama's UN ambassador, and who had served on Clinton's National Security Council during the Rwanda genocide, attacked the Bush administration's Sudan diplomacy and called for military action to stop the Darfur atrocities.[65] Obama also appointed Gayle Smith, a long-time advocate on southern Sudan, to the National Security Council and later as head of USAID. Hillary Clinton as Secretary of State and Joe Biden as Vice President had also been outspoken on southern Sudan and Darfur. But once the Obama administration was in office, positions like the special envoy to Sudan and South Sudan, ambassador to South Sudan, and assistant secretary of state for African affairs, were left vacant for extended periods. Although unwilling to challenge the narrative of the lobbyists after coming to power in January 2009, the administration initially assumed a low-key approach to South Sudan.

However, with pressure mounting, Obama appointed a retired military officer and major contributor to his presidential campaign, General J. Scott Gration, as his special envoy to Sudan and South Sudan. It was not until 19 October, though, that Hillary Clinton, together with Gration and National Security Advisor, Susan Rice, announced Obama's new policy on Sudan. It had three core principles: first, achieving a definitive end to the conflict in Darfur, human rights abuses, and genocide in Darfur; second, implementation of the CPA that resulted in a peaceful Sudan or two separate viable states at peace with one another, and third, ensuring that Sudan did not provide a safe-haven for terrorists. This newly announced policy was held to represent a broad engagement with Sudan, albeit not with Bashir, who was ostracized because of the International Criminal Court (ICC) charges against him. It also reflected a desire by the Obama administration to distance itself from the failed policies of its predecessors and recognition that the level of violence in Darfur had been reduced.

However, the Obama doctrine proved to be a failure: the war in Darfur continues, although at no time has there been evidence of genocide; there has been no sustainable peace between the successor states, neither of which can be considered viable, and there is no evidence that Sudan was a safe-haven for terrorists. Part of the difficulty in developing a coherent policy was because of the internal struggles within the administration between Rice, who advocated a hard line against Khartoum, and Gration, who believed the regime had to be engaged to achieve US objectives in South Sudan and Darfur. Because Gration's approach followed that of Bush, which Obama had attacked during the election campaign, he alienated virtually everyone he worked with, and was fiercely opposed by advocacy groups like the Enough Project, Save Darfur Coalition, and Genocide Intervention Network, who urged Obama to dismiss him for his perceived accommodating approach to the government of Sudan.[66] In the face of this opposition, Gration was appointed ambassador to Kenya, where he received one of the worst internal ratings of any US ambassador in the world and was removed from that position as well.[67]

Obama faced more internal dissent when Susan Rice ran afoul of Kerry and Power, the US Congress, France and Britain, and many international NGOs,[68] for opposing an arms embargo or sanctions against the South Sudanese belligerents. Rice claimed that such measures would undermine the capacity of Salva Kiir's government to defend itself against the forces of Riek Machar, who she considered guilty of war crimes.[69] There were also fears that Russia and China might veto these measures because they wanted African unity, but even when later it appeared they could be brought on board, Rice still objected. It was also suspected that Uganda's Yoweri Museveni would continue to provide weapons to the SPLA irrespective of any UN resolution. As a result, Power's actions on the Security Council were erratic and inconsistent, sometimes appearing to support an embargo and sanctions and then abruptly withdrawing.

Despite divisions among the policy makers, the generally pro-SPLM policy of the previous Clinton and Bush administrations continued under Obama. Although the Child Soldiers Prevention Act of 2008 banned the provision of military assistance to nations that use child soldiers – the SPLA routinely employed child soldiers both before and after South Sudan's independence – in 2012 the White House issued a waiver that ensured the flow of aid. Obama declared the waiver to be in 'the national interest of the United States'.[70] The decision, however, was initiated by Secretary of State Hillary Clinton, even though she had spoken publicly in 2011 against child soldiers in South Sudan.[71] In 2013, only months before the outbreak of war, the White House with a new Secretary of State, John Kerry, supported another presidential waiver.

The 2012 Country Study of South Sudan issued by Clinton's State Department recorded many SPLA abuses that had been widely known since her husband's administration had opted to provide it with support. The study reported politically motivated abductions, government restrictions on the press, speech, assembly and association, harsh prison conditions, inefficient and corrupt judiciary, restrictions and harassment of NGOs, widespread violence against women and girls, discrimination and violence against ethnic minorities and homosexuals, government incitement of tribal violence, and child and forced labour.[72] Likewise, the United Nations reported 159 incidents of recruitment and use affecting 2,596 children in South Sudan, of whom nearly 70 per cent were attributed to the SPLA.[73] Worse, according to the State Department Country Study, 'The government seldom took steps to punish officials who committed abuses and impunity was a major problem'.[74]

Justified by the need to help South Sudan carry out necessary security sector reforms in its transition to a democratic state, the waiver ensured that the US was able to deliver $620 million in military assistance to South Sudan in 2012 and $556 million in 2013.[75] This support, according to the State Department's 2013 Congressional Budget Justification, was designed to promote 'a military that is professionally trained and led, ethically balanced, aware of moral imperatives, and able to contribute positively to national and South–South reconciliation'.[76] That rationale looked decidedly weak in light of the systemic killing of thousands of civilians by units trained by the US military, including the presidential guard.[77]

Although Obama had little to do with the IGAD peace process, he was happy to bask in the attention given to the birth of the world's newest state and in the view of Republicans to take credit for the achievements of the Bush administration. Appreciating that South Sudan's independence was due to US support and that its future security was dependent on maintaining that support, the Salva Kiir-led government went to great lengths to win its approval, including strongly endorsing American policies internationally, supporting economic integration with the US-dominated states of East Africa, and developing relations with Israel. The SPLA, however, had no doubt as to whom it owed a debt and Salva Kiir sent virtually his entire cabinet to Washington to thank out-going President George Bush at a time when he had become a virtual pariah in his own country.

Despite the dependence of the fledgling regime on the US for both its creation and continued existence, Salva became enamoured with his own status, which undermined US relations.[78] Thus, Salva kept Obama waiting on the sidelines of the UN General Assembly for over half an hour for their first meeting in September 2012, and in a later personal phone call denied that South Sudan was providing support for Sudanese rebels even though US intelligence services had evidence that it did. Relations between the two presidents further deteriorated in April 2013 when Salva assured Obama that the SPLA would not attack Heglig, a disputed oil field on the Sudanese border, but then proceeded to do so in coordination with Sudanese rebel forces, thus provoking international outrage.

Despite such treatment and increasing evidence of the failures of the regime, Obama did not change a policy of many years standing in support of the SPLM, and instead issued a presidential order permitting US military exports to South Sudan. Obama neither had the interest, nor probably the capability, to challenge assumptions about Sudan and South Sudan that had become mainstream, particularly when two of the strongest proponents of this thinking, Rice and Power, were leading members of his administration. Susan Rice was the key link between the failed policies of the Clinton administration on Sudan and those of the Obama administration. As one critic noted, 'During both the Clinton and Obama administrations, Susan Rice displayed a remarkable ability to cast the confusion in Sudan in black and white, and to push the United States away from hard choices and toward simple, moralistic policies'.[79] As a result, although the pro-SPLA lobbyists had less influence in the Obama administration, the narrative they had popularized which supported the secession of South Sudan was pursued by Rice and other ideologically driven officials, but not necessarily US diplomats.

Conclusion

Nowhere outside of South Sudan was the country's independence in 2011 more widely welcomed than in Washington, which not only placed great hopes in the new country and its political masters, the SPLM, but also took considerable – and justified – credit for the peace process which produced this result. At a time when the US was in conflict with a host of Moslem countries, Sudan represented a unique success story. The US-dominated peace process not only appeared to end a long-standing humanitarian disaster, but also established a loyal client state in the south that was keen to move from Khartoum's orbit into that of the US friendly states of East Africa. In its desire to win American favour the new government in Juba courted Israel at a time when Tel Aviv was throwing its fleeing citizens into detention camps. It was also claimed that the peace process not only defanged the Islamist government in Khartoum without military engagement by the US but laid the basis for ending numerous conflicts in the north. That kind of success does not come often for a Washington that in recent years has lurched from one foreign policy failure to the next, and there were congratulations all around among the diplomats, politicians, NGOs, and lobby groups who had pushed forward the peace process through to South Sudan's independence.

Alas, it was too good to be true and any close observer of the SPLM during its long years of armed struggle knew that it was incapable of administering its captured territory, much less govern a sovereign state. The glorification of the SPLM and its leader, Dr John Garang and the demonization of the Islamist government of Sudan and President Omar al-Bashir – the dualistic portrayal of good and evil that figures so often in American political life – first came to the fore under the Clinton administration, which supported the SPLM's quest to overthrow the regime. A climate of opinion that viewed the US as the 'exceptional country' with the right and even duty to intervene in Sudan, together with the efforts of powerful individuals that moved freely between government and civil society, made this policy possible. However, despite initial massive support from the Eastern Bloc, later from the US and its regional allies, successive rounds of sanctions against Khartoum, and international efforts to isolate the Islamist regime, the SPLM was unable to overthrow the Islamists. That should have alerted the US government to the fundamental weaknesses of the SPLM, but instead the US supported a peace process which led to the independence of South Sudan.

The US Government is largely responsible for catapulting the SPLM into power even though it controlled less than half of southern Sudan and much of that was captured by neighbouring states, never defeated the Sudan Armed Forces, proved itself unable to administer the territory it controlled during the war, and at the time of independence was still officially committed to a united reformed Sudan. Although there was a wealth of information available to conclude that an SPLM-led South Sudanese government would be a disaster, US policy was not informed by it and instead was pulled along by lobbyists and civil society groups that placed their moral principles above fact-based analysis. As Chester Crocker noted, 'breaking up a country out of sympathy for the oppressed and on the strength of one visionary leader's promise was a dubious choice by southerners and their outside champions'.[80] Those outside champions were convinced that an independent SPLM-led South Sudan would overcome its many obstacles and be a crucial first step in overthrowing the demonized Islamist government in Khartoum. But the NCP held on to power and these conflicts on the periphery continue to rage. More upsetting and surprising to SPLM supporters was that violence between South Sudanese steadily increased with independence.

That the US was still bragging about its foreign policy success only months before the country descended into civil war speaks to policies that went badly off track. That kind of failure is not simply the result of negligence, since the brutality and incompetence of the SPLA were widely known. Support of the SPLA was the counterpart to the demonization of Sudan, which although weak, challenged American interests in the region. In that context and against the background of doctrines like the Responsibility to Protect and the US as the indispensable nation the secular and religious lobby groups had a major influence in propelling a disastrous US policy forward.

The failure of the 'Friends of South Sudan' and the narrative they had popularized became evident even before the outbreak of war in December 2013. Concerned with the near collapse of the government they had done so much to put in power on 24 June 2013 the 'Friends', minus Brian D'Silva, wrote to Salva Kiir as people who had 'committed more than two decades of our lives to the great cause of a just peace for the people of South Sudan [and who had] lobbied government officials, student organizations, media and nongovernmental groups to build a strong constituency for South Sudan in the United States' complaining about the dire situation the country had sunk to.[81] The fact that the 'Friends' felt the need to write such a letter should have served to highlight their failings in making the commitment of two decades, but it did not, and in good part because of the narrative they had helped make mainstream, the US continued to give tacit support to the SPLM government of Salva Kiir and oppose the Riek Machar-led movement.

3 | THE DESCENT INTO CIVIL WAR

Introduction

The Sudan peace process created the illusion that South Sudan's problems were a result of its subjugation by the north and that with secession conflict would end. If the six-year transition and two-and-a-half years of independence did not discredit that notion, then the descent into a brutal war after 15 December 2013 surely did. Instead of reducing conflict, independence served to intensify the country's internal divisions as the SPLM elite competed over control of the state. The divisive war that broke out calls into question the entire Sudan peace process and its principle outcome – the independence of South Sudan.

Although endlessly repeated by political pundits and the basis of the peace process, South Sudan's civil war was not a direct result of a power-struggle by the ruling SPLM elites. Power struggles form part of the background to the breakdown of the state, but the civil war did not begin when Salva dismissed his government, including Vice President Riek Machar, in July 2013. The Nuer did not consider Riek's dismissal a collective assault on the tribe and it was not something for which they were prepared to take up arms. Nor was the immediate cause of the insurgency the announcement by Riek and other SPLM leaders in late 2013 of their desire to displace Salva as president in the scheduled 2015 national election. And if a leadership power struggle was – as is claimed – the cause for war then it begs the question of why until its final phase did the war largely take the form of a tribal conflict between the Dinka and Nuer when Riek was only one of a number of SPLM leaders from different tribes, including Dinka, who voiced their discontent with President Salva and made clear their political ambitions?

Nor in repeated conflicts prior to December 2013 did the Nuer collectively rise up against the government. Although angry at the lack of development, the Unity state governor Taban Deng, and the disarmament of the white army by the SPLA, these were not seen as existential threats to the Nuer tribe as a whole. It was only after the wholesale attack by Dinka elements within Salva's Presidential Guard and his private militia against Nuer civilians in Juba in mid-December 2013 that the tribe collectively, virtually spontaneously, and at least initially without the leadership of Dr Riek Machar and his colleagues, launched their rebellion against the government.

The root cause of the conflict was the granting of independence to South Sudan and the hand-over of state power to the SPLM by IGAD, with the endorsement of the US. This, when the party was unable to gain military control of South Sudan, was incapable of governing its liberated territories, and repeatedly demonstrated its inability to peacefully resolve conflicts within its own ranks. During the war with Khartoum problems of administration and leadership within the SPLA could be justified as being due to a lack of resources and other priorities. But with the advent of supposed peace under the CPA and flush with oil revenues, the SPLM continued its multi-decade pattern of human rights abuses, corruption, militarism, and mal-administration.

Civil War

The AU Commission of Inquiry on South Sudan provided the most thorough examination of how the conflict unfolded and noted there were two competing explanations of what caused the outbreak of violence in the Presidential Guard, which then spread to the community at large. The first explanation held that there was a disagreement on orders for the Nuer component of the Guard to disarm and this caused a fire-fight between the two, although it was never clear why the Nuer were ordered to disarm. The second explanation, as put forward by Salva Kiir, clad in military fatigues, at a press conference on 16 December, was that the violence in the military barracks was due to an attempted 'coup' led by Riek Machar, who he called 'the prophet of doom', a reference to his 1991 rebellion.

This latter position became the government rationale for the subsequent killing of Nuer civilians in Juba who were somehow linked to Riek's coup attempt. It was also endlessly repeated by government ministers loyal to Salva and by those passing as disinterested intellectuals, such as Dr Jok Madut Jok, chairman of the Western-funded South Sudan Sudd Institute think tank. According to Jok, 'Riek Machar is not new to this militaristic avenue to power' and went on to hold troops loyal to Riek responsible for the resulting carnage.[1] Not surprisingly, Ted Dagne concluded of his former boss that, 'President Salva Kiir was elected democratically and he did his best to keep the country united and democratic, despite some setbacks [while] Machar by his own admission is now attempting to overthrow a democratically elected government'.[2] Eight days after the onset of fighting Eric Reeves was quoted in *The Washington Post* as saying, 'It clearly is an attempted coup now'.[3]

In addition, Reeves suspected a 'military intervention' by Khartoum on Riek's behalf 'to seize the most productive oil regions in northern Unity'.[4] A few days later John Prendergast said, 'Given Riek's long history of collaboration with the Khartoum regime, it is reasonable to be alert to the potential for reengagement over oilfield security'.[5] As one wit had it, 'This must be the first time in history that the coup leader carried out his actions in his pyjamas and arranged to have his own house attacked and body-guards killed'. Likewise, the claim that Khartoum was from the outset in league with Riek and had intentions of capturing the oil fields has proved bogus.

Not only did frequently expressed fears that Khartoum would strangle the fledgling state not prove true, but the equally hated Riek was not held responsible by the AU Commission, which concluded, 'the evidence does not point to a coup'.[6] Indeed, the evidence suggests that rather than carrying out a coup, Riek was the target of an assassination attempt by forces loyal to the president and these same forces were responsible for the attack on the Nuer civilian population of Juba. Riek, still living in the government-provided vice presidential mansion, was forced to flee along with his wife, Angelina, and other members of the household late on the evening of 15 December, after it was attacked. Soldiers returned to attack Riek's house on 17 December and, according to Angelina, nine people in the house were killed and her son arrested.[7] Along with Angelina and Taban Deng, Riek headed north to Mangala where he was rescued by Peter Gadet. Gadet said he viewed Riek like other Nuer fleeing Juba in those troubled days and not as the leader of the resistance movement as IGAD would soon announce.[8] Indeed, as the leading public figure in the insurgency against the government, Gadet not unreasonably assumed that he was the closest thing to an overall opposition leader since Riek was not able to command the disparate forces then fighting the government.

A UN human rights investigation found:

[A]s early as 8:00 a.m. [i.e. on the morning of 16 December], SPLA-elements of Dinka origin reportedly began targeting civilians of Nuer origin, who were beaten, arrested, and killed, notably after house-to-house and hotel-to-hotel searches. By the end of the day, about 800 civilians had taken shelter at the UNMISS Tongping compound in Juba. By the next day, that number had swollen to over 10,000 [and even days later] SPLA soldiers and heavily armed civilians were reportedly still conducting house-to-house searches for Nuers, who were also targeted on their way to and from safe havens.[9]

Who were the people carrying out these killings? According to the Minister of Defence, Kuol Manyang Juuk, a shadowy 'group that organized itself as *Rescue the President* (Dut ku bany in Dinka) killed most people here [i.e. in Juba] from 15th to 18th'.[10] Major-General Mac Paul, Chief of Military Intelligence at the time, also said the killers of 16–18 December were mainly from the Rescue the President group. (Mac Paul was dismissed in May 2014 for rejecting the government's allegation that the December 2013 killings were the result of a coup attempt by Riek Machar.) Similar testimony was made by Major-General Pieng Deng, the head of the national police service, who said that the SPLA was disorganized, lacking orders, and thus presumably incapable of organizing the massacre. It also seems unlikely that the then SPLA Chief of Staff and a Nuer, James Hoth Mai, would lead or be involved in the mass killing of fellow Nuer, some of whom were close relations. Pieng attributed the killings to a private militia led by Bol Akot, a retired SPLA Lieutenant-General from Warrap, Salva's home state. James Hoth told the AU Commission that a militia associated with the president carried out the massacre and he has repeatedly insisted that its funding did not come from the SPLA, he had no control over it, or indeed any knowledge of its activities.

James subsequently told the author that although a witness to the killings (a number of Nuer fled to his house for security and some were killed literally on his doorstep) he feared that any action, such as trying to take state power, would be interpreted as a Nuer power grab at the behest of Riek.[11] He also said that a false move by him would put at risk 30,000 Nuer resident in Aweil and other parts of Greater Bahr al Ghazal.

In his separate submission to the AU Commission, Mahmood Mamdani reported that a 'senior intelligence officer' attributed the killings to the Rescue the President group.[12] This officer said that the soldiers had been recruited in Bahr al Ghazal and were led by Major-General Bol Akot, but the organizers of Rescue the President were made up of 17 Dinka elders under the country's former chief justice, Ambrose Riing Thiik, who coordinated closely with President Salva Kiir. This group was known as the Jieng Council of Elders. It was widely reported that Paul Malong Awan, then governor of Northern Bahr al Ghazal and subsequently SPLA chief of staff, served as the coordinator of the militia and according to various witnesses was seen directing the activities of the militia during their assault on Nuer in Juba. Meanwhile, the Minister of the Interior, Aleu Avieny, told the AU Commission that the militia carrying out the attacks on the civilian Nuer was not part of a government apparatus but a 'local initiative' without a budget organized by Paul Malong. Various sources indicate that in the absence of funding from the SPLA, Salva's office provided the budget for this group.

After dismissing his ministers in July 2013 Salva began a speaking tour of Greater Bahr al Ghazal where, according to testimony given to the AU Commission, he said, 'I have now decided to fight my enemies, and my nickname is Tiger'.[13] Salva subsequently acknowledged his role in creating a militia known as *Mathiang Anyoor*, but called it a 'reserve army' rather than a private army and at a public address on 15 February 2014 said that it was recruited in the four Dinka-inhabited states of Greater Bahr al Ghazal.[14] At another event on 24 November 2014 Salva said that because the SPLA refused to feed and train the force the responsibility was assumed by the governors of these four states. Salva also claimed that this force saved Juba from a mutiny: 'Ok, if I didn't bring Mathiang Anyoor from Bahr al Ghazal, would we [i.e. the Dinka] be staying here in Juba now?'[15]

Mathiang Anyoor was originally organized to protect and expand South Sudan's territory along its northern border with Sudan during a period of tense relations with Khartoum. The militia was recruited in two batches in 2012 and another in 2013, and was sent to Pantit Military Training Center in Aweil West County of Northern Bahr al Ghazal state. Estimates of the number of soldiers range from 3,000 to 15,000. Former Deputy Defence Minister Majak D'Agoot told the AU Commission that the force was 15,000 strong, while Presidential Guard Commander Major-General Marial Chanuong confirmed they were trained in Pantit and said they numbered 12,000. Salva acknowledged that 6,000 had been recruited in Bahr al Ghazal to 'diversify' a heavily Nuer SPLA and that rogue elements subsequently gained control of the soldiers.[16] Mamdani attributes the Juba massacre to 320 soldiers drawn from the Mathiang Anyoor as well as some members of other security agencies and civilians who were based at Salva's ranch in Luri just outside Juba.[17] This force was then mobilized as Rescue the President. There is circumstantial evidence that soldiers from this group constructed a profile of where Nuer in the city lived a week before the massacre under the cover of a Juba clean up drive.

Human Rights Watch concluded that Dinka elements from various security forces in Juba coordinated with about 1,000 Dinka cattle-herding youth, organized in part by Northern Bahr al Ghazal Governor Paul Malong, to carry out the killing of Juba's Nuer.[18] According to Human Rights Watch, some Nuer women were killed and a number raped, but most of the victims were Nuer men who were shot or arrested during neighbourhood sweeps that targeted the entire Nuer community. This campaign also involved the destruction of property, theft from Nuer and other ethnic communities, and widespread torture by the security forces. The worst single investigated abuse was of 200–400 Nuer men and boys arrested, hoarded into a room at the Gudele Juba police station, and shot on the evening of 17 December, as confirmed by the AU Commission.

The AU Commission of Inquiry concluded that, 'these crimes [i.e. those against Nuer civilians in Juba] were committed pursuant to or in furtherance of a State policy'. The method under which these crimes were committed proved the 'widespread or systematic nature' of the attacks. The evidence also shows that it was an organized military operation that could not have proved successful without concerted efforts from various actors in the military and government circles. 'Therefore, the element of the existence of a State policy can be deduced therefrom'.[19] Although not highlighted, this was the most significant – indeed explosive – finding of the Commission, even if the notion of state policy is problematic since neither the vice president nor minister of defence were aware of the policy.

That the killings were very likely organized by the Rescue the President group and that this group was organically linked to Salva Kiir seems almost certain in light of the testimony reported to the AU Commission and other sources. The AU Commission, however, chose not to explore links which suggested that Salva was the ring-leader in the mass killings and that Paul Malong was his main agent. Nor did it specifically link the Dinka Jieng Council of Elders to the killings even though the Commission heard testimony that 17 Dinka elders under the country's former chief justice, Ambrose Riing Thiik, coordinated with the president and that he is the head of the powerful Jieng Council.

Despite the AU Commission's finding that the 'ethnicized killings' of Nuer were linked to 'state policy' and that 'crimes against humanity' were committed, it rejected – without any explanation – the widely held Nuer conviction that they were victims of genocide. The failure to address this issue seriously has proven to be a major weakness of the Commission's study and one compounded by the failure of other organizations to pursue this line of inquiry. As a result, there remains a major gap in our understanding of how to characterize the Juba killings and why they were carried out. Ignoring the problem has not made it go away and most Nuer have little doubt that they were victims of a government-orchestrated genocidal attack.

The Commission also failed to consider why large numbers of Nuer civilians were attacked by Salva's militia. Even if it is assumed that militia members believed they were protecting the president from a Riek-led coup it begs the question as to why they systematically killed innocent Nuer civilians or what their leaders hoped would be accomplished by ordering the killings. In the absence of forthright testimonies by those behind the massacre one is reduced to speculating that the conspirators wanted to provoke a tribal war between the Dinka and Nuer in which the Dinka with their larger numbers, control of the state, and foreign friends would win and thus eliminate the Nuer threat. In attacking only the Nuer they were anxious not to bring other tribes, notably Equatorians, into an anti-government alliance. The governor of Central Equatoria, Major-General Clement Wani, together with the governor of Western Equatoria, Joseph Bakosoro, met Salva on 17 December to complain that the killing of Nuer civilians in Juba was continuing despite widespread knowledge that Riek had left the city.[20]

The conspirators almost certainly did not expect the rapid mobilization of the opposition, which might have overthrown the government in the first week of the war were it not for the timely intervention of the Ugandan army. But it is also possible that Salva had gained assurances of support from President Museveni before he unleashed his attack on the Nuer. Initially, the rapid arrival of the Ugandan army in Juba was explained as due to the need to evacuate Ugandan nationals. It was then expanded to include safeguarding strategic infrastructure, and then to directly engaging the rebels on behalf of the government. This expanded mission was sometimes attributed to a mutual defence treaty between Uganda and South Sudan, but no such treaty exists and instead there is only a status of forces agreement between the two countries.

Although the evidence is not there, given the role Museveni has played in supporting US interests in the region and the reluctance of the US to condemn the actions of his army in the Congo and elsewhere it seems highly likely that the US was made aware of, approved, or even encouraged the Ugandan army intervention in South Sudan. As noted earlier, the Salva-led government of late 2013 was made up of many pro-NCP members or officials with close relations to the government in Khartoum and had close intelligence and security cooperation with Sudan. This cannot have failed to alarm President Museveni and his decision to rapidly bring his troops to Juba and other centres was not simply due to the need to protect Ugandan nationals, but to ensure that Khartoum would not be able to use the crisis to further increase its influence over the beleaguered government.

The Commission did not examine this issue, but its failure to follow up on testimonies, draw conclusions, and name the suspected guilty persons is all the more surprising given it found that there could be no reconciliation until 'those with the greatest responsibility for atrocities at the highest level should be brought to account'.[21] That finding in turn must be set against the decision of the Peace and Security Council of the AU to only release the Commission's report late in the day due to enormous pressure, and in doing so to not reveal crucial information on the identity of those accused of the state-orchestrated mass murder.

The United Nations Mission in South Sudan has rightly been applauded for opening the doors of its bases to displaced and fleeing Nuer and later those from other tribes. This undoubtedly saved many lives. However, its role is not without fault. Although the UN Mission has a mandate to use force to 'protect civilians under imminent threat of physical violence' it consistently emphasized its other mandate of assisting state-building, which involved working closely with the government, including the security forces. Indeed, as a spokesperson for the UN Department of Peace-keeping Operations explained, 'The primary responsibility to protect civilians is with the government, and our job is to support the government'.[22] The problem in December 2013 and in numerous examples after was that it was government soldiers who killed, maimed, tortured, and raped its own citizens and as a result of UN policy they were effectively given a free pass.

According to Human Rights Watch, 'the mission [i.e. UNMISS] has showed itself to be unwilling to criticize the government publicly, including when government forces committed serious human rights violations and authorities failed to provide justice for victims. This contributed to a lack of accountability for abusive soldiers and their leaders'.[23] AU Commissioner Mahmood Mamdani made a similar point:

> Were the UN and the special representative of the secretary-general to be applauded for this action [i.e. providing a sanctuary for fleeing citizens], or rather held responsible for not using the troops at their disposal to stop the killing of civilians outside the gate of the UN compound? In other words, was this a latter-day Srebrenica? What if anything had the UN learnt from the Rwanda genocide?[24]

Human Rights Watch also criticized UNMISS for stopping its radio Miraya FM broadcasts on human rights abuses early in the crisis, and the reduction of its news service.

Moreover, despite the enormous resources available to UNMISS in comparison to other organizations in South Sudan, it made no effort to identify who or which group within the SPLA or 'armed civilians' was carrying out the killings or under whose orders they operated. It repeated the allegation of a coup by Dr Riek but made no attempt to determine if the allegation was true. Like many of the analyses of the conflict there was no attempt to come to terms with the cause of the insurgency. Instead, the UN move seamlessly between the killings in Juba and those subsequently carried out by the 'opposition' without any appreciation that the Juba killings were the cause of the second round of killings in the Greater Upper Nile towns of Bor, Bentiu, and Malakal. According to its own mission statement, UNMISS has a 'robust mandate … to monitor, investigate, verify, and report regularly on human rights'. Nonetheless, as Mahmood Mamdani has pointed out, neither UNMISS nor any other organization with the infrastructural capacity to estimate the number of dead has come up with a global estimate.[25]

Hilde Johnson, then Special Representative of UN Secretary-General in South Sudan (SRSG), told the AU Commission regarding the numbers killed that, 'We say thousands, but we do not know. We are deliberately not flagging figures in any of our reports'.[26] In other words, the problem was not one of not knowing the true number killed, but of not wanting to know. This was presumably because of the political implications involved, how it would impact on the peace process, and perhaps also out of fear that such figures would anger the government which was attempting to scale down the numbers killed. This kind of covering up of information has long been characteristic of the paternalistic and elitist approach of the international community to peace-making in Sudan and South Sudan. And along with it goes hypocritical appeals by the internationals for transparency and the end of impunity.

Failures of UNMISS must ultimately be placed with its head, UN Special Representative, Hilde Johnson, for her misplaced priorities. These can be attributed to her long-term support for the SPLM, the South Sudan independence project, and close personal relations with leading SPLM and SPLA figures. Indeed, so close was the relationship between Johnson and leading figures in the SPLM, including Garang and the 'sons of Garang', that the in-coming government lobbied strongly for her appointment to head the UN Mission. Instead of having someone in charge of UNMISS who could call the SPLM government to account, this crucial post was held by a major cheer leader for the SPLM. Johnson left her post shortly after the war broke out and wrote a book on the conflict which absolved herself of responsibility and, following other internationals, held it to be entirely due to the failures of the SPLM leadership. This was a leadership that she had actively supported when they came into power and then helped evade responsibility for mass murder when, as head of UNMISS, she refused to have her officials count the number of victims of the government-orchestrated killings in December 2013.[27]

The South Sudan National Assembly played no role in investigating the revolt in the army barracks or the subsequent large-scale killing of civilians in Juba, and did not make any attempt to stop it, even though some of its own Nuer members and their families were attacked and had to flee to the UNMISS Protection of Civilian (POC) camps. The inadequate excuse given was that the Assembly was pre-occupied with consideration of the budget. The Assembly should have been the core institution in a democratic South Sudan defending the citizens of the country and holding the executive to account, but instead it proved to be subject to the machinations of the presidency rather than exerting control over it. Its performance will forever undermine the legitimacy of this CPA-created institution.

Also notably silent during the outrage in Juba was the Church. This is all the more surprising given the high profile it holds in South Sudan and its efforts to present itself as the conscience of the nation. During the war with Khartoum the New Sudan Council of Churches based in Nairobi played an important role as a critic of human rights abuses of both the government and the SPLA, but that role faded after the 2010 national elections when many religious leaders ran as SPLM candidates and others joined various government bodies. As a result, its officials did not publicly criticize the government nor the president when forces loyal to him carried out mass murder in Juba. Nor did they organize a defence of the unarmed victims. Instead, the Church's role was largely limited to its leaders assuming high positions in a subsequently appointed government reconciliation commission that to date has accomplished little.

The international community repeatedly claims that it wants to end impunity in South Sudan, but the same international community has been involved in what can only be called a cover-up surrounding the killing of the Nuer in Juba in mid-December 2013. The internationals, however, are deluding themselves if they think that ignoring the Juba killings will make them disappear. The Nuer Council of Elders claims that 20,000 Nuer were killed in Juba and is endeavouring to put a name to each of those it said were killed.[28] Whether right or wrong, it is that figure that is widely accepted among the Nuer and given the failure of the international community to come up with a convincing estimate it is not easy to reject.

In 1991 a Riek-led force which included the white Nuer army killed an estimated 3,000 Bor Dinka. Despite the passing of many years and numerous public apologies by Riek the issue continues to weigh heavily on South Sudanese politics. Those killings were carried out in a haphazard manner by a rag-tag army of youths in the context of a war over a long period, while the December 2013 killing of the Nuer was done systematically during a period of ostensible peace as a result of state policy according to the AU Commission and under the collective noses of the international community in the country's capital. The ineffectualness of various components of the international community in addressing this issue in a forthright manner exacerbated the problem, refuting its claim to want to end impunity, and probably figured in the thinking of the people that organized the next round of Nuer killing in Juba in July 2016.

The White Army Insurgency

To the extent that the internationals defend their failure to highlight the Juba killings in the peace process it is by linking these killings and abuses with those later carried out by Nuer forces, especially the white army, and to then issue a blanket condemnation of all ethnic based killings. It was the Juba killings, however, that motivated the Nuer youth of the white army to respond across Greater Upper Nile with revenge attacks against government positions and to free Nuer civilians still under the government. The virtual consensus in the literature on the causes of the South Sudan civil war, as well as by the most authoritative studies – the AU Commission of Inquiry and the separate submission to the Commission by Professor Mahmood Mamdani – is that it was a result of rivalry between the SPLM factions. That was also the conclusion of IGAD and the Troika. Almost alone, the International Crisis Group concluded that 'systematic targeting of Nuer civilians in Juba in the days following 15 December was perhaps the most critical factor in mobilizing Nuer to join Machar's movement'.[29]

IGAD and the Troika also mistakenly determined that Dr Riek Machar was in control of all the forces that began attacking government positions almost immediately after the Juba killings began.

Riek said in testimony to the AU Commission that he was in control of the armed opposition forces, including the white army, from the time he reached Panyagor near Bor on 17 December 2013 after escaping from Juba.[30] Although widely accepted, the claim was patently false and as a result the international community both misunderstood the nature of the insurgency and who was carrying it out.

White army fighters interviewed by the author found the suggestion that any outside group mobilized them to fight when they had a duty to carry out revenge against the killers of their people insulting. In response to claims that the white army was mobilized by Riek a Nuer chief said, 'Anyone who said that is lying' while a young fighter said that Riek could not have organized them because he 'doesn't like to fight, he doesn't like the army'.[31] That conclusion was confirmed by Duir Tut Duir, former SPLM Commissioner for Olang in Upper Nile and later SPLM-IO Commissioner for Sobat, who after three months travelling in IO occupied Upper Nile said neither he nor any other politician had any influence over the white army.[32] A similar view was expressed by John Kong Nyuon, former defence minister, Salva loyalist, a Nuer, and governor of Jonglei state when its capital, Bor, was attacked by the white army. In his testimony to the AU Commission John Kong said, 'The white army are not soldiers, they are people mobilized from their own houses, with their own guns. Riek made a mistake, you cannot mobilize people who are not under the command of anyone because you cannot control them'.[33]

Organization of youth-based groups to defend their communities and property is common throughout South Sudan, but the Nuer white army stands apart from other groups by its autonomy from external military and political forces, lack of a formal hierarchy, and provision of its own leadership. While not overtly political it has repeatedly demonstrated a capacity to fight for broader objectives outside its home area. As a result of the greater authority of the chiefs and limited access to modern weapons the Nuer white army is not found on the west bank of the Nile in Unity state and instead is concentrated in three clans – Jikany, Lou, and Gawar – on the east bank of the Nile in Jonglei and Upper Nile states.

The white army first came to prominence in the Riek Machar-led attack on Garang's home base of Bor in 1991 after he defected from the SPLA. The Bor attack gained the white army an enduring reputation for being ruthless, cattle thieves, murderers, and beyond the control of government. After Riek returned to the SPLA fold in 2002 the various branches of the white army frequently made common cause with the SSDF, the largely Nuer group which continued to fight the SPLA until the signing of the Juba Declaration in 2006. In the march to independence competition intensified between the Nuer and Dinka and took the form of repeated violent – and ultimately inconclusive – attempts by the SPLA to forcefully disarm the various branches of the white army.[34] The animosity, however, did not stop the Nuer from probably voting for Salva Kiir as president in the 2010 national elections, supporting the independence of South Sudan in 2011 under a Dinka-dominated SPLM, or from considerable inter-tribal marriages with the Dinka. And in the period immediately before the civil war the Lou white army made common cause with the Bor Dinka, and reputedly on occasion even with the SPLA, to attack the Murle who stole cattle and abducted children from both tribes.

Like traditional Nuer governance, which Evans Pritchard characterized as almost anarchist with its weak structures and largely powerless chiefs, authority in the white army was also widely diffused. The white army is made up of 'youth' (a term that refers to males between the ages of about 15 and 40) and is organized on a clan and sub-clan basis. However, membership has less to do with age than whether the person can run fast and for long periods, an important requirement when launching attacks. Each clan elects its own leader by consensus and conducts its own operations. Below the clan are the sub-clans, each of which also has its own representatives elected by consensus, who can be removed at any time and do not hold formal ranks. Criteria for leadership include being brave, consistent, a powerful speaker, and given the fractious nature of the youth, having the skills to resolve internal conflicts. Mobilization and support, such as food for the fighters, is organized at the sub-clan level by the community. Further emphasizing the diffuse power of the white army, each sub-clan must agree to military action before the clan as a whole commits to it – that includes collaborative operations with the regular forces of the SPLM-IO.

While the traditional authorities do not exert direct influence over the white army fighters and are not involved in decisions to go to battle or the organization and leadership of the campaigns, when not at war the fighters fall under the authority of the traditional leadership.

Thus, the white army is organically linked to the broader Nuer community. According to numerous reports the outbreak of the civil war served to increase the authority of the traditional leaders and subsequently the civil authorities of the SPLM-IO in their common struggle against the government.

The term 'white army' is simply a means to distinguish it from black or regular forces, in this case those of the SPLM-IO, who the fighters view with disdain, in part because they have little control over their activities and are paid to do what the fighters think they should do out of loyalty, namely defend the Nuer when the tribe is facing an existential threat by a Dinka government. The fighters also contend that the regular forces played a negligible role in the fighting in Eastern Upper Nile and while that appears to be over-stated there is little doubt that the brunt of the initial opposition fighting was carried out by the white army. Only clan leaders have direct contact with the SPLM-IO military leadership. While Riek has no direct control over the white army, he has some influence because the chiefs listen to him, he appoints the senior IO officers with whom the white army clan leaders meet, and in the context of the war, and the attempt by Dinka forces to kill him in December 2013, he became to some extent a symbol of the tribe.

The insurgency against the Salva Kiir government mirrored that of the 1991 attack on Bor in that the fighters were motivated by a desire for revenge against the Dinka for the killing of their compatriots in Juba, to free Nuer still in government-held towns, and to loot the towns, particularly for weapons which were in short supply. The striking difference in the two attacks, however, is that the white army, and indeed almost all Nuer, saw the government attack on the Juba Nuer civilians in December 2013 as a threat to the survival of the tribe as a whole. They were also quick to appreciate that in the resulting war they would have few friends. Although Equatorians might be sympathetic to their plight they would not take up arms unless they were themselves attacked, while the only potential foreign support could come from Khartoum and as experience would prove that assistance was limited and calculated.

The white army has no ideology other than the preservation of the tribe and it had no stated political objectives other than to cause pain to those who had carried out the attack on the Nuer civilians. Nuer civilians had often been killed in intra and inter-tribal conflicts and many youths had been killed by the SPLA in the course of its various disarmament campaigns. These events caused anger and reinforced the view that the SPLA was a Dinka organization designed to advance Dinka interests to the detriment of the country. But they did not serve to mobilize the entire tribe in a war against the government. Nor were the revolts in the wake of the flawed 2010 elections effective in mobilizing large number of Nuer in armed opposition to the government. Indeed, the record of failed Nuer rebellions and the misplaced attempt by a host of would-be saviours of the Nuer to launch a sustained rebellion makes clear that local-level grievances did not prove sufficient to mobilize the tribe in a war against the government.

The mobilization of the tribe to fight the government took place because forces under the command of Salva Kiir carried out an attack on Nuer civilians without distinction of clan for no discernible reason other than Riek was one of a number of SPLM leaders who challenged Salva for the presidency. Attacks within a clan- or sub-clan-constituted security nexus could be responded to at the local level by the aggrieved parties, but the Juba attack was understood to be against the Nuer as a whole, and it was the Nuer collectively that responded violently. The civil war that ensued took the form of that response. The international community then went to great lengths to reduce the conflict to a power-struggle between competing factions of the SPLM which could then be taken up by their cookie-cutter peace process and resolved by power-sharing.

Militarily events unfolded at a bewildering pace after the Juba killings, which were known to South Sudanese within minutes of their occurrence because even common cattle herders can now possess cell phones, while some have the latest smart phones provided by diaspora relatives. Peter Gadet led a mutiny of Nuer SPLA soldiers and together with the Lou white army under clan leader Borduang Lieh from Uror County in Jonglei attacked and captured Bor on 18 December after most of the defending SPLA soldiers fled. An older fighter than most, Borduang had participated in the 1991 Bor attack after the SPLA killed his father and he continued to fight the SPLA in numerous contests down to the Juba massacre. After the capture of Bor these forces, numbering perhaps 25,000, began to march on Juba.

Near hysteria developed in the national capital at the prospect of revenge-seeking Nuer youth murdering and raping the citizenry, and these sentiments quickly infected the international community, including the US, which gave Ugandan President Yoweri Museveni a green light to send his army first to Juba and later to the towns of Greater Upper Nile. In keeping with current fashion, Museveni presented himself as a humanitarian, but as noted above his real concern was that Khartoum, which at the time had the most influence over the Juba government, would take advantage of the situation to exert even more control. The threat posed by the Ugandan army and appeals by Riek Machar, who was under enormous pressure from the international community to stop the Juba attack, appears to have been crucial in the decision by Gadet and the white army to abort the advance. Gadet told the author that Riek promised that stopping the attack would only be temporary until he could better supply the fighters with logistics. Gadet later realized this commitment was a lie and as a result he now thinks he made a major strategic error.[35] While the government forces appeared vastly superior to those of the rebels, poor morale, the element of surprise, the collapse of the SPLA, and the fear engendered by the white army may well have overcome the imbalance.

Riek, though, feared a military victory of Nuer forces over whom he exerted little control almost as much as the government, because he worried the atrocities they might commit in the process of winning that victory – crimes for which he would be held responsible by the international community. After the Ugandan troops arrived the window of opportunity of an early and conclusive opposition military victory over the government faded. It is an open question whether the supposedly humanitarian intervention of the international community saved lives or exacerbated the conflict and cost more deaths in the long run. What is clear is that the Salva government quickly became dependent for its survival on Museveni and the carefully constructed alliance with Khartoum was cast aside.

White army fighters insist they have no fears before going into battle and did not need the kind of morale boosting that other armies, including the regular forces of the SPLM-IO, used. According to one fighter, 'The black army needs such lectures because they are not brave, but we [in the white army] do not fear death and don't need them'.[36] Whether bravado or not, fighters held that if they died in battle neither their families nor friends would mourn them. The latter claim is hard to confirm, but observers of white army fighters in battle were struck by their apparently fearless charges. This is even more surprising because unlike fighters in other parts of Africa white army fighters do not use stimulants before going into battle, although after a town was captured discipline often broke down and drinking was common. In keeping with the traditional values that guided their approach to war white army fighters would neither attack at night nor conduct guerrilla operations because they were considered dishonourable. With only light and traditional weapons white army fighters had no means to overcome artillery, tank and aerial attacks, and simply tried to avoid them.

The primary concern of fighters was with acquiring modern weapons, since in the early period of the war they often went into battle largely dependent on spears and knives. Firing with the few modern weapons in their possession only took place in the final moments of charges on government front lines. The rapidity and ferocity of the charge, which bordered on the suicidal, by large numbers of youth frequently proved sufficient to overcome the regular soldiers of the SPLA. Where the white army advance was detected and the SPLA was able to use artillery or call upon the Ugandan air force, its prospects were much reduced and the attack could rapidly turn into a disorganized and rapid retreat. When successful, the white army fighters set about killing anyone identified as a 'Dinka', a term which meant any male in a government garrison irrespective of his age, tribe, whether in military or civilian attire and not in the UNMISS POC camp and prisoners were not taken. This is freely acknowledged by white army fighters, although they deny – despite evidence to the contrary – that sometimes women and children were beaten, killed, and sexually abused. Freed Nuer Internally Displaced People (IDPs) from the UNMISS Protection of Civilian sites often joined the fighters in looting or abusing the resident civilians who may have previously abused them and forced them to take refuge in the POC sites. All the brutality was justified on the grounds of revenge after the Juba killings.

To be sure, elders and religious leaders like the Nuer prophet Dak Kueth warned fighters against abusing women and children in war zones, condemned those that did, and made the guilty suffer humiliation before their families and communities. In their condemnation of abuses the elders were not liberal humanitarians, but representatives and defenders of the values of their community, and thus they were notably silent about white army killing of men, whether combatants or not, suspected of aligning with the government. Like the Nuer community, the elders were committed to the war against the Dinka, both as revenge for the Juba killings and because, as many said, 'if we lose the war we will be slaves of the Dinka'.

As well as the killings, the capture of a government town was a signal for a breakdown in order and looting which again had the support of the community. This typically went on for two to four days after which, loaded down with stolen goods and having no vision of how to proceed militarily, the white army fighters left. The much smaller contingent of regular SPLM-IO forces was then left in the unenviable position of defending the town against vastly superior SPLA and Ugandan forces. More often than not the vulnerable regular forces also looted and followed the fleeing white army fighters to security in the countryside. This ensured the return of the government and the restocking of the town, which encouraged yet more white army attacks and as a result the government-garrisoned towns of Jonglei and Upper Nile changed hands at a bewildering pace.

The white army typically dominated the campaigns in Jonglei and Upper Nile, with the regular IO forces assuming a supporting role. In Jonglei, the white army worked closely with Peter Gadet's forces to capture Bor and in other operations until he was transferred to his home state of Unity. In Eastern Upper Nile, the white army captured the government-held towns of Mathiang, Jamam, Tangrail, and Maban on their way north to receive weapons and supplies from the IO based along the border of White Nile state in Sudan. The white army then cooperated with the regular IO forces in the capture of Melut.

Despite the ferocity and fearlessness of its charges, it repeatedly failed to capture such centres as Nasir and Ayod, apparently because of the superior defences, which included deep trenches and razor wire. With their light weapons the white army fighters had no effective means to deal with tanks and heavy artillery. Not only did the fighters not know how to use captured tanks, but typically their IO-aligned soldiers also did not have the necessary skills. While a handful of wounded white army fighters were transported to hospitals in neighbouring Ethiopia, most of those injured in battle received little more than first aid treatment and many needlessly died. With experience the SPLA and the Ugandan army became more adept at confronting white army tactics, which never changed from the first attack on Bor in 1991. The psychology of the white army fighters, including their lack of discipline and failure to develop long-term and political objectives, help to understand how they could repeatedly overwhelm technically superior forces in entrenched positions, but then be unable to consolidate their victory, much less administer the captured towns and guarantee the security of the inhabitants.[37]

These failures can ultimately be attributed to weak leadership. White army leaders with their close links to the villages of Nuerland were remarkably effective in quickly mobilizing large number of youth, feeding and equipping them, and getting them to a battlefield which might be a week's walk away. But it was a leadership incapable of building on its military victories or using them to advance its political objectives which – when deconstructed – amounted to ending Salva's presidency, removing Dinka soldiers and administrators from Nuer-inhabited lands, and collectively punishing the Dinka for the Juba killings. The failure of the white army is also a failure of Riek Machar and the SPLM-IO leaders. Dependent on the white army to carry them into the negotiations and present themselves as the primary opposition to the government, Riek and the IO had little influence over the fighters and were anxious to limit their association with the white army and not be tainted with their human rights abuses.

The IO made no effort to politically educate the white army fighters. This is surprising because they are not the ruthless and mindless village idiots they are often portrayed to be. Their campaign against the government had widespread support among the Nuer and when not engaged in combat the fighters were integrated into the local security organs of their villages and the SPLM-IO administration. In recent years, many fighters have gained a formal education because of the vast expansion of Ethiopian schools to which the people of Eastern Upper Nile have had access, the establishment of some schools in their territory since the signing of the CPA, and because white army ranks have been supplemented by defecting Nuer SPLA soldiers, educated refugees from Jonglei and Upper Nile, and members of the diaspora.

The educated and more experienced white army fighters have become increasingly upset at their marginalization in the IGAD peace process and by the Riek Machar-led SPLM-IO, as well as the failures to capitalize on their great sacrifices and the fact that the major towns of their homeland remain occupied by a largely Dinka SPLA.[38]

Conclusion

The SPLA apologists were quick to claim that the cause of the December 2013 violence was an attempted coup by Riek Machar, a favourite target since his rebellion against John Garang in 1991. But no one outside of a small core around President Salva Kiir continues to make that claim. The initial widespread reporting of this false charge, however, coloured the way many would view and frame the conflict, as well as making clear the biases of those 'experts' that the media and the US government looked to for objective analysis.

From the outset, the international community made no distinction between the Dinka killing of Nuer in Juba and the subsequent Nuer killing of Dinka in Greater Upper Nile, condemning all ethnic-based killing. This position could be morally defended from the Western perspective, and even African leaders of IGAD adopted it, but it made no sense to the tradition-minded participants in the war. It is not simply that the internationals were intellectually lazy in not appreciating that the Juba killings were the cause and provided the rationale and justification for the subsequent Nuer retaliation. By ignoring the tribal imperative which held that a crime must either be revenged or reconciliation proceed on the basis that those who carried out the crime acknowledge their guilt and be prepared to atone for it, the internationals ensured that their peace process would not succeed.

The peace-makers also suffered from ethno-centrism: although politically dressed up with moral language the GWOT was not based on a very different logic from the Nuer insurgency, since it too began as largely a war of revenge for the 9/11 attacks on New York and Washington. At the time of the Juba killings the repeatedly heard complaint of Nuer intellectuals was that the West treated them as Africans, different than Europeans. They noted that the West strongly condemned the supposed killing of a hundred demonstrators by the Ukrainian government of President Viktor Yanukovich, following this up with support for a coup which overthrew his elected government and brought to power the pro-NATO and neo-fascist government of Petro Poroshenko. However, when far more innocent people were killed in Juba by a government supported by the West, the US was not prepared to identify the guilty party or impose sanctions, much less endorse its overthrow. Instead, it issued a blanket condemnation of ethnic killings by both sides and continued to give tacit support to the government.

The Nuer intellectuals – like their counterparts in the rest of South Sudan – viewed the United States as a world model, but this lack of concern about the facts surrounding the outbreak of war and the continuing support it provided to a government which carried out a massacre of its own civilians was a shock. What these intellectuals failed to appreciate was that South Sudan had little or no strategic significance to the West, unlike Ukraine which could be used to justify the growing US-led conflict with Russia. Moreover, the Salva-led government came to power because of a US-led peace process, while Riek and the Nuer collectively had long been demonized because they threatened Garang's leadership and were held to be in league with Khartoum.

4 | THE ESTABLISHMENT OF THE SPLM-IO

Introduction

In response to the Juba massacre and the crisis within the SPLA, many Nuer SPLA soldiers went home or to the UNMISS Protection of Civilian camps for security, a handful remained loyal to the government of Salva Kiir, and some joined the white army. Others, though, left the SPLA and despite many obstacles and a lack of logistics were mobilized remarkably quickly. Despite additions and defections, these soldiers formed the core of what became the military wing of the SPLM-IO. What united these forces was a desire for revenge, the overthrow of Salva's Dinka regime, and Nuer solidarity – sentiments similar to those that motivated the white army fighters. In the initial phase of the war they were led by SSDF generals who made a tactical alliance with Riek Machar, but never trusted him or the SPLM party he espoused.

The politicians that formed the core of the SPLM-IO came together more slowly than the military. Some were Nuer leaders of their community that managed to flee the government's pogrom, some were from the diaspora, many were opportunists looking to Riek Machar to take them to power, and others were selected by Riek because they represented important ethnic interests and were needed to construct a pan-South Sudanese party. None represented traditional society. Although some were accomplished leaders, with very few exceptions they assumed the role of agents of Riek, often going against their own community to support him and keep their positions. Ideological issues were never a concern for the leadership and the IO's political programme rarely went beyond clichés and appeals for reforms.

While an outwardly sophisticated party structure was created, like Garang's SPLM, in practice decision-making was made by the leader, sometimes in consultation with selected advisors, particularly

Taban Deng, and outside the formal institutions. But given the democratic character of Nuer society much effort and many resources were directed to mass consultations with party supporters, which was in sharp contrast with the government. Ultimately, however, the views of IO supporters on key issues like the commitment to the peace process versus war, the parallel negotiations to achieve SPLM unity, and the considerable power assigned to Taban were ignored.

Although Riek contended that he was leader of the insurgency, in fact it was already under way and he initially had no control over it. However, IGAD and the Troika needed a leader of the opposition to pursue their peace process and never seriously concerned themselves with whether he really controlled the forces he claimed, nor if his views and those of Taban Deng Gai reflected those of the people carrying out the insurgency. As a result, Dr Lam Akol's statement to the AU Commission that Riek 'took over a rebellion that was not his' is an accurate assessment of the state of affairs.[1]

Riek Machar Takes Control of the Insurgency

At the time of the Juba massacre some of the future SPLM-IO commanders defected from the SPLA and others had been forcefully retired, demoted, or recently jailed. It would quickly become clear that the party he claimed leadership of was bitterly divided over the goals of the insurgency, how to conduct the war, and the best means to advance the peace process. Failing to understand the character of the insurgency, though, and devoted to elite accommodation, the IGAD and Troika peace-makers were initially largely unaware of the disparate interests in the SPLM-IO.

Major-General Simon Gatwech, who would become the SPLM-IO chief of staff, had been imprisoned for eight months because of doubts about his loyalty. Released four months before the Juba massacre took place he was staying in his house 200 metres from the National Security Agency headquarters, spending his time meeting guests and studying English. Immediately before the Juba massacre Simon was being watched closely, expected war, and told me that although not an educated man he had the ability to mobilize, feed, and lead a division in the bush.[2] In the event, he was to do just that in his Lou Nuer homeland in Akobo, Jonglei state.

Meanwhile, Major-General Gabriel Tang-Ginya and Brigadier-General Thomas Mabor had only recently been released from two years in prison for allegedly opposing the government. They were being re-integrated into the SPLA, and after being given their ranks were fêted by the government which clearly – and mistakenly – concluded they had been neutralized. When the war broke out they were dispatched to the curiously named World Focus International Hotel and effectively placed under arrest. But they managed to flee Juba and return to their homeland in Fanjak in northern Jonglei, there beginning to mobilize opposition to the government.

Forcibly retired from the SPLA and bitter as a result, Major-General Chayot Nyang (known by his field name 'Saddam') had spent the previous year doing little in Malakal when the fighting broke out, but he too quickly returned to his home in Longochuk Upper Nile, where he began mobilizing his forces. At the time of the Juba massacre Major-General Gathoth Gatkouth was serving as an advisor to the government of Upper Nile after he had been removed from his position as a commissioner in his home area of Nasir due to being implicated in an earlier white army attack on the SPLA. He too deserted his position, went to the bush, and began mobilizing opposition to the government among his Jikany clan. Another former SSDF leader from Upper Nile, Chuol Gakah, had his house on the outskirts of Juba (where I had three interviews with him over the previous two months before the killings) flattened by a tank, but he escaped the pogrom and walked hundreds of kilometres to join the rebels. At the same location, I met Lieutenant-Colonel James Lounge, former aide to Paulino Matiep, grandson of the Nuer prophet, Ngundeng, who likewise anticipated war and would join (and subsequently leave) the SPLM-IO.

Despite his earlier rebellion against the government another former SSDF senior officer, Major-General Peter Gadet, was commander of SPLA Division 8. When the Juba massacre took place he left Juba and brought most of his forces in Panpandier, 30 kilometres from the Jonglei state capital of Bor, over to the rebels.

The only initial senior Nuer IO commander that did not come from an SSDF background was Major-General James Koang, a Jikany Nuer from Nasir, a respected career officer in the SPLA, and the commander of Division 4 in Unity state. Two non-Nuer generals joined the rebels: Major-General Dau Aturjong, a Dinka and former SPLA deputy chief of staff from Northern Bahr al Ghazal who felt robbed of the governorship in the 2010 elections by Paul Malong, and retired Lieutenant-General Alfred Ladu Gore, a Bari from Juba, who was fraudulently defeated as a candidate for governor in Central Equatoria in the 2010 elections. After initially failing to mobilize his fellow Bari in Juba, Alfred was largely carried by Nuer soldiers to safety in Unity state, from where he went on to Addis Ababa.

While the Nuer white army and the forces of Peter Gadet began their march on Juba, the main towns of Greater Upper Nile were repeatedly attacked by white army forces or, in the case of Bentiu, by the Nuer forces of James Koang. After this, Koang declared his loyalty to Riek Machar even though no formal opposition movement had yet taken form. Conditions remained highly unstable for the next four months, but with the assistance of the Ugandan army and air force by late April 2014 all the major towns were securely in government hands, while the countryside was largely under the Nuer forces of what was now the SPLM-IO.

Making the situation worse for the rebel forces, the large Bul Nur clan of Unity state joined the government forces, marching south and west in a campaign characterized by massive civilian displacement, widespread atrocities, and theft of cattle, all of which created famine conditions. Most of the victims of the Bul Nuer attacks were Nuer from other clans, including those of Riek and Taban Deng, whose defection to the rebels fed into the long-running hatred of many in the state for him. By the end of May, government forces, together with those of Sudan's Justice and Equality Movement, which the government of South Sudan hosted, controlled most of the northern parts of the state, which served to disrupt IO supplies from Khartoum. In this offensive, the SPLA also gained control of the Unity state oil fields, even if they were not able to bring them into production. JEM's involvement in South Sudan's conflict upset Khartoum, but that did not serve to increase its paltry support for the SPLM-IO. The two countries were in a stalemate situation, able to support proxy wars in one another's territory,[3] but not able (and in the case of Khartoum not willing) to decisively change the status quo.

The tribal configuration was equally complicated in Upper Nile. In the white army attacks on Malakal and its surrounding area in December 2013 and February 2014, large numbers of Shilluk civilians were killed, driving many youths into the militia of Major-General Johnson Olony, himself a Shilluk. With Olony fighting the white army and IO forces an alliance with the government was cemented. He became the beneficiary of an enormous amount of weapons and was crucial to the defence of Malakal. The alliance, however, was never stable because, with the assistance of the SPLA, Dinka in the state had displaced many Shilluk to the east bank of the Nile and the two tribes were in dispute over possession of the state capital of Malakal. Tensions developed after one of his senior commanders was killed by the SPLA and Johnson took his forces and military supplies into an alliance with the IO.

Johnson's militia and the IO forces captured Malakal, bringing large amounts of military hardware and munitions as well as Chinese-made gunboats over to the opposition. With them they were able to occupy a string of towns north along the Nile to Melut, where they linked up with the white army. What could have been a turning point in the war if the IO forces and those of Johnson and the white army had captured the oil fields of Paloich, only a day's march from Melut, instead petered out and Melut and then Malakal again fell to government forces. The SPLM-IO leadership attributed this reversal to being out-numbered and out-gunned by government forces acting in concert with the Sudanese rebel groups. Many IO and white army fighters interviewed by the author, however, were convinced that their failure to capture the oil fields was not simply due to the forces they faced, but because Riek and Taban had bent to American and Chinese pressures not to attack.[4] Supporting that hypothesis, within weeks of the failed campaign a previously destitute IO suddenly appeared to have finances that were widely assumed to come from Chinese sources. Thus, for the second time – the march on Juba was the first – Riek may have stopped his own forces from achieving the military ends to which he was supposedly committed.

SPLM-IO forces began carrying out guerrilla operations in selected parts of Aweil West and North near Sudan's border state of East Darfur, and in Western Bahr al Ghazal IO forces began guerrilla operations in Wau but were unable to hold territory. Western Equatoria was a regional centre of resistance to the government, with IO forces operating around Mundri, which they briefly controlled and in the Nimule area on the Ugandan border, home to their leader, Major-General Martin Kenyi. Like the Nuer components of the IO they suffered from a lack of weapons and munitions.

Just as Riek and the interim political leadership he appointed had only marginal control over the revolt of the white army, initially he had little control over the rebelling military commanders, who came from radically different origins than Riek. Most of these generals came from traditional backgrounds, were first members of Anyanya 2 and then the SSDF and were not loyal to Riek and even less to the SPLM, only to the Nuer cause. They had few political skills and largely derived their legitimacy from the capacity to mobilize their communities to fight.

The SSDF generals readily fit the definition of warlords, operating in a pre-capitalist environment where the state was either weak or even absent. Initially, the generals made a mutually beneficial alliance with Khartoum and then attempted to negotiate their way into the SPLA through the Juba Declaration of January 2006. But the breakdown of that agreement left the generals increasingly marginalized, angry with the Dinka rulers, and anticipating a return to war with the SPLA even before the Juba massacre. Although retaining a corporate identity, the SSDF generals responded individually and largely spontaneously in revolting against the Salva government. The generals had no ideological convictions to speak of and never anticipated a protracted guerrilla war as part of a liberation struggle, as was the case in neighbouring Ethiopia, Eritrea, and Uganda. With each general having many wives and dozens of children, they were also constantly in need of money and this as much as strategic concerns often pre-occupied them.

While often tactically highly skilled, the generals lacked a strategic vision; nor did they have a taste for the cut and thrust of politics and did not make alliances in the IO with similar minded groups, which could have strengthened their influence. The parochial character of the early formal IO army and the white army and the lack of a coherent vision from Riek made it difficult to formulate, much less implement, long-term military goals. For example, after the SPLA captured the IO centre of Nasir in Eastern Upper Nile, the large number of displaced people exerted pressure for repeated and failed attempts to recapture the town, instead of focusing on more important strategic targets such as Juba and the oil fields.

The former SSDF generals grudgingly accepted Riek as their leader despite distrusting him, and their initial operations were conducted without his knowledge. They did, however, have to conform to the imperative of the Nuer who demanded unity of their leaders. The generals thought that although Riek was formally the leader of the opposition, their field level control of the armed forces meant they could organize and conduct the insurgency without much interference by him and Taban. They were mistaken: in a context where the Nuer concluded they faced an existential threat as a tribe they demanded that disputes between the generals and Riek be peacefully and internally resolved, and that there be no public challenges to the tribal unity they felt was key to their survival. Furthermore, in the early days of the war the generals acquired a plentiful supply of weapons and crucially munitions by repeatedly capturing government garrisons. With the SPLA and Ugandan army consolidation of power in the main towns of Greater Upper Nile, they became increasingly dependent on the political leadership for munitions. This served to strengthen Riek and Taban.

Riek was equally distrustful of the generals and considered them to be a constant threat to his authority, the more so because their thinking, values, and Nuer parochialism was much closer to the tribe than was Riek. While Riek used tribal values and symbols, particularly his claim to be the leader of South Sudan anticipated by the great Nuer prophet Ngundeng Bong, he personally had little taste for them. He was more comfortable in a Western world, was married to a white woman, and was frequently criticized by his tribesmen for his lack of embrace of Nuer culture. He was in these respects very different from Salva, who is neither educated nor worldly. However, too much emphasis on *Nuerism* would threaten to undermine Riek's efforts to broaden his appeal to other tribes.

Riek's background in the SPLA and under John Garang held that military and political power were to be centralized in one person who had virtually uncontested authority. This was something that would never be accepted by the former SSDF generals. The IO was constructed on a fragile alliance between various Nuer groups and the primary internal contradiction during this period was between a small politically sophisticated political component led by former SPLM officials and a military component largely made up of former SSDF generals.

Attempting to increase his authority over the independent-minded generals, Riek refused to establish a formal institutional military hierarchy and instead served as both de facto minister of defence and chief of defence staff of the IO. However, there were limits to how far Riek could go in humiliating the generals because, unlike a conventional army, the former SSDF generals had their own constituencies that could potentially be mobilized to undermine his authority. For Riek, the sooner the former SSDF generals could be dispensed with, marginalized or tamed the better, because almost as much as the government they were a major threat to his authority. Following Garang, Riek and Taban had learned that the best means to contain and control ambitious generals was to manipulate their access to logistics, but this made them increasingly angry. The generals appreciated that Riek only wanted to use them to achieve his political ambitions but failed to understand that in the right circumstances he was prepared to expel them.

Despite his long years in the military Riek is not a man of war, never looked to war on its own to carry him to power or anticipated a lengthy war, and, as his actions would subsequently demonstrate, looked to the international community to end the conflict peacefully. As a means to both limit the war and exert the maximum control over his generals Riek also wanted to keep the war contained to Greater Upper Nile, but that meant his own Nuer people bore the major cost of the war in terms of lost lives and livelihoods. Given the extensive role of the international community in the internal affairs of South Sudan, Riek correctly anticipated a quick move to a peace process that he hoped would end the war and bring him back to power, ideally carrying the mantle of a democratic reformer. This would also rid him of his dependence on the generals. In the event, he was able to displace some of the generals and tame those remaining, but the road back to power has proven much more challenging than he anticipated.

Rise of the SPLM-IO Political Leadership

Riek inherited his generals, but he also faced problems with the IO political leaders and they were largely of his own making since he appointed them. While the military leadership of the IO and the white army almost spontaneously mobilized their communities and fought the government in multiple locations, those that became the IO political leadership took longer to organize. Indeed, the route of most of them to the IO political leadership was as displaced persons. After being saved from almost certain death by Peter Gadet, Riek, Angelina, and Taban Deng were escorted across South Sudan, and while Taban went to Addis Ababa and became the IO's chief negotiator in the IGAD negotiations, Riek and Angelina attempted to organize the IO forces from the Nuer centre of Nasir in Eastern Upper Nile.

Meanwhile, another group of the SPLM leadership opposed to the Salva presidency, led by the party's Secretary-General Pagan Amum, was put on trial for participating in Riek Machar's alleged coup. The former Minister of Higher Education, Dr Peter Adwok, was also briefly held before being released because of poor health and placed under house arrest. IGAD and the Troika launched a major campaign to have the Pagan Amum group (who would subsequently be called the Former Detainees) released. Because they were close to Garang and known to the pro-SPLM groups abroad, the Friends of South Sudan also strongly advocated for their release, so they could undermine the IO and serve as the base for a third force. Riek also pressed for their release under the assumption they would join him, and that Pagan would serve as his chief negotiator. While Riek sang the praises of the Former Detainees, the membership of what became the IO, and particularly the military leadership, wanted nothing to do with them. This was because they were tainted both by their relationship with Garang and because they were widely viewed as being among the most corrupt officials when they were in government. In response to international pressure seven of them were turned over to the government of Kenya on 29 January 2014, but to the surprise of Riek they proceeded to Addis Ababa where IGAD accepted their separate participation in the negotiations. The four remaining detainees – Pagan Amum, Oyai Deng, Majak D'Agoot, and Ezekiel Lol – were kept in detention until May 2014, when they too were released.

At the time Riek told me that he would object to the separate participation of the Former Detainees in the negotiations, and since Salva also opposed their participation it seemed likely they could abort the schemes of IGAD and the US. However, Taban supported the participation of the Former Detainees in the negotiations and his voice carried the day. Briefly, they became a useful tool for the peace-makers because, having no armed supporters, they were fully committed to a peaceful resolution of the conflict. In time, though, the mediators appreciated that because they had no forces they also had little political weight.

Meanwhile, after his release from prison the former SPLM representative to the US, Ezekiel Lol, a Nuer from Upper Nile, joined the IO, although from the outset many in the IO felt he was still loyal to the Former Detainees. Peter Adwok Nyaba had publicly disowned the SPLM after being released from prison and even publicly burned his party card, but Riek nonetheless appointed him to lead negotiations being organized in Arusha to unite the party. Rebecca Nyandeng, widow of the late John Garang, initially sided with the IO before increasingly associating with the Former Detainees. Her son, Maboir Garang, however, joined the IO and was appointed a spokesperson. This was a boost for Riek, who was anxious to make inroads among the Dinka and gain the allegiance of the son of the founding father of the country.

Peter Parr had been education minister in the Jonglei government and, after he made his way to Addis Ababa, Riek put him in charge of education. Hussein Mar, the long-serving deputy governor in Jonglei who had been acting governor at the time of the Juba killings, fled Bor for Addis Ababa where Riek appointed him to the humanitarian commission. Dr Dhieu Mathok Diing Wol, a Dinka academic from Northern Bahr al Ghazal, and former NCP official, was appointed the IO director of foreign relations and Ezekiel Lol initially served as his deputy. Gabriel Changeson, an Eastern Jikany Nuer and head of the United Democratic Salvation Front-Mainstream, spent the early months after the Juba massacre in the UN displaced camp in Juba before fleeing the country. Gabriel had held a number of cabinet portfolios in Juba, including minister of finance, after the previous SPLM Dinka minister was forced to resign for allegedly stealing $60 million. After refusing Riek's demand that he join the SPLM, though, he was dismissed as minister of finance.[5] As befitting that background, he was put in charge of finance and appointed to the IO negotiating team.

Riek was anxious to win the favour of Equatorians and thus appointed retired Lieutenant-General Alfred Ladu Gore as his deputy and deputy commander-in-chief, thus making him number two in the SPLM-IO hierarchy even though he was old, infirm, and carries little political weight within his own Bari community, as demonstrated by his failure to mobilize them to fight the government. He is also foremost an Equatorian, and was suspicious of a Nuer-led revolt. As a result, his role was one of window-dressing for the IO and he largely stayed in the background. In addition, Dr Richard Mula, from Mundri and a former MP, was appointed head of the IO's Justice Commission, while Ramadan Hassan Laku, former NCP official, a Mundari, and former MP, served as director for organization in the office of the chairman.

Some of Riek's Equatorian allies proved to be a mixed blessing because, in a war that focused on the two dominant tribes, Equatorians feared they might be marginalized and some of Riek's closest colleagues have worked behind his back to advance their personal and tribal interests. Thus, Alfred Ladu Gore, Ramadan Hassan, and Adel Elias Sandani, the party's representative to Kenya, and others met with their government counterparts in May 2015 in Nairobi, leading to a further meeting unknown to Riek in Kampala, where they met with Ugandan security officials. Not only did they receive money from the South Sudanese government, but they attempted to gain Ugandan support to establish a separate Equatorian movement. Museveni's officials turned them down since Uganda was the main supporter of the Salva regime. All of this caused an uproar in the IO and many called for their dismissal. In the event Riek ignored what could be considered rebellious acts by his colleagues. This was presumably because he would lose more politically by forcing them to leave the IO, after which they might establish a separate movement or join the government. The entire episode, however, made clear the capacity of the government to infiltrate and cause divisions in the IO, while many Nuer felt the Equatorians were only in the IO to pursue their personal interests and were not paying the price in blood on the battlefield that they were.

Many of the SPLM-IO leadership, not unlike that of the government and the Former Detainees, hold foreign citizenship, mostly in Western countries, particularly the US, Australia, and Canada, but also in Sudan and East Africa. As a result, even before the war broke out few had their immediate families in South Sudan. Although Riek has a number of wives, Angelina's children were born, raised, and live in the UK. The Nuer diaspora have contributed financially to the IO war effort, supported war-afflicted families, in some cases joined the regular forces or more often the white army, attended IO conferences, and in places like the US states of Nebraska, Iowa, and Minnesota have attempted to bring their concerns to the broader political community. Belatedly, the IO appreciated that the Nuer diaspora could be a major source of funding and in May–June 2015 Gabriel Changeson toured the Nuer-inhabited areas of the US to mobilize financial resources.

In practice, the number two in the IO was Taban Deng Gai, who grew up in the household of Riek's wife, Angelina. Although an accomplished political operator, businessman, and negotiator, he is a notorious schemer. When governor of Unity state he alienated most of the inhabitants and single-handedly created a Bul Nuer armed opposition to his government (the SSLA, see above). When he concluded that more was to be gained by an alliance with Riek he joined his rebellion, but kept on good terms with senior government officials and the Former Detainees to the extent that rumours persisted that he would defect.

Taban drew the ire of the former SSDF generals because, in addition to his role as chief negotiator with the government, Riek gave him responsibility for the acquisition of arms and munitions. It is hard to imagine an appointee to this crucial position that would be more loathed by the generals. He was also viewed with suspicion in Khartoum, the only potential IO arms supplier, because as governor of Unity state he had played a key role in the transit of arms from Uganda and Juba to rebel forces in Sudan. There are also numerous reports, albeit unconfirmed, of Taban sabotaging negotiations with Khartoum for weapons and their delivery.

Cynics think that Riek's selection of Taban as his first lieutenant was based on the principle of keeping one's enemies close, while others think he was influenced by Taban's money. As well as distrusting the former SSDF generals, though, the two men shared a fear of the international community, an ability to conflate their interests with the Nuer tribe, and a desire to reach a negotiated agreement with the government, even if it did not meet the needs of their constituents. In addition, Riek viewed his military as posing a major threat to his leadership and wanted someone interfacing with the generals who distrusted them as much as he did. Given their mutual loathing, there was little possibility of Taban and the former SSDF generals making common cause to overthrow him.

Beyond Taban, Riek's ambitious and intelligent wife, Angelina, effectively became number three in the informal SPLM-IO hierarchy. In addition, she became head of the party's security committee, despite never having served in the military. As a result, she was opposed by the generals and many others in the IO, as much because she is a woman as because her power derives solely from being Riek's wife. She is more astute, less diplomatic, and tougher than her husband, and in the context of the traditional culture of the Nuer brought a needed feminist perspective and the espousal of women's issues to the top echelons of a generally unsympathetic SPLM-IO.

However, absent in all three leaders is any philosophy or ideology beyond calls for 'reforms'. Riek never proposed the kind of far-reaching changes that would give any hope of making South Sudan functional and governable. Late in his academic studies he became involved in politics, but never displayed any interest in the socialism that was popular at the time.[6] Although Riek kept to an ideologically centrist-right and inoffensive path, he never won the favour of the US government and was hated by the Friends of South Sudan and Susan Rice, who never forgave him for his betrayal of their hero John Garang and alliance with the NCP.

Ideological debate was rare in both the SPLM and the IO, and this explains why the party's political strategies are typically ill thought out, opportunistic, and not based on any concern to address the practical needs of the people. Change for the leaders of these organizations is about altering the leadership in government, giving more political weight to their tribe, and acquiring jobs. The SPLA's initial support for state communism was designed to win the favour of the Ethiopian Derg. But with the end of the Cold War, when Garang needed support from the West, the SPLA developed important links with American Christian missionaries and the Friends of South Sudan. The lack of any motivating ideology led the SPLM to jump from a long-held commitment to a united reformed New Sudan to endorsing secession. The SPLM-IO under Riek is cut from the same cloth.

Worst of all for his followers, Riek insisted on a commitment to a united SPLM. This strategy was consistently opposed by most IO members, who contended that the SPLM had proved itself unworthy to rule South Sudan after being responsible for the virtual collapse of the country and the killing of thousands of Nuer in Juba. Instead of reforming the SPLM most SPLM-IO members wanted to organize an alternative party. Like his boss, Taban was equally insistent on preserving the SPLM and working through it, which made personal sense because he had no hope of winning popular support. What Riek refused to acknowledge, though, was that the hard-core Dinka SPLM leadership would do anything, including murder, to prevent him from ruling South Sudan.

Democratic Governance and Autocratic Rule

The SPLM-IO's formal hierarchy and many committees suggest accountability, but the practice followed that of Garang where SPLM committees in practice rarely met, held little genuine power, and decisions were made informally and unilaterally by the leader or in consultation with a handful of advisors. Day-to-day IO administration took the form of Riek sitting in a small room of his large house in Addis Ababa with seven cell phones, a couple of satellite phones, and two laptops, which he regularly turned to while holding non-stop meetings from 9 AM until late in the evening with leaders, military officers, chiefs, followers, diplomats, IGAD officials, journalists, analysts such as the author, business people looking for contracts, and assorted others. Tea and water were regularly served and many were provided excellent meals prepared by Angelina, although no alcohol or tobacco was consumed in the house. The meetings, alternately conducted in Nuer, English, and Arabic, were good humoured, and Riek was invariably approachable and a good listener. He thus met the Nuer cultural requirement of the leader being accessible to his followers, to such an extent that Riek told me he was once followed into his bathroom by an over-zealous official. Riek is tolerant but unbending when he has made up his mind and has an excellent memory, but is rarely alone or has the time to consider the many interviews he conducts, much less read or write.

But crucially the voices of the Nuer masses were frequently either not heard, ignored, or over-ruled. Moreover, although seemingly open to debate, what was most striking at the morning-to-night meetings I attended was that virtually no one challenged Riek. After a couple of meetings senior IO officials thanked me for arguing positions with the leader that they supported but feared to take. Peter

Adwok was a notable exception, but his leftist views were routinely dismissed by Riek and the conservative IO leadership. Although a seemingly diverse and generally intelligent group, the people Riek brought to the leadership were motivated more by opportunism and job-seeking than concern for their community or building a strong politically and ideologically coherent organization with a realistic programme.

The second level of IO governance was pursued through mass conferences held in the liberated territories, beginning with Nasir, which officially inaugurated the organization and later a series of meetings in Pagak Upper Nile State, which became the party and military administrative headquarters. The Nasir conference held 15–18 April 2014 was initially organized so that Taban Deng could brief the then field-based Dr Riek on progress in the negotiations. However, at the suggestion of Riek the conference became a founding convention of the IO attended by approximately 1,000 people, mostly displaced Nuer government officials, church leaders, civic society members, observers from other parties, but – to their later regret – only a handful of senior military officers. The key resolutions rejected Salva's claim of an attempted coup by Riek, endorsed the IGAD mediation, and rejected the proposed Protection and Deterrent Forces because it would compromise IGAD's neutrality as a mediator, condemned the Juba killings, declared Salva's government 'illegitimate', and called for a federal South Sudan.[7] The conference mandated the negotiating team, called for the immediate withdrawal of the Ugandan army and the various Sudanese armed groups assisting the government in South Sudan, supported the formation of the AU Commission of Inquiry, and called for the establishment of an independent Truth, Justice, and Reconciliation Commission.

The conference approved the establishment of the National Leadership Council made up of the chairperson, deputy chairperson, head of eight provisional committees, and the governors. At the impetus of the military it was agreed to establish a Military and Security Council which included the commander-in-chief, deputy commander-in-chief, heads of relevant provisional committees, governors, front commanders, and heads of military and security organs. Not surprisingly the conference endorsed Riek as leader, but significantly only as the *provisional* chairperson of the SPLM and commander-in-chief of the SPLA-IO and other organized forces, without setting any date for an official leadership conference to be held.[8]

The most significant debate was over the position of the SPLM in the insurgency, with representatives of other parties in attendance arguing for an SPLM-IO-led front that would include other parties and forces. This position was forcibly argued by Gabriel Changeson, who wanted to bring together all groups opposed to the government in an alliance headed by the IO and to end any pursuit of SPLM unification. This approach was probably that of the majority of people at the conference and Riek was only able to gain the conference's approval to defer a final decision on the matter. The conference concluded that 'the Intra-SPLM party dialogue has been overtaken by national events and the current crisis has moved beyond the SPLM Party [and therefore] the environment for such a dialogue shall be conducive after a final peace agreement has been signed'.[9] Despite the clear opposition to SPLM reconciliation, Riek, Taban, and Angelina would ignore the popular sentiments and continue to press for party unity.

From the start of the conference Riek, Taban, and Angelina were on the defensive for the failure of the IGAD peace process to consider the root causes of the conflict and the Juba killings, while their negotiating committee was criticized for supporting SPLM reconciliation, a peace process concerned almost solely with elite accommodation, sympathy for the SPLM detainees, and emphasis on a negotiated settlement of the conflict. These differences were a continuing source of tensions and reflected competing interests and approaches to the conflict, which even at that early stage threatened the IO's dismemberment. Despite these complaints, the leadership was generally supported. This was due to a concern with maintaining an appearance of unity and not challenging Riek in a public forum, as well as the political weakness of the former SSDF generals, who were unable to provide an alternative political leadership.

Pagak I Conference

There were a series of SPLM-IO conferences held at Pagak, which gave the party a democratic veneer entirely lacking in the government, which only held tightly orchestrated meetings of selected supporters. The most significant Pagak conference, in terms of numbers that attended and diversity, was the first one held in late November and early December 2014. Officially it was meant to consult the IO membership on the state of the peace process and the way forward but was in fact organized after Riek requested that IGAD break from negotiations to give him the opportunity to convince his followers to accept their proposal on the formation of a government headed by Salva, in which he would serve as an executive prime minister. Such a proposal, if posed directly, would almost certainly be opposed by the conference attendees since Salva was viewed as the person most responsible for the Juba massacre.

What ensued was the best and worst of the IO. Riek and the conference promoters faced many obstacles ranging from organization to lack of finances to the difficulties of arranging for people from six continents to attend. Another obstacle was posed by the high-handed actions of the Ethiopian security agency, which expelled journalists who wanted to cross the border from Gambella to Pagak and even stopped a small group of IGAD and UN diplomats headed by a former Ethiopian ambassador for two days from attending. In the event, only two independent internationals attended the conference – a journalist from Khartoum and the author.

The attendance of more than 3,000 delegates from South Sudan, Australia, Canada, United States, Europe, Egypt, and hundreds of others who took week-long bus trips from Nairobi and Khartoum to Pagak speaks to both the interest and commitment of those attending. In addition, there were representatives from every state in South Sudan and all these groups, together with the military, elders, and traditional leaders, had their own meetings and submitted resolutions to be considered by the conference as a whole. Best, Riek's late arrival limited any opportunity for the leadership to manipulate conference attendees, at least until they arrived.

Although ethnically diverse most of those in attendance were Nuer and perhaps half came from Upper Nile state, the site of the conference, and thus the outcome of its meeting chaired by Gathoth Gatkouth, the military governor of the state, was critical. The Upper Nile delegates accused the IGAD mediators of bias, refused to participate in any Salva-led government, and called for Salva to relinquish the presidency, thus undermining Riek's primary reason for holding the conference. The delegates demanded that the IO withdraw from any SPLM unity talks, that the killing of the Nuer in Juba be taken up in the negotiations, that the root causes of the conflict be considered, and that there be a 30-month transitional period during which the IO military would maintain a separate existence.[10] These resolutions reflected the views of Gathoth and the former SSDF generals, but they were also broadly representative of the majority of the Nuer. However, were these positions to be sustained Riek would be in a difficult position with IGAD and the Troika. Other state conferences reached their own conclusions, with some endorsing those of Upper Nile and others contradicting them. The non-Nuer states were usually less militant, and those meetings chaired by Riek loyalists managed to temper any radicalism.

If the high point of the Pagak conference was the open and widespread debates and discussions, the downturn began with Riek's inauguration speech. Speaking entirely in English (with Nuer and Arabic translation) Riek spoke over the heads of his followers to the absent international community. He rejected the allegation that he had attempted to carry out a coup against Salva and emphasized his commitment to the IGAD peace process and a peaceful end to the armed struggle. He asked his followers to forgive their transgressors for their abuses, which led to audible groans. Most of his lacklustre speech was spent itemizing the government reforms to which he was committed without explaining how he was going to make them in a government in which the IO would be – according to the proposal he was making to the conference – a minority and led by Salva. Riek spoke without emotion, never drew attention to either the Nuer killed in Juba or the tens of thousands killed, maimed, and displaced in the war, and failed to acknowledge the role of the military in keeping alive the hopes of victory. Instead of exciting the delegates, Riek bored them; instead of inspiring them, he dampened any expectations they might have had. This was a key opportunity for Riek to highlight both the struggle for which his people had paid dearly and his leadership, but so intent was he on impressing the international community with his moderation and commitment to the IGAD peace process that he failed his people. His speech ended with only polite applause.

Worse was to come when Riek's speech was followed by that of Taban Deng. Although the conference delegates thought they were there to be part of the SPLM-IO decision-making process, Taban bluntly informed them they had no choice but to endorse the decisions already made in the negotiations, including the acceptance by the IO negotiating team of a Salva-led transitional government. This was typical Taban, contemptuous of the masses and always insisting on the right of elites to make decisions above and for the people and this is probably why he was respected by the international peace-makers and hated by his own people. Despite his condescending and even disdainful view of the conference attendees his speech was treated respectfully, and it was left to General Gathoth to articulate the view of the majority and refer to the Upper Nile state resolutions which contradicted Taban's views. Gathoth was supported by Generals Peter Gadet and Chayot Nyang, both popular leaders, with Gadet receiving more applause for his speech than either Riek or Taban. The diplomats in attendance could not have been happy to be confronted by the views of the people, which throughout the peace process they had gone to great lengths to ignore. Though these sentiments could not have been a surprise to Riek and Taban, they no doubt thought that they could either massage the final resolutions of the conference or just ignore them, counting on the support of the international peace-makers.

Not surprisingly the conference endorsed federalism. The Nuer viewed federalism as state-level Nuer control in Greater Upper Nile and an end to Dinka domination of these governments, although at the time of the outbreak of the civil war all three governors of Greater Upper Nile were Nuer, albeit highly unpopular among Nuer constituencies.[11] The Equatorians had always been strong proponents of federalism. Although the SPLM had long championed federalism, after taking power the enthusiasm for devolving power evaporated and the states simply functioned as agents of the national government. The conference attendees never attempted to define the powers of the proposed federal states, their relationship to Juba, or why the many non-Nuer in GUN would accept Nuer hegemony.

Also, not considered was Riek's proposal for a federalism based on the 21 districts established during British colonial times. Riek's model was designed – he said – to bring government services closer to the people, did not increase Nuer territories, and was not strictly speaking ethnic-based, although that is what most Nuer favoured. When asked why more time was not devoted to considering this critical issue, what actual powers would be devolved, and even how South Sudan could afford 21 states, I was told by conference attendees that the important thing was the endorsement of federalism and that the details, including Riek's proposal, could be resolved later. As a result, few conference attendees even understood the federal proposal they endorsed.

At the insistence of the generals, who had little faith in the peace process, a 30-month interim period was agreed to in which the IO military would retain its independence, there would be a joint command, and Juba would provide the rebels with logistics. Such provisions would never be agreed to by the government and it was also unlikely they would gain the support of the peace-makers.

Riek's leadership was never challenged at the conference (the best Riek's critics could do was attack his first lieutenant, Taban Deng), and the final 'Communiqué' 'reaffirms total and undivided loyalty to the leadership of Dr Riek Machar Teny-Dhurgon' and also recommitted to the 'peaceful resolution of the South Sudan civil war through the IGAD mediation process that addresses the root causes of the conflict [and] stands for a federal system of governance which restores power to the people'.[12]

With the conference over, Riek met the senior generals in closed-door meetings to consider their repeated demand that the military be organized in a professional manner. It spoke to Riek's fears of them that even after a year of intense warfare the IO did not have a formal military structure. Confronted by their collective resolve Riek had little choice but to accept their demands. The generals also complained about their lack of weaponry and munitions to conduct the war, but there was no resolution on this crucial issue and they returned to the field. After more delays Riek appointed Simon Gatwech Chief of General Staff. Simon would report directly to him and there would be no defence minister as the generals wanted. In addition, Riek appointed Simon's deputies and divisional commands.[13]

The military problems did not end, however, because Riek did not provide either job descriptions or resources for the generals to carry out their responsibilities. Although Gathoth was in charge of logistics he did not have the authority or capacity to acquire weapons and did not work with Taban, who did. While Gadet was in charge of operations he had little control over the divisional commanders. Dau Aturjong could not organize the training of the IO army while he was in Northern Bahr al Ghazal and in any case was not given any money. Moreover, the General Staff lacked a consensus on the way forward and the authority and capacity to formulate a suitable military strategy. While the leadership structure looked impressive it is difficult not to conclude that Riek designed it to be a mere façade and had no intention of granting the generals real power.

Riek used the changes he was pressed to make to marginalize key critics like Gadet and Gathoth, shifting them from their previous field positions as military governors and divisional commanders to the Pagak headquarters. Keeping Gadet, who is not a strategist, in Pagak was, as a senior IO politician put it, placing him in a 'virtual prison'. To be fair, Gadet would be a problem for any leader since with his seniority he would be expected to hold a leading position in the General Staff despite his talents lying at the field level.

Pagak II

Another conference was held in Pagak 19–23 April 2015, due to the continuing frustration and anger of the generals – indeed, Gathoth sent out a radio message in March to field commanders threatening to create his own faction unless a meeting of the high command was held. For public consumption, though, the conference was supposed to review the peace process. The generals contended they were unable to fulfil their responsibilities, the system did not work, power was still centralized with Riek and Taban, Chief of Staff Simon Gatwech did not have sufficient authority, and Riek continued to go over their heads and issue orders directly to field commanders. The generals also held that the weapons and munitions shortages had reached a critical stage and that new approaches to Khartoum be initiated. In addition, they complained about the unnecessary loss of life because of a lack of medicines and qualified medical personnel, and of the priority given to negotiations over armed struggle when the peace process was going nowhere.

The private meetings got very acrimonious and at one point Gadet threatened to shoot Taban, accusing him of deliberately not acquiring the necessary weapons so that there could be an alignment with the

Former Detainees to reach a negotiated agreement that betrayed the IO armed struggle. Chief of Staff, Simon Gatwech supported his colleagues, but was more restrained. In addition, the generals complained about the centralization of authority under Riek, who was chairman of the SPLM-IO, commander-in-chief, served as his own defence minister, oversaw the acquisition of logistics, and even had to approve the issuing of bus tickets. The senior military officials left the conference increasingly angry that they had attained little.

The leadership repeated its call for the Peace and Security Council to release the AU Commission of Inquiry report and that an independent judicial body be established to try perpetuators of human rights abuses in the South Sudan conflict. While there was little doubt that the vast majority of the IO membership were opposed to SPLM unity, and the conference repeated the formula that 'the implementation of SPLM Reunification was not possible without first reaching a negotiated peace settlement', under pressure from the leadership the conference endorsed the efforts of their negotiating team to achieve party unity in negotiations in Arusha.

Until the signing of the peace agreement in August 2015 there were five SPLM-IO conferences held at Pagak and they became integral to SPLM-IO governance, giving the appearance of democratic accountability. Although Riek was not authoritarian like Garang, Salva, and most of the SPLM leadership, when his views conflicted with the masses – as they did on a range of issues – it was his view that almost always prevailed. This was more easily done than imagined because the conference decision-making process was typically poorly organized, dominated by senior officials under Riek, there was an unspoken prohibition against challenging Riek and thus showing divisions in the ranks, and Riek and a couple of close colleagues wrote up the decisions reached at the conference. Ultimately the IO was shaped by the command military culture of John Garang's SPLM with its formal speeches, lack of genuine debate, unanimous votes, and adoration of the leader. While the pre-conference Pagak I debates were admirable, democracy in the SPLM-IO has been limited to the outer reaches of the organization, and given the lack of political skills of those opposed to the Riek and Taban leadership and the disorganized state of the majority the leaders almost always got their way.

Riek Dismisses His Leading Critics

From the early days of the war the former SSDF generals made clear their unhappiness with the IO political leaders, all three of whom are from Unity state and related, and as a result some have complained about the party being led by a 'Unity state mafia'. But the most consistent complaint of the generals was over the lack of supplies, for which the generals held Taban chiefly responsible.

Out of frustration Simon Gatwech, the IO's chief of staff, on behalf of Gadet, Gathoth, and Tang Ginya, wrote directly to President Omar Bashir on 20 June 2015 asking for support. Simon praised Bashir, noted the generals' frustration with Riek and Taban, and requested that logistics supplied by Khartoum not go through Taban but directly to the senior field commanders. Simon wrote that he was sending Gabriel Tang Ginya, a former SAF officer, to Khartoum to facilitate arrangements. The letter does not appear to have influenced Bashir, but its public release embarrassed the IO by making clear the party divisions and providing evidence of Khartoum's support for the rebels, although also that Khartoum was very parsimonious in the supply of logistics.

To satisfy lobbyists in the West, and notably the US and the Enough organization of John Prendergast, a number of generals (including two from the IO – Peter Gadet and James Koang) were sanctioned by the US, EU, and Canada. It is unlikely, though, that these generals have bank accounts or property in these places, and they can easily avoid these parts of the world.[14] In any case, the sanctions are largely viewed as a joke by the generals and have had no discernible effect on their behaviour. Indeed, singling out these generals gave them an inflated view of their importance and this was reinforced by the decision of IGAD's chief negotiator, Seyoum Mesfin, to meet them without the knowledge of Riek. The IGAD mediators viewed such meetings as a way to demonstrate their frustration with Riek by exacerbating divisions within SPLM-IO ranks. At their meeting with Seyoum, Simon Gatwech repeated the generals' widely known complaints and demanded that Riek and Salva be kept out of the transitional government, and that they conduct direct negotiations with the SPLA leadership. Seyoum told the generals he would ensure that military representatives from both sides were at the negotiating table since it was clear Riek's refusal to have anyone from the high command at the negotiations was designed to marginalize them. But Seyoum's promise begged the question of what right the IGAD mediators had to determine the composition of the IO negotiating team and if successful in forcing Riek to have a military representative at the table it could be anticipated that the person would simply echo the positions of Riek and thus undermine Seyoum's intent.

In ending the meeting Seyoum requested that the generals repeat their complaints in a letter and they obliged, thus deepening the division between them and Riek. In the letter Simon wrote,

> Any peace agreement that confirms President Kiir as the head of the Transitional Government of National Unity and Dr Riek Machar as first vice President during the transitional period is not acceptable to us and cannot be saleable to the people of South Sudan. Because they are seen by the people of South Sudan as symbol of hate, division and failed leadership in South Sudan and therefore cannot reconcile and heal the Country.[15]

Simon also rejected efforts at SPLM unification 'because Juba Massacres were perpetuated by the same SPLM government' [and his IO forces] 'are not fighting for the re-unification of SPLM party because all of them [i.e. the IO generals] are not members of SPLM party'. In addition, Simon argued against returning to the pre-December status quo and – like Riek – said there should be no resumption of peace talks before the AU Commission of Inquiry had released its report.

Ultimately, what the mediators' irresponsible intervention proved was that if they continued to make demands on Riek they might get him to go to Juba, but the generals would be left behind, thus making the resolution of the conflict even more difficult. Indeed, although the IGAD mediators virtually encouraged the IO generals to challenge Riek, after they defected the mediators ignored them. The internationals went full circle: they bestowed legitimacy on Salva and Riek by blessing the flawed 2010 elections to keep the Sudan–South Sudan peace process on track (and that did not work), recognized Riek's leadership of the armed opposition to the Salva-led government (at a time when he was not in control), and then at the instigation of the US encouraged talk of having both Salva and Riek removed from the peace process when they did not do their bidding.

While Riek was weak, vacillating, contradictory, and disingenuous, he had the support of the majority of ordinary Nuer and going behind his back indicated both desperation and a failure to consider the implications of such an approach. The call for the removal of Riek and Salva made a certain amount of sense if – as the internationals assumed – the war could be reduced to a conflict among the SPLM elites. This proceeded from the assumption that the legitimacy of these leaders was dependent on the international community which could remove that legitimacy. If, however, the immediate stimulus for the war was the Juba massacre and the root causes included a failed Sudan peace process, then removing these two leaders could make reaching a sustained peace even more difficult. Altogether, it was simplistic thinking that made clear the amateurship of the IGAD and Troika approach to peace-making.

Things came to a head on 21 July 2015 after Gathoth, with Gadet in attendance, told a church gathering in Gambella Ethiopia that 'I am no longer under Riek'. IO leader Duir Tut witnessed the statement and immediately phoned Riek to complain. Many Nuer refugees in Gambella held Gathoth's comments to be a threat to SPLM-IO unity and sided with Riek. Gathoth, however, held that it was not his words about serving under Riek that upset the refugees, but instead his further statement that under the peace agreement Riek would serve as vice president under Salva.[16] Be that as it may, things were falling into place for Riek, who had long wanted to be rid of the generals. The present circumstances provided him with the opportunity to dismiss his biggest critics, Gathoth and Gadet, and in this he was strongly supported by Taban and Angelina. The danger was that their dismissal would herald a full-scale revolt by other like-minded generals, particularly the IO Chief of Staff, Simon Gatwech, who authored the letters to Omar al-Bashir and Seyoum Mesfin condemning Riek.

To the surprise and anger of Gathoth and Gadet, Simon sided with Riek. This appears to be due to two factors: first, as a Lou Nuer far from his homeland Simon only had a handful of personally loyal troops in Pagak to protect him from arrest by Riek, and second (and this is likely key) his fellow Lou urged him not to make an open break with Riek and divide the SPLM-IO. Chayot Nyang, who had also been close to the dissenting generals, did not defect even though he had sufficient troops, apparently out of respect for Nuer concerns to maintain unity.

Concerned that Gathoth and Gadet could breed insecurity in the perennially unstable Gambella, they were placed under house arrest by the Ethiopian authorities, but slipped away and turned up in Khartoum. The Sudanese government's response to the arrival of their uninvited guests was to provide them with accommodation, but ensure they maintained a low profile, and give no indication it was prepared to sponsor their hopes of launching an anti-Riek rebellion. Although the core of the IO military leadership stayed loyal to Riek, a number of generals and other officers followed Gathoth and Gadet to Khartoum.

Also quick to side with the dissenting generals was the leading section of the Nuer Council of Elders, who had long been a thorn in Riek's side. Led by its chair, Gabriel Yuol, together with Gabriel Changeson and others, they had an 11-hour non-stop meeting with Riek where they discussed the dismissals of the generals, Changeson's role in the affair and allegations that he was their leader, the chairman's unilateral decision making, the IO's failure to establish institutions, Riek's continuing support for SPLM reconciliation despite widespread opposition, the inability of Riek and Taban to provide military logistics, and the demand for a wide-ranging IO reconciliation. Although dutifully listening to their concerns, according to Changeson 'Riek absorbed all the shocks' and in the end made no concessions beyond a vague commitment to reconcile with the generals.[17] As a result, the elders agreed to part company and Changeson told Riek that he had little choice but to form his own party. On 7 August Riek formally relieved Changeson of membership in the SPLM-IO for anti-party activities and the others were also dismissed, measures strongly argued for by Taban who claimed – wrongly – that Changeson was the leader of the dissenting generals.

In the wake of the dismissals the crucial question was whether Riek or the generals would be held responsible for undermining Nuer unity, but it quickly became apparent that the generals had over-played their hand. On almost all the areas of confrontation between Riek and the generals the Nuer sided with the generals, but when the issue was one of tribal unity in face of the external threat loyalty to the leader was demanded and the generals were isolated.

The dissenters soon concluded that Riek was not committed to reconciliation, and that opened the door to forming a separate party. What held them back were first, most Nuer favoured reconciliation and not the formation of another party, and second, the two factions could not agree on the form the party would take and who would be its leader. Gadet, as the senior military officer, was designated the head of the military wing, but he had no political ambitions. Gathoth did harbour political ambitions, but along with the other generals did not want to share power with a politician and after months of discussions there was a de facto agreement for unworkable separate and autonomous military and political wings.

Changeson had the political skills to assume the leadership, but in South Sudan the only politicians that carried weight were those who commanded soldiers, and unable to gain the acceptance of the generals he found himself reduced to writing press releases condemning Riek, thus further reducing any prospect of reconciliation. The generals were in a potentially stronger position than Changeson because they had supporters in the military across the Nuer territories and hoped to use their positive relations with the Sudanese leadership to acquire weapons. But soldiers in the field were only bound to leaders able to supply them with weapons and munitions, and while Khartoum was prepared to host the generals it was not prepared to provide the weapons on a scale sufficient to challenge the Juba government and thus gain the ire of the international peace-makers, particularly the US.

Riek and his supporters attempted to minimize the damage done to the SPLM-IO by the departure of the generals, but a weakened IO was ill-placed to deal with their loss if it had any hope of winning the war or convincingly confronting the government in the negotiations. Indeed, the government concluded that the departure of the generals represented a major loss for the IO and so did many Nuer, who were now prepared to make concessions to the government that would have been considered treasonous only months before. In the event, Gathoth returned to Juba and continued to oppose Riek, Gabriel Yuol returned to Juba to resume his position as an MP, and Thomas Maboir returned to the IO military, but Gadet, Tang Ginya, and the other generals remained in Khartoum opposed to both Salva and Riek. Gabriel Changeson continued his lonely battle from Nairobi.

Conclusion

Hurt, anger and a desire for revenge in the wake of the Juba massacre provided the stimulus for a popular insurgency by the Nuer against the government, but they could not supply their own leadership and with the intervention of IGAD and the Troika that gap was filled by Riek. The fact that years of peace-making in Sudan based on elite collaboration and power-sharing had produced a litany of failures did not result in a change in approach when civil war broke out in South Sudan in mid-December 2013. Once again peace-partners in the form of Riek and Salva and their respective parties were required, and no serious consideration was ever undertaken to determine why the war broke out, who fought it, or the make-up, character, and divisions of the SPLM-IO and how they impacted on the peace process. Crucially, the question of why the Nuer civilians in Juba were killed was never addressed. Just as the internationals followed a script during the Sudan negotiations, which assumed South Sudan to be a liberal society in the making and the SPLM a worthy group to whom state power could be given, many of the same internationals assumed that Riek and a small group around him represented the Nuer tribe while Salva represented and controlled the government. Both assumptions were wrong.

The SPLM-IO is a big house with many factions and if Riek is to be credited with encouraging the formation of this coalition and keeping it largely intact, he also bears responsibility for never producing a coherent political and military leadership with objectives that met the needs of his constituents. Riek has a PhD in management, but this does not constitute a personal skill. He also draws back from organization, mobilization, and institutionalization, both because – like Garang – he fears they will pose a threat to his leadership and he also views such processes as leftist and inconsistent with his generally right-wing philosophy.

From the outset, the IO was at war with itself and to the extent the peace-makers were aware of the tensions they deliberately tried to exacerbate them. Riek was thus pulled between the peace-makers who were singularly focused on power-sharing (IGAD/Troika) and re-uniting the SPLM (Arusha) on the one hand, and on the other, his constituents who demanded attention to the Juba massacre, the root causes of the conflict, and the need to remove an SPLM government that had failed the citizens of the country.

Riek sided with the internationals against his own people, thus deepening the tensions in the IO and producing its first major schism in

June 2015. Two things kept the party from disintegrating: first, the commitment of the Nuer to tribal and SPLM-IO unity, and second, a leadership devoted to self-aggrandizement which concluded was best pursued by sticking with Riek. The peace-makers' devotion to finding formulas for dividing the spoils of government among the opportunistic SPLM factions was not mistaken if the objective was solely to get a signed agreement. But if the peace-makers wanted a sustainable agreement that addressed the needs of the people it could not be achieved by catering to the interests of weak, grasping, and unrepresentative elites. In addition, to the extent that the IO had been noticeably weakened by its divisions, the government was less willing to share power and increasingly entertained the idea of militarily defeating its opponents, as will be made clear in the next chapter.

5 | LAYING THE GROUNDWORK FOR FUTURE FAILURES

Introduction

IGAD–Troika peace-making in South Sudan suffered from all the problems associated with the model of international peace-making that took form in the post-Cold War era, as well as the legacy of the CPA which effectively created obstacles that could not readily be overcome. But the biggest weakness of the peace process and agreement is that it did not proceed from any understanding of what caused the conflict. Power-sharing was simply rolled out to solve the problem of violence, but absent in the final agreement was any statement by the peace-makers of what caused the endemic violence and mal-governance and why power-sharing would solve these problems. The same absence of analysis or explanation of why there was a war is evident in the Sudan peace process and the CPA, but in that case the granting of a referendum on national self-determination suggests that the national oppression of southern Sudanese was considered the cause of the conflict. The continuing wars in the rump Sudan, the civil war in South Sudan, and tensions between the two countries make clear the error of that analysis. And the break-down of the August 2015 peace agreement premised on power-sharing among the SPLM elites 11 months after it was signed leads to the conclusion that an almost exclusive reliance on power-sharing has failed to stop the violence in the country.

The US was responsible for placing southern Sudan on a trajectory towards independence and subsequently supported a peace process to overcome a problem largely of its own making. Although faith in the SPLM had been declining and by late 2014 American diplomats were calling for both Salva Kiir and Riek Machar to be removed, US policy continued to oppose the Riek-led insurgency. Peace-making in Sudan and South Sudan was conducted by elites for elites. In the case of the Sudan the peace-makers used democratic rhetoric, while there was no commitment to democracy in the South Sudan peace agreement, presumably because the peace-makers did not see a connection between South Sudan's endemic violence and a lack of accountable government.

This chapter considers the organization of the IGAD peace process, the leaders of the process, controversy around the selection of the participants to the peace process, and the tensions within IGAD that made it difficult to serve as an impartial mediator. When the focus on power sharing did not produce results, and in response to their constituencies, the internationals began sanctioning individuals – an entirely symbolic exercise that had no impact.

Also to be considered in this chapter are the parallel talks conducted in Arusha, Tanzania, that had the objective of unifying the SPLM factions but got bound up in efforts by different countries to advance their national interests or, in the case of Uganda, to take the pressure off their South Sudan government allies at the IGAD negotiations. Although there was considerable symbolic progress made at Arusha it never translated into stopping or even reducing the conflict.

Despite little progress being made in the IGAD negotiations this did not lead the mediators to conclude that their approach warranted critical review. Instead, they concluded that additional countries and organizations needed to be added to bring more pressure on the belligerents to reach an agreement. Indeed, this had the desired result: Riek signed on to an agreement he had previously rejected, while Salva also eventually signed despite noting a long list of reservations. These reservations, however, left little hope that the agreement would prove sustainable.

Organizing the IGAD Peace Process

Given the SPLM's dismal record in government and the instability that continued seamlessly after the signing of the CPA, the outbreak of the December 2013 civil war cannot have been a surprise to any close observer of the country. However, the form it took, with the attack on Nuer civilians, was a shock and even more shocking was the AU Commission finding that the attack was 'committed pursuant to or in furtherance of a State policy'. In other words, responsibility lay with the head of state, Salva Kiir. IGAD and the Troika, however, did not pursue that line of inquiry and instead were intent on rolling out a peace process designed to stop the violence and return the country to the pre-war period. But beginning with the six-year transition, through two years of independence, South Sudan was beset with violence and why that was the case and whether it was a consequence of a flawed CPA was never considered. Given the speed with which the peace process took form, the mediators could not have had the time to carefully examine either the nature of the war or who were the leading actors. Also, not questioned was whether the countries of the region with their multiple and competing interests in South Sudan were best suited to lead the peace process. However, belief in their capacity as well as fear that the AU, UN, or the West might take up the process all played into the decision of IGAD to lead the process and crucially the US gave its approval.

As a result, the many layered tensions and conflicts between the various peace-makers were simply ignored. Some of the leading actors in the Sudan peace process, including General Lazarus Sumbweiyo, simply shifted from Nairobi to Addis Ababa, where the former Ethiopian Foreign Minister, Seyoum Mesfin, took the lead in a tense relationship with his Kenyan counterpart. Western diplomats reported that Sumbweiyo deliberately undermined the efforts of Seyoum. Still basking in the glory of his supposed achievements in overseeing the CPA and the secession of South Sudan, Sumbweiyo held that he should lead the peace initiative and the process should again be pursued under the auspices of the Kenyan government. Not welcomed by the US and assuming a low profile throughout the peace process was the third and final member of the team, General Ahmed Mustafa from Sudan.

The participation of Salva Kiir's government in the peace negotiations was not controversial but, as noted, the assumption made that Riek Machar fully controlled the Nuer white army which carried out the initial attacks on government positions in Greater Upper Nile was mistaken. However, the peace-makers were committed from the outset to power-sharing among the SPLM belligerents and a more complex rendering of the conflict and how the negotiations might be focused was beyond their imagination or capability.

This helps explain the participation of the Former Detainees in the negotiations since they were not in rebellion against the government – as they repeatedly affirmed – and nor did they at any time during the war control armed forces opposed to the government. They were also politically weak, with almost no constituencies and were widely hated in the country for their corruption, mismanagement, and role in increasing tensions with Khartoum by their support of northern rebel groups. They were nonetheless made part of the IGAD negotiations because of US pressure and to a lesser extent by Kenya's President Uhuru Kenyatta who hoped – mistakenly as it turned out – that by hosting them he would play a leading role in the peace process and have leverage over the post-conflict government. Support for the Former Detainees as a separate participant in the negotiations also undermined Riek's hopes that if the six Dinka among the 12 Former Detainees had joined the SPLM-IO, what initially took the form of a Nuer–Dinka war would have become a national war against a small Dinka clique surrounding Salva. The US and Kenya efforts to enhance and give a separate political representation in the negotiations to the Former Detainees helped exacerbate Nuer–Dinka tensions during the first two years of the war.

IGAD and Its Contradictions

IGAD brought together a diverse group of countries with often conflicting interests that were played out during the peace process. Most tense were Uganda–Sudan relations. Sudan had supported dissident groups in Uganda, notably the LRA since the 1990s, in response to Museveni's assistance to the SPLA and Darfur rebels. Tensions between the two countries further developed when Museveni sent his army to save the faltering government of Salva Kiir. Salva's replacement of the Garangists from his government with ministers who had previously been loyal or had close relations with Khartoum meant that the NCP had an investment in his government. Bashir's support for the Salva-led government also convinced some SPLA Nuer generals at the start of the war not to defect to the IO because they would not be supported by Sudan, and without that support they could not defeat the government. However, even the presence of Khartoum-friendly ministers in Salva's government was not able to stop the continuing logistical support of northern Sudanese rebels by Uganda. Fearing Museveni's influence over the Salva government, Khartoum felt compelled to provide the SPLM-IO with some support, but not enough to be decisive, despite claims to the contrary by the Juba government and its friends in the US.

Complicating its position, the NCP had good reason to distrust Riek. He had repeatedly called for the contentious border territory of

Abyei to be united with South Sudan, was a strong supporter of stopping the transit of oil to Sudan to leverage higher payments, and tried to win the allegiance of the Garangist Former Detainees who were perceived as a threat. Meanwhile, Taban was a key supporter of rebel groups in Sudan when he was governor of Unity state; he was also close to the Former Detainees and opposed to the former SSDF generals who had historical links to the Sudanese army. The NCP also knew that Riek and Taban were anxious to return to Juba and thus there was a danger that any weapons supplied might be turned over to the SPLA, as was the case when Khartoum provided the South Sudan Liberation Army enormous amounts of military equipment, only for it to make peace with the government (see above).

None of these subtleties, however, was appreciated by the Friends of South Sudan, who repeatedly held that the SPLM-IO was under the control of Khartoum, which was providing it with massive supplies of weapons and was either intent on taking back South Sudan or more likely its oil fields. In reality, as noted, the white army went to war with few weapons while Khartoum's meagre supply of weapons to the IO's regular forces was a major bone of contention between the former SSDF generals and Riek and Taban. Khartoum provided the IO with sufficient weapons to stave off outright military defeat, but not enough to completely jeopardize its relations with the Salva government – to which in the early period of the war it continued to sell weapons – or unduly upset the US.

Indeed, fear of the US, a desire to end the sanctions, and to drop the ICC charges against Bashir informed key foreign policy decisions by the Sudan government. Thus, Sudan assumed a by no means insignificant role in the Western-led war to overthrow Muammar el-Qaddafi (even though the UN resolution gave it no such right), ended relations with Iran, stopped serving as a conduit for weapons (largely from Iran) to Hamas in Gaza, and joined the Gulf-led war against the Yemeni Houthis which had never posed any threat to the country. While the US, Britain, and other Western countries supported the Saudi war against Yemen, sold weapons to the Gulf states, assisted in the illegal sea blockade of the country, and provided targeting information for Gulf air forces, Omar Bashir sent soldiers to assist the war effort. Sudan's participation in the war was foremost about gaining badly needed foreign reserves and investment from the rich

Gulf Arabs, acquiring regional support, and reducing the regime's isolation. All these actions were welcomed by Washington, even if it was not in a hurry to end the sanctions against Sudan. Washington was also reluctant to acknowledge the key role Khartoum must play in any sustainable peace in South Sudan, not only because of its many faceted links with the country, but also because President Bashir knew Salva and Riek better than other leaders in the region.

While slowly being rehabilitated internationally, the killing of more than 200 unarmed demonstrators in September 2014 made clear Khartoum's continuing brutality, while the paltry turn-out at the April 2015 national elections indicated its lack of public support. Having invested considerable political capital in reducing its isolation and improving relations with the US, however, Bashir was reluctant to risk open-ended support of the feckless Nuer and their even more distrusted leaders. That decision, however, was always subject to review and could be reversed if it looked like the SPLM-IO could be defeated, the Ugandan army was threatening Sudanese security, or if the Former Detainees with their New Sudan sympathies again assumed a dominant position in the South Sudan government.

While Museveni's crucial support for the Salva regime was in the first instance due to fears of Khartoum's influence over the Juba regime, he was also concerned about losing the enormous cash cow South Sudan had become for Uganda. While Ethiopians and Eritreans largely controlled the major hotels, restaurants, and hospitality industry in South Sudan, Kenyans ran the banking and some of the high-end services, and Somalis the supply of petrol and water, Ugandans in their thousands dominated petty trade and the supply of basic and luxury goods. Thus, the fish eaten at one of Juba's upmarket restaurants on the Nile would invariably have come from Uganda. In addition, key members of the Ugandan regime, including Museveni's brother, General Salim Saleh, had important investments in the country. And crucially the costs of Uganda's army were borne by the South Sudanese government. The loss of such labour and markets would have dealt a serious blow to the Ugandan economy and in turn politically weakened Museveni. Even before the start of the war, though, oil prices began their downward curve, and with its outbreak many of the country's oil fields were put out of production, seriously undermining the economy and the ability of South Sudan to pay for the services and goods from Uganda.

The Ugandan army had been deployed in Western Equatoria since 2005 to fight the LRA in collaboration with the SPLA, together with support and special forces provided by the US. Since 2010 the LRA has not been present in Western Equatoria, but the Ugandan army and US logistical support continued and Museveni's brother, General Salim Salih, said that even if the Ugandan army was withdrawn as a result of a peace agreement they could quickly return if the security situation in South Sudan required it.[1]

Museveni also feared that a Riek-dominated government would open the door to more influence by Khartoum in South Sudan, a position that mirrored that of the US government. Museveni claimed that Riek supported the LRA and its leader, Joseph Kony, when he led the LRA–Uganda peace process. In addition, Museveni distrusted Nilotics, who he had fought on his road to the presidency, and was suspicious of Riek's friendship with the Luo-Kenyan opposition leader, Raila Odinga. Museveni always feared subversion along Uganda's borders and takes a keen interest in the affairs of the Equatorians who are closely linked to the adjacent tribes in Uganda. Colonial borders arbitrarily divided peoples, but cultural and familial continuity was unaffected and the massive movement of South Sudanese refugees to Uganda could be expected to evoke sympathy and raise questions as to why Museveni supported their oppressors.

During the August 2015 IGAD peace negotiations in Addis Ababa, Riek directly confronted Museveni about persistent rumours from Kampala that he supported the LRA. Riek argued that Khartoum linked reaching the CPA to ending the problem of the LRA and this was the stimulus for him taking up the issue. He pointed out that he encouraged the Ugandan army to set up a base in Western Equatoria to hunt the LRA. Riek also rejected allegations that because he had signed agreements with Khartoum (notably the Khartoum Peace Agreement of 1997) and once had close relations with the NCP leadership that he had any influence over Khartoum's support of the LRA.

Although a Riek presidency would have diminished Museveni's influence in the country it would not have seriously jeopardized Uganda's role in the economy, for which there was no alternative, and there was no political appetite to expel Ugandans. Moreover, while most of Riek's generals, and probably his followers as well, opposed supporting Sudan's rebels, Riek had taken a hard line on

Abyei and had been one of the strongest proponents of cutting the oil to Khartoum, so there was little reason to imagine that as leader of the country he would have become a tool of the NCP. Despite not being based on any tangible evidence, Museveni's hard-line approach to any Riek-led insurgency reinforced similar negative assessments of Riek in Washington.

Meanwhile, Ethiopian Prime Minister Meles Zenawi, who died in 2012, reportedly said that because his country was between war-ravaged South Sudan and Somalia and their conflicts would inevitably cross the borders into the Gambella and Somali regions, it had no choice but to be a leader in the search for peace. Gambella is a multi-national lowland state that culturally, economically, and in its ethnic make-up, more closely resembles South Sudan than highland Ethiopia. While the Anuak had long been the largest ethnic community and had dominated the state's government, even before the war the Nuer surpassed them in numbers and with the war and arrival of hundreds of thousands of fleeing South Sudanese, Nuer are now double the number of Anuak. Moreover, many Ethiopian Nuer have family and friends in South Sudan and have joined the fight against the government, particularly by participating in the white army. Meanwhile, the IO military and administrative base was in Pagak Upper Nile, less than a stone's throw from the Gambella border. As a result, the EPRDF initially viewed the war through the lenses of its impact on Gambella.

For this reason and the considerable participation of the Ethiopian army in UN forces in South Sudan and Abyei, Addis Ababa and the Ethiopia-led peace process were viewed by Juba with suspicion. To balance Ethiopia's influence, Juba attempted to develop relations with Asmara, but this was a dangerous game, not only because it threatened to upset Addis Ababa, but also the Troika because Eritrea had been locked out of the IGAD mediation and was under sanctions because of its support of *jihadi* groups in Somalia.

The EPRDF views Ethiopia as the regional hegemon and was angered at the involvement of the Ugandan army in the South Sudan conflict. Contrary to assumptions in Kampala and claims by the Eritrean government, which is itself sometimes accused of supporting the IO, there is no evidence of EPRDF support for the SPLM-IO. And while the IO has carried out political activities in Gambella, so has the South Sudan government and later Taban Deng, who has also accused the IO of providing weapons to the Ethiopian Nuer in their frequent conflicts with the Anuak. There is no evidence, however, to substantiate the allegation, and the IO would have to be very stupid to threaten its relationship with the EPRDF by interfering in domestic politics.

Beyond the IGAD region, but a crucial participant in the politics of north-east Africa, is Egypt, which began by assuming a neutral position in the South Sudan conflict and was courted by both sides. But Egypt's national interests primarily relate to the Nile River. It wants to restart the discredited Jonglei canal diversion which would destroy the Sudd and undermine the economies of the pastoralist Dinka and Nuer, in order to bring more water to Egypt. More immediately, it is involved in a dispute with Ethiopia over construction of the Renaissance Dam on the Blue Nile, which it contends would reduce the flow of waters into the main branch of the river. When proposals were made for the establishment of a Regional Protection Force (see next chapter), with the support of Juba, Egypt pressed for involvement. This was strongly opposed by Addis Ababa, whose nightmare is to have Egyptian troops on the upper reaches of the Nile. There is growing evidence, however, that the failure of Egypt to stop construction of the Renaissance Dam and Uganda's inability to defeat South Sudanese rebels has provided a basis for collaboration in which Uganda supports Egypt's efforts to undermine Ethiopia's project in return for Egypt supplying weapons to the Juba government through Uganda,[2] a view supported by President Omar Bashir, whose country is in an increasingly tense relationship with Egypt.[3] In these circumstances there is the potential for a conflict involving Egypt, Ethiopia, Uganda, South Sudan, and Sudan.[4]

Against the background of these conflicting interests the question must be asked as to whether IGAD could possibly be a neutral or effective instrument in resolving the problems of South Sudan, rather than exacerbating tensions between the member states? IGAD is part of a bigger security network constructed by the US and its Western allies that involves regional organizations to deal with problems at that level and the African Union at the continental level, all based on the premise of African solutions to African problems. But this is disingenuous, since the West provided the stimulus for the establishment of IGAD, paid for IGAD and later encouraged and paid for the establishment of its peace committee, while the African Union receives much of its financing from the European Union. Not only are IGAD and the African Union subject to considerable Western control, the repeated failures of IGAD-led peace-making in Sudan, South Sudan, and Somalia draw into question the Western security architecture for the region and the continent.

IGAD Peace Talks

On 9 May 2014, Salva Kiir and Riek Machar signed an agreement calling for the talks to be broadened to include other stakeholders: the Former Detainees, other opposition political parties, civil society, and faith-based groups. In June, opposition- and government-supporting political parties formed their own delegation led by Dr Lam Akol. In these talks, Riek opposed the separate representation of the other stakeholders and held that the talks should be between the warring parties and the government, and that the other parties should side with either one or the other. IGAD took the contrary view and talks were adjourned. Talks resumed in August, but angered at the position of the political parties, a split developed and the government refused the participation of Lam and the other opposition parties, after which Lam was restricted to Juba. The government then attempted to limit political party participation to only its supporters under the leadership of Dr Martin Elia, Minister of Cabinet Affairs, but this was rejected by IGAD. As a result, after September 2014 the political parties other than the government and the SPLM-IO were not represented in the talks.

The participation of civil society proved equally problematic. Most of civil society in politically immature South Sudan was created by the international community to facilitate their aid and development efforts and was weak, dependent on the West, and primarily viewed as a source of jobs. The various branches of the South Sudan church once had a semblance of independence, but have become increasingly close to the government. Traditional authorities were the closest to the people, but SPLA efforts over many years to banish this potential threat to its authority left many chiefs powerless, displaced, corrupted, or subservient to whatever gun-carriers dominated their particular fiefdom.[5] While South Sudan's civil society was heavily weighted in favour of the government, neither the government, nor the IO, was keen on their presence at the negotiations. As a result, the mediators did not defend the participation of civil society and instead concluded that it complicated the peace process and its role should be diminished.

In response to criticisms, IGAD organized a special session on the root causes of conflict in the northern Ethiopian city of Bahr Dar. Government representatives, however, refused to attend, presumably because they feared it was a means by which the IO would introduce consideration of the Juba killings. IGAD did not press the matter and this potentially fruitful approach was dropped and never taken up again.

The Juba killings were the motivation for the insurgency and Riek and the IO negotiators had little option but to press this fundamental issue if it did not want to alienate its followers. However, the government objected and IGAD and the Troika did not back up the opposition. In a private meeting with Ethiopian Prime Minister Haile Mariam Dessalgn, Riek was told that the issue was too disruptive to consider during the formal negotiations.[6] This evasion of difficult issues is reminiscent of the refusal of the Sudan negotiators to permit the SSDF to participate in the mediation. As with that ill-fated decision it can be expected to have negative repercussions for years to come. The Juba killings were instead to be considered by an AU Commission of Inquiry headed by former Nigerian President Olusegun Obasanjo. Instead of the focus being restricted to the Juba killings, though, it included all abuses of civilians by the belligerents, thus ensuring that the immediate cause of the war would be down-played, while the cause and effect link between the Juba killings and those elsewhere would never be made.

Obasanjo's report was presented to an AU Heads of State meeting in Addis Ababa in January 2015, but was not publicly released by the Peace and Security Council until 24 July 2016 despite demands from various quarters, including Dr Riek and the Troika. When it was finally released the section which identified the individuals responsible for the crimes against civilians, and hence subject to prosecution, was kept secret. Meanwhile, a separate draft submission to the AU Commission by Professor Mahmood Mamdani was leaked to discredit the author because of his conclusions that the Troika handed over power to the criminal SPLA and that in the circumstances the best approach was to place the territory under the administration of the AU.[7] But such radical ideas were never entertained by a peace process stuck on finding power-sharing formulas acceptable to Salva and Riek.

Restricted to elites, refusing to address the issues people had fought over, and instead devoted to finding acceptable formulas for the elites to continue looting the state, the negotiations marginalized the South Sudanese. Nuer supporters of the IO were particularly aggrieved that the international community reduced the conflict over which their families and friends had died to power-sharing and re-imposing Salva, the person they held responsible for those killings.

The failure of the negotiations to make progress and the refusal of the belligerents to honour repeated cessation-of-hostilities agreements opened the door to demands for other means to be exerted on the parties to reach an agreement. Most popular here and taken up early by the American pro-SPLA lobbyists of the Enough organization was sanctions. While an arms embargo was widely called for, the US feared it would disproportionately harm the government and thus opposed it. There was also little reason to believe that the states of the region would end or freeze their economically profitable and military engagements in the country.

As a result, sanctions were only applied against four generals – two from the SPLA and two from the IO – by the US, EU, and Canada. However, there is no evidence that such sanctions have in any discernible way influenced, much less constrained, the activities of these individuals or anyone else. This is hardly surprising given the provisions restricting them from travelling or holding financial assets in these countries are irrelevant. Indeed, being sanctioned became something of an honour, to the extent that one IO general, Gabriel Tang, complained that the imposition of sanctions against another IO general, Peter Gadet, had made him more popular and he too demanded to be sanctioned.[8] Riek's response to the repeated threats to have sanctions laid against him was, 'We Sudanese [sic.] have been in wars for a long time and will not be moved or intimidated by the international community',[9] but all indications are that he personally feared such measures. The UN passed Resolution 2206, which called for its Sanctions Committee to designate individuals and entities while the Peace and Security Council of the AU appealed to the UN Security Council for the immediate imposition of an arms embargo on the belligerents.[10] But with the region divided, comprehensive sanctions were never possible, individual sanctions unworkable, and the US repeatedly opposed an arms embargo.

It is a mark of US frustration that in late 2014 its diplomats began calling for the removal of Salva and Riek from the peace process (a 'battle of the egos' was how one American diplomat put it), who they simplistically held responsible for the war. How Riek caused the conflict was never explained. Also not explained was how they would be removed, who would replace them, and why their replacements would be more likely to accept the peace-makers' demands. While nominally supporting a neutral peace process, the US government and the lobbyists had no doubt as to who bore the major responsibility for the conflict. Responding directly to the equivalency rhetoric of Eric Reeves of the Friends of South Sudan (see above), Secretary of State John Kerry said, 'we do not put any kind of equivalency into the relationship between the sitting president, constitutionally and duly elected by the people of the country, and a rebel force that is engaged in use of arms in order to seek political power or to provide a transition'.[11]

Feeling the pressure, IGAD and the Troika tried to pull together the various points of agreement and put before the parties a detailed proposal. These efforts did not provide the break-through the mediators had sought, however, and running out of steam they issued another proposal, 'Key Provisions and Justifications for the Agreement on the Resolution of the Conflict in the Republic of South Sudan' in March 2015.

Riek attacked this proposal for its weak commitment to federalism, which only called for the Transitional Government of National Unity (TGoNU) to 'Initiate a Federal and democratic system of government that reflects the character of South Sudan'. He also objected to the absence of a ceasefire for the non-GUN states, failure to provide for the demilitarization and cantonment of forces in all state capitals and – consistent with the demands of his military – that unification of the armed forces be completed in 30 months.[12] Voicing long-held IO demands, Riek insisted that the Ugandan army and Sudanese rebel groups be withdrawn before a ceasefire could be approved. Meanwhile, the failure to bring the IO components in Equatoria and Bahr al Ghazal into the peace process was reminiscent of the sidelining of the SSDF during the Sudan peace talks, which became a precipitating factor in the outbreak of South Sudan's civil war. In addition, for Riek the absence of these two areas in the peace agreement reduced him to a Nuer tribal leader when he wanted to project himself as a national leader. The Nuer, however, were only lukewarm about building a national organization and were happy with the 53 per cent share in the governments of Greater Upper Nile allotted to the IO by the IGAD proposal.

After repeatedly saying that he could work with Salva Kiir in government, Riek now said that the government had lost legitimacy by over-staying its term of office and by killing civilians in Juba, and he could not serve as vice president under Salva. This threw a spanner into the works of the mediators, but Riek was trying to defuse the claim of the defected generals that the war was being fought so that he could again serve under the person held most responsible for the December 2013 Juba killings by his Nuer followers. Riek also opposed the Former Detainees being granted 7 per cent representation in the central government, even though they had already joined the government.

In opposition to the government, Riek and the IO leadership strongly endorsed IGAD's proposal for a Joint Monitoring and Evaluation Commission (JMEC) headed by a former president of Botswana, Festus Mogae, which would oversee and evaluate the progress of the transitional government in implementing the provisions of the agreement. The proposal for the JMEC was based on the limited capacity of the belligerents to implement the agreement, opposition to its provisions, and went part of the way to responding to those calling for an international trusteeship. The SPLM-IO also endorsed the proposal for a hybrid court to put on trial those deemed guilty of abuses against civilians during the war, even though there was no doubt that some senior IO officials, including probably Riek, would be candidates for charges.

Arusha Talks

Talks, as opposed to negotiations, were held in Arusha in parallel to those in Addis Ababa, in order to reconcile the three branches of the SPLM. This was based on the premise that the conflict had its origins within the ruling SPLM and could be resolved by agreement at the party level. These internal party talks were also justified by the failure of the IGAD negotiations to make progress. They were sponsored by the ruling parties of Ethiopia (Ethiopian People's Revolutionary Democratic Front or EPRDF), Tanzania (Chama Cha Mapinduzi or CCM), and South Africa (African National Congress or ANC). From the outset, it was made clear that the Arusha talks would supplement and support the Addis Ababa negotiations and not serve as an alternative venue for achieving peace.

However, after being slow to endorse the process, the EPRDF withdrew when it realized that Arusha was being used to undermine the Addis Ababa-centred peace process and instead highlight the roles of South Africa, which wanted to project its presence on the continental stage, Kenya, aggrieved at Addis Ababa's domination of the peace process and which wanted to use the Former Detainees to reinforce its role, and Tanzania, which wanted to play a greater role on the regional political stage. Meanwhile, Uganda's Museveni supported Arusha because it served to take pressure off Juba in IGAD negotiations dominated by Ethiopia, which was held to be sympathetic to the SPLM-IO. The Former Detainees supported Arusha because their lack of military capacity would not be so debilitating in this forum and they assumed they could employ their supposedly superior political skills. With his lack of popularity and links to the Former Detainees, Taban Deng was a keen supporter of Arusha and it was only through the party that he could manoeuvre his way to the heights of power. Riek supported the Arusha process to build a relationship with then Tanzanian President Jakaya Kikwete that he hoped would undermine the influence of Museveni in the region. He also appeared to be under the illusion that SPLM reconciliation was a useful means to pursue his leadership ambitions, although the Dinka who have dominated the organization from its inception were unlikely to accept any Nuer for the leadership, and certainly not Riek. The US, however, did not support the Arusha initiative, fearing it would undermine the IGAD negotiations and serve as a means for the belligerents to 'forum-shop'.

The continuing failure of the rancorous Addis Ababa negotiations provided a sharp contrast with Arusha, where the talks were usually conciliatory and led to the signing of a framework agreement on 23 October 2014, which committed the three SPLM factions to work together peacefully and acknowledge their shared responsibility for the crisis. Progress continued to be made and on 21 January 2015 the Intra-SPLM Dialogue produced an Agreement on the Reunification of the SPLM signed by Dr Riek Machar, President Salva Kiir, and the Former Detainee's Deng Alor. The agreement concluded that 'the reunification and reconciliation of the SPLM is the key to the resolution of the current crisis'.[13] The parties also agreed to restore peace and stability, apologize for past atrocities, embrace policies that encourage tolerance and democracy, promote political pluralism, refuse to let those who committed atrocities in the war hold office, and expedite the conclusion of a peace agreement.

The SPLM-IO leadership was under the gun from its membership for even participating in a process designed to reconcile with the hated SPLM, since it flew in the face of repeated IO resolutions that SPLM reconciliation must be dependent upon the outcome of the IGAD negotiations. The former SSDF-IO generals were particularly upset at the course of the Arusha process, fearing that since they opposed the SPLA they would become its sacrificial lambs. Nonetheless, IO negotiators trumpeted the agreement's promise that the SPLM apologise for the country's conflict and contended this was a major concession, since Salva as president bore the primary responsibility and as a result should step down.[14] That was never going to happen, and it could well be argued that Riek as vice president should also resign on that basis. The various detailed provisions on the re-organization and democratization of the SPLM were equally the product of the dreamland environment in which these talks were held.

Even this unrealistic approach to stopping South Sudan's civil war ended in late May 2015 when President Uhuru Kenyatta reached the end of his patience with the Former Detainees, whose expenses he assumed, and called for the Arusha process to be merged with the IGAD mediation. Never popular with either Ethiopia or Sudan, in June 2015 the IO leadership and Riek concluded that the Arusha process had reached an impasse and for it go forward there must be a comprehensive peace agreement[15] – that is, the position the IO reached in 2014 in Nasir. Despite the collapse of the initiative five Former Detainees went to Juba on 2 June 2015, accompanied by the Deputy Chair of the ANC, Cyril Ramaphosa, the Secretary-General of the CCM, and the foreign ministers of Ethiopia and Kenya. The Former Detainees claimed their return to Juba was a success and in the view of their many critics it was, because Salva reinstated them as members of the party and allowed these avid businessmen access to their bank accounts. Calling for peace and reconciliation the Former Detainees then went on to Addis Ababa where they met Taban, but Riek refused to see them.

The Former Detainees' leader, Pagan Amum, returned to Juba to resume his position as secretary-general of the party, but Majak D'Agoot and Oyai Deng stayed abroad.

Back to IGAD

The failure to reach a peace agreement led IGAD and the Troika to conclude that their approach was correct, but – and this is strange for a mediation process – that they were not able to exert enough power to force their agreement on the belligerents. The mediators also said privately that they felt constrained by the agendas of Bashir and Museveni, particularly the latter, contending that increasing the size of the negotiating team would dilute their influence. They thus organized IGAD Plus, which took the same approach, but vastly expanded the international presence at the negotiating table. It now included representatives from the AU, five African states, the European Union, China, and the IGAD Partners' Forum. But mindful of the developing cold war, Russia was not invited.

Meanwhile, the Salva government set about getting its house in order by dismissing five state governors during the negotiations – including Joseph Bakosoro of Western Equatoria – to ensure that Riek and the IO could not find any potential allies among the governors. The dismissals went into effect just before the signing of the peace agreement, after which governors could not be removed. The government also continued its repression of the private media and, among its more bizarre actions, organized anti-peace demonstrations in Juba and the regional capitals.

On 24 July 2015, the mediators presented the parties to the conflict with a 'compromise agreement' and gave them until 17 August to either reach an understanding on their differences or have the agreement imposed on them. This 'take it or leave it' agreement included virtually the same provisions that the government and SPLM-IO had rejected in March 2015. The only significant difference was that it included provisions for compensation for the victims of the violence, something long advocated by the IO. Since the agreement had not changed, the only thing that could have led to a change of heart on the part of the government or the IO was an alteration in the political and military situation, and the added pressure on the belligerents.

Indeed, the IO's limited supply of munitions meant that the IO insurgency in Jonglei and Upper Nile had largely petered out. All the capitals and major towns were under the control of the SPLA and Ugandan army, and even the IO headquarters at Pagak was in danger of falling. By late April 2015 most of Unity state was under the government, and the IO leadership was further depressed by the failure of their colleagues in Greater Equatoria and Bahr al Ghazal to launch major insurgencies. The only thing that kept the IO from complete collapse in its heartland was the fortuitous defection of the Shilluk war lord, Johnson Olony, to the opposition.

The IO's inability to build on the momentum of the first Pagak conference and galvanize country-wide opposition to Salva's increasingly authoritarian regime, and the opposition of the US-led international community left the SPLM-IO isolated, largely restricted to a Nuer core in Upper Nile, Jonglei, and parts of Unity, and dependent upon Khartoum's parsimonious supply of weaponry. By August 2015 an IO military victory over the government appeared further away than at any time since the commencement of the war, hopes for the development of a nation-wide resistance movement had declined, and SPLM-IO leadership morale was at an all-time low. Against that background Riek's self-appointed IO leaders met in Pagak Upper Nile and after only two days of debate formally approved almost the same IGAD agreement they had rejected only months before. The IO's declining fortunes rather than international pressure or the flurry of diplomatic activity in the run up to the signing of the agreement is what brought the party to accepting the agreement.

Most attendees welcomed the IGAD proposal, which gave them power and positions in the Juba government and effective Nuer control of the states of Greater Upper Nile. They justified selling out their colleagues in Greater Equatoria and Greater Bahr al Ghazal by contending that the Nuer had paid the price of the war while their counterparts had achieved little militarily. At Riek's behest, though, they passed an amendment calling for 33 per cent IO representation in these two regions. This was not sufficient for the Equatorian Major-General Martin Kenyi, who was the strongest opponent of the agreement at Pagak, but other Equatorians supported the agreement because they held it was the best route to achieving federalism. Martin, however, made clear his intention to continue the war in Equatoria irrespective of the outcome of the peace process. In the event, a number of Equatorians and a representative from Western

Bahr al Ghazal wrote a memorandum to Riek demanding that the IO not go forward with the implementation of the peace agreement unless the issue of government recognition of IO forces in Greater Equatoria and Western Bahr al Ghazal was resolved.[16] Riek refused, but said he would make the issue of cantonment a priority upon his return to Juba and if it was not resolved he would consider it a breach of the agreement and withdraw. The Dinka component of the IO had little to say and supported the agreement.

In response to the concerns of the military, the delegates objected to IGAD's proposed 18-month army integration and passed an amendment that it be extended to 30 months. The agreement's commitment to federalism was welcomed, but delegates demanded that it be accomplished during the transitional period and further that the government take the name of the 'Transitional Government of the Federal Republic of South Sudan'. Since virtually all the attendees had opposed any agreement that called for a Salva-led government and almost as many opposed SPLM reconciliation, they had to perform intellectual contortions to justify their now contrary position.

With the attendees largely of one mind on the agreement they had little to do and – to 'keep them busy' as one delegate put it – Riek assigned them the task of examining the 106-page submission of desired reforms he had recently submitted to Kenyan President Uhuru Kenyatta. The attendees approved an IO constitution and Dr Peter Adwok's proposed party's manifesto after making major changes due to its mildly social democratic tone offending their right-wing sentiments. According to Riek, these documents would serve as templates for the reconciled SPLM constitution, after which the IO would be dissolved. This despite most of the IO membership opposing SPLM reconciliation and not wanting to dissolve their organization.

Based on interviews of about 20 attendees in the immediate aftermath of the Pagak conference, it would appear that most would accept the IGAD agreement even if their amendments were rejected, so keen were they to reach an agreement. In meetings with Riek on 8 August and Taban on 9 August they said that some of the IO amendments – such as those on power ratios in Greater Equatoria and Bahr al Ghazal, federalism, and a longer army integration period – were very important, but they never threatened to withdraw from the negotiations if they were not accepted.

Although Riek claimed that the latest IGAD effort would not produce an agreement and that the parties would return to war, he was remarkably unconcerned at the poor organization and morale of his army, and how ill-equipped it was. Indeed, there was a steady trickle of IO officers and soldiers going to UN camps, returning home, or even joining the SPLA, while even senior IO officers were spending an increasing amount of time away from the field in Addis Ababa. Without ammunition or leadership, the white army fighters had largely returned to their cattle herds. Despite the IO's military vulnerability, Taban was dismissive of any attempt to reconcile with the dissident generals, arguing that they were an insignificant minority with no popular base. While demoralization was encouraging support for a peace agreement among Riek's colleagues, it was leading the Juba regime to conclude that advancing the war offered more opportunities to achieve their ends.

Since Taban consistently supported a negotiated end to the conflict, there was little doubt he would sign the agreement, but Riek professed ambivalence. Apart from his battlefield losses and the lack of support for war by his IO colleagues, Riek wanted to sign the agreement to embarrass the government, which most had concluded would not sign, based on the anti-peace campaign it was carrying out at the time. Unlike some of his Nuer colleagues Riek is not a natural warrior, always looked to the peace process and his political ability to take him to power in Juba, and never appreciated that most of the Western diplomats reviled him, especially those from the US.

Fearing that his Juba allies would not sign the agreement and he would be left internationally isolated, President Museveni brought Prime Minister Haile Mariam, President Kenyatta, and Sudanese Foreign Minister Ibrahim Ghandour (Bashir did not attend out of a fear that his old enemy Museveni would have him arrested and turned over to the ICC) to Kampala on 11 August, where he insisted that the 'white man's deadline' of 17 August for the IGAD-Plus agreement be extended, the IO's 53 per cent share of power in the state governments of Greater Upper Nile be withdrawn, power only be shared at the executive level in the central government on the basis of 53 per cent for the government and 33 per cent for IO, and Juba and the regional capitals not be de-militarized. He also demanded the elimination of 15 per cent IO representation in the non-Nuer states, and urged the governments of Uganda, Kenya, Ethiopia, and Sudan to assume responsibility for security arrangements and integration of the forces, and that these tasks be completed within three months. No one doubted Museveni's power over Salva because of South Sudan's military and economic dependence on Uganda, but his late-in-the-day attempt to derail the peace process was still shocking and many blamed the US for not reigning him in. Indeed, one IGAD official said, 'Despite Seyoum's efforts to pressure Museveni he could not get over his hatred of Bashir and the US supported Uganda through the entire peace process because of their unity in opposition to the Sudanese Islamists'.

Salva refused to negotiate with Riek for their scheduled 13 August meeting or attend the IGAD Heads of State Summit two days later because of fears that if he did not sign the IGAD agreement he could be arrested, a conclusion his cabinet reached after Seyoum Mesfin said that he would not permit the belligerents to leave Addis Ababa until an agreement was signed.

Seyoum briefed Riek on 14 August on the impending changes to the peace agreement, with Riek expressing his shock at Museveni's demands and the indications that IGAD was going along with him. The peace-makers had repeatedly emphasized that the IGAD-Plus agreement was written in stone and could only be altered with the shared approval of the belligerents. Unable to accept the altered proposal Riek tried to reassure a meeting of the IO leadership on the same day that the party had faced isolation before and it could weather this storm if the IO refused to sign. But Riek's comparison was false and the IO was now divided and isolated to a degree not seen since the start of the insurgency. This could largely be attributed to his leadership, which produced divisions, the breakaway of generals and politicians, military losses, and led the government and regional leaders to conclude that the IO was on the ropes and were thus prepared to weaken the agreement. Meanwhile, Taban assured the author that the IO would not walk away from the peace process and instead would demand that IGAD stick to the original agreement. He also said that if the IGAD process collapsed he looked to the Arusha process to reconcile the SPLM factions, which again emphasized the gap between his thinking and most IO members.

In the event, the US rolled back some of Museveni's changes to the original document. Under the latest power sharing provisions, the

IO was allocated 40 per cent of the executive positions in the states of Greater Upper Nile, 15 per cent in the other seven states, and the governorships of Upper Nile and Unity state. The powers of the Ministry of Federalism, a key concern of the IO's Equatorians, was increased and the IO gained representation on the Council of Ministers, but Jonglei was kept under the government in response to the demands of the powerful Bor Dinka community. The Former Detainees who were effectively part of the government were given 7 per cent representation in the national cabinet.

The optics of the government-orchestrated rejectionist campaign, with people on the streets of Juba screaming against peace and the refusal of Salva to go to Addis Ababa, cast the government in such a negative light before the international community that Museveni pressed him to attend the negotiations. In response, Salva did go to Addis Ababa, but some of his closest colleagues were seen trying to physically stop him from attending the negotiations, presumably because Salva is considered even by his closest colleagues as so unreliable that they could not be assured he would follow government policy. Although the international community had long pressed for face-to-face negotiations between Riek and Salva,[17] and Riek had wanted such negotiations, the mediators kept them apart. Government sceptics were proven correct when at midnight on 16 August Riek and Salva reached an agreement on the IGAD proposals. They could have signed it then but were advised to wait until morning when an official ceremony was being organized. That proved another error in judgement by the mediators and while Riek maintained the unity of his followers in support of the agreement, government opponents threw up so many objections that by morning their acceptance of the agreement was in doubt and by mid-day on the 17th agreement between the SPLM-IO and the government had collapsed. The best that could be done was to extract a promise from Salva – one that few thought he would keep – to return to Addis Ababa in 15 days to sign the peace agreement, i.e. 15 days after the mediators' deadline.

Dlamini Zuma, leading the AU delegation, together with the region's Uhuru Kenyatta, Yoweri Museveni, and Haile Mariam were very upset with the failure of the peace process and feared that the 'white men' (ironically the 'white man' they most feared was President Barack Obama) would usurp their process. To salvage the best of a bad situation, the diplomats engineered an agreement between Riek and Pagan Amum, who as Secretary-General of the SPLM again assumed the role of leader of the Former Detainees. The fact that the Former Detainees were effectively part of the government and controlled no armed forces, and it was far from clear how many of the Former Detainees Pagan represented, was glossed over. Pagan's signature was presented as a major achievement and an important step on the road to sustainable peace. The weakness of what was awkwardly called the Agreement for the Resolution of Conflict in South Sudan (ARCSS) was demonstrated by the Former Detainees' fear they would be arrested if they went to Juba, and some did not return. Others that signed included Salva's presidential advisor and liberation hero, General Joseph Lagu, while Dr Lam Akol indicated he would sign as leader of the SPLM-DC if the agreement was brought to Juba, because he was not permitted to leave the city.[18] The peace process had not only run up short, but everyone – except Riek – had egg on their face. Although long held up as the main obstacle to peace, and as his critics would have it even the cause of the war, Riek for a brief period basked in the glow of a peace-maker. This was in sharp contrast to Salva, who fled Addis Ababa for Juba and a hero's welcome from his government of peace rejectionists.

The IO leadership was pleased with the agreement since the party had not fractured during the process, escaped international condemnation, and looked forward to watching the pressure mount on Salva and his government to sign. Moreover, given the IO's weak political and military position, the IO had come out of the negotiations better than could have been expected. Riek also claimed that the peace agreement represented a vindication for the IO insurgency because it included a commitment to federalism, hybrid courts, the Joint Monitoring and Evaluation Commission, agreement to reform the judicial system, reparations, and transitional justice. Riek was to be proven wrong in each of those claims, but there was no denying that signing the agreement had transformed him overnight from being a war-monger to a peace-maker, winning the support of South Sudanese civil society and the interest of a host of businessmen who now descended on his house in Addis Ababa.

Almost alone in the IO, Riek had directed his energies to reaching a negotiated settlement, but he was now dependent on an unreliable international community and, as the late-in-the-day watering down of the agreement had demonstrated, that was a reckless move. Not a few in the IO also asked whether the limited gains of the peace agreement could ever justify the enormous loss of life and destruction of the previous 20 months. While considered a hero immediately after signing the peace agreement, Riek would follow the trajectory of Omar Bashir, who went from being a figure of hate to an upholder of the CPA, before reverting to a monster upon completion of the agreement. Unfortunately for Riek, his hero status only lasted 15 days.

To the surprise of many, Salva signed the peace agreement on 26 August in Juba. But duly prepped by the rejectionists around him he read out a statement listing nine major areas of objection to the agreement, which he described as 'neither the Holy Bible nor the Holy Koran'. He made clear he was signing under international duress, which made it difficult for IGAD and the Troika to claim any success and most observers were left doubtful about the viability of the agreement. To summarize the key elements of the Agreement on the Resolution of the Conflict in South Sudan, both parties committed to an immediate cessation of violence, Riek to be reinstated as first vice president, troops in Juba to be scaled down and jointly provided, the creation of a transitional government for 30 months, presidential elections to be held 30 days before the end of the transitional government's mandate, and the establishment of a hybrid court to try those responsible for abuses committed during the conflict.

Three elements were meant to reinforce the peace process and keep the SPLM factional leaders in line: first, an AU-conducted investigation into the causes of violence which would identify the guilty parties (although the chapter in which these individuals are named has yet to be released); second, the formation of a US-funded hybrid court where those identified in the report and others could be brought to trial (although to date this court has not been established), and lastly, a Juba-based Joint Monitoring and Evaluation Commission with the authority to oversee the implementation of the peace agreement. That too would not live up to expectations. Having undermined his own party's capacity to militarily challenge the government, Riek looked to the international community to ensure government compliance with the agreement. Meanwhile, the government viewed the JMEC with horror, contending it undermined national sovereignty, and that the mild-mannered chairman and former president of Botswana, Festus Mogae, was in effect a Paul Brenner, who served as the US pro-consul in Iraq. It would not take long before the positions of the belligerents were reversed: Mogae was tamed, little more than an agent of the government, and all sections of the opposition would call for his dismissal.

The biggest weakness in the agreement as far as the SPLM-IO dissidents were concerned was its failure to address Nuer demands for Salva to step down and to end SPLM rule. Thus, it gave them a big stick with which to bash the agreement and Riek. Indeed, Riek told me that once ordinary Nuer found out that Salva would remain president and he would serve under him they would reject the agreement. In the wake of the signing of the agreement Gathoth Gatkouth and Peter Gadet said by phone from Khartoum that the IGAD document was a 'surrender agreement', and the newly formed Federal Democratic Party under Gabriel Changeson concluded it was a 'doomed so-called peace agreement'. Both these groups said they would continue to fight.

Surprisingly, the many divisions in the IGAD region appeared to have been set aside during the final days of the process when the heads of state came together and tried to oversee an agreement, albeit after Museveni had thrown a wrench into the works by pressing for last minute changes. The cooperation shown between the leaders, especially between Bashir and Museveni, stood out. Within a couple of days, however, the Sudan ambassador to South Sudan contended that the Ugandan leader was playing a two-faced game and that Salva would not have withdrawn from the peace process without assurances that his back was covered.[19]

Indicative of the regional concerns was the provision in the agreement requiring the components of the northern rebel groups supporting the government in South Sudan 'be disarmed, demilitarized, and repatriated by the state actors with whom they have been supporting within the Pre-Transitional Period'.[20] If enacted this would involve these rebel groups serving as sacrificial lambs to the South Sudanese process. This provision was introduced by Bashir and while unlikely to be implemented it was used by Khartoum for leverage. This measure also made clear that a sustainable peace in South Sudan was dependent on Sudan and Uganda's security interests being met.

Lastly, while the collapse of the peace agreement would lead the US to try to distance itself from the agreement and place responsibility on the South Sudanese, as made clear by the Senate Committee on Foreign Relations holding a panel on 'Independent South Sudan: A Failure of Leadership', Special Envoy Booth was correct in claiming 'the agreement would not have come about without the intensive diplomatic efforts of the United States'.[21] He also emphasized the role of President Obama, who met regional leaders in Addis Ababa in July 2015 to convince the parties to sign an agreement, Secretary Kerry's efforts in October to reinforce US expectations, and how administration officials kept up a 'drumbeat of calls ... to keep the peace process moving forward'.

Conclusion

IGAD's approach was directionless, sometimes dependent upon the whims of the belligerents, and subject to the conflicting interests of the countries of the region. What passed for analysis was holding President Salva Kiir and IO leader Dr Riek Machar solely responsible for the conflict and sometimes calling for their removal, but at the same time constructing a peace process and agreement in which they assumed a central role. Under the peace agreement 93 per cent of the executive positions in Juba and the states were turned over to components of the SPLM, while the president and two vice presidents all came from the SPLM. Thus, for the third time – the first was the CPA and the second the 2010 fraudulent elections – the international community bestowed legitimacy on South Sudan's one-party state. And not just any party, but a party that had politically and economically bankrupted the country, driven it into an unnecessary war, and was now abhorred by most South Sudanese. The most important constituency for peace – the South Sudanese people – were not there to be mobilized because they were denied participation in the peace process. Despite an enormous investment in political capital over two years and the experience that should have been drawn from the interminable Sudan peace process, the best that the peace-makers could come up with was some modifications in the allocation of power among the SPLM elite. While the government and South Sudanese state needed far-reaching reforms the IGAD peace process endorsed the status quo.

With the mediation focused on a conflict between the government and the SPLM-IO, which was understood mostly to be between the Dinka and the Nuer, other parts of the country, notably the

Equatorians, were largely ignored. As a result, the signing of the peace agreement set in motion the revolt of the Equatorians, which would bring a new phase to the war. Summing up, de Waal said, 'They frame the conflict as solely between the two belligerents, ignoring the fact that any deal that rewards and privileges the two will set in motion additional conflicts'.[22]

Equally alarming, there was no indication that the peace-makers had a common understanding of the causes of the conflict and thus what problem they were attempting to resolve. As a Nuer elder noted, 'I looked in the agreement to find the IGAD mediators' understanding of the problem and never found it'. The endemic failures of government and finally the outbreak of the December 2013 war proved that judgement mistaken and even the AU Commission of Inquiry concluded that 'the flaws of the CPA (in terms of process and outcomes) as well as implementation' led directly to the next war.[23] And the same pattern followed with this peace agreement.

6 | THE COLLAPSE OF THE PEACE AGREEMENT

Introduction

It did not take long after the peace agreement was signed for it to begin falling apart. In the first instance, this was because the agreement failed to address the structural problems that underlie South Sudan's descent into civil war. The problems continued with the failure of IGAD, the Troika, and JMEC to ensure implementation of the agreement in the face of government efforts to dismantle it. IGAD-Plus brought to bear the pressure of a large section of the international community on the belligerents to sign the peace agreement, but after it was signed that authority withered and the government drew the not unreasonable conclusion that, with the US opposed to the Riek Machar-led SPLM-IO and unwilling to directly confront the government, it could operate with impunity.

The government cast aside the core power-sharing formula based on the existing ten states and created 28 states. The peace-makers complained but did nothing. More alarmingly, the government ignored security arrangements provisions on the demilitarization of Juba, hid soldiers in the capital, and SPLA Chief of Staff Paul Malong secretly brought a Dinka militia into the city. Despite knowledge of these breaches and widespread predictions that they would produce a conflagration, the US-led international community insisted that Riek return to Juba and take up his position as first vice president in the TGoNU.

The question must be asked as to why under these circumstances did the US put so much pressure on Riek to return to Juba? In light of subsequent events, some have concluded that key officials in the US government saw him as an obstacle to the peace process and would not be unduly troubled if he was killed. The first part of that contention is clearly true, but it would appear that – at this stage – the only option the US could entertain was fulfilment of the peace agreement and that meant not only ignoring the danger that Riek's return to Juba would pose, but also down-playing other blatant breaches of the peace agreement by the government. However, this approach by the US government was interpreted by the Salva government as indicating that the US not only favoured the government over a Riek-led IO, but that it was being given licence to pursue an agenda which focused on war and not fulfilment of the peace agreement. What at this stage was a 'give Salva a chance' position by the US government would after the collapse of the peace agreement in July 2016 become support for 'give war a chance'. Circumstances, frustration, personalization of the conflict, hatred of Riek, and a series of incremental steps led the US government to shift from being the leading backer of the peace process and peace agreement to tacitly supporting war as the best means of bringing peace to South Sudan.

South Sudan Government Creates 28 States

The peace agreement stipulated that the government be granted 46 per cent representation in the three existing states of Greater Upper Nile, the SPLM-IO 40 per cent in Greater Upper Nile and 15 per cent in the other states, with the remaining 14 per cent in Greater Upper Nile split between the Former Detainees and the independent political parties. In addition, the agreement stipulated that the IO would nominate the governors for Upper Nile and Unity states and the government would nominate the governors for Jonglei and the other seven states. Agreement on the form of federalism was to be the result of a constitutional review process that would take place at the end of the 30-month transitional period.

As a result, President Salva Kiir's announcement on 2 October 2015 that the government was replacing the ten-state system with a 28-states decentralized system was a shock. The government claimed its plan would 'devolve power closer to the people', but the same government had opposed all proposals for federalism during the IGAD negotiations and for a time had banned South Sudanese journalists from even using the word federalism because it feared Riek's popularization of the term. In addition, the government's Dinka leaders held that any genuine devolution of powers to the states would undermine their dominance in the country, and were opposed.

Appreciating that opposition to federalism was no longer tenable, though, Salva and his advisors came up with their own federal arrangements, which transferred oil production areas in Upper Nile and Unity states from the SPLM-IO to the SPLM. Under the 28 states system Dinka territory expanded from 25 per cent of the country to a commanding 42 per cent,[1] and by almost tripling the number of states under Dinka control, vastly increased the scope for patronage. Salva's arrangements did not change the overall land base of Equatoria or touch the Murle (important allies he could not risk alienating), and Nuer territory was only reduced by 2 per cent, but the Shilluk lost half of their land base, including the Upper Nile capital of Malakal. Meanwhile, minority communities like the Bul Nuer and Fertit of Western Bahr al Ghazal had their land reduced from 20 per cent of the country to a mere 5 per cent.[2]

The government's elimination of the states on which the power-sharing arrangements were based, creation of new states, and ignoring of the requirement that the type of federalism suitable for South Sudan be a result of a country-wide consultation at the end of the process, were all clear and fundamental breaches of the peace agreement.

Although the peace agreement took precedence, Salva's order was also in breach of the Transitional Constitution. Under the Constitution, the president does not have the power to either create states or alter the boundaries of existing states.[3] Article 162 (1) of the Transitional Constitution stipulates that 'the territory of South Sudan is composed of ten states' and any amendment to that provision could only be decided upon by the National Legislature, not the president. Moreover, articles 162 (3) and (4) grant authority to the Council of States alone to alter boundaries. While the President has the authority to initiate an amendment to the Constitution, Salva did not do that. If there was an independent judiciary in South Sudan – which the AU Commission of Inquiry concluded there was not – the presidential order would have been quickly set aside.

Upon coming to power under the CPA, the SPLM made the ten states mere appendages of the central government and the establishment of 28 states continued that trend. Moreover, the lack of planning and consultation before implementation, failure to establish state boundaries, as well as confusion over the powers of the additional states is creating additional problems that an already lawless South Sudan is ill-equipped to cope with. For example, in Upper Nile, the government turned over Shilluk land to the Dinka, including the contested capital of Malakal, and relegated the Shilluk to the less developed western bank of the Nile. The displaced and threatened Shilluk found refuge in the UN POC camps, but even here they were not safe. On 17 and 18 February 2016 the UN forces stepped aside while SPLA entered the camp, separated the Dinka from the Shilluk and Nuer, and killed 30 and wounded 123 from the latter group.[4]

A government which could not provide the necessary financial and human resources for the effective functioning of ten states then committed to provide resources for 28 states, in a context where the war and the collapse of oil prices has drained it of revenues. Only 15 per cent of the national budget was allocated to the states and most of it was consumed by the salaries of SPLM functionaries, leaving little for programmes.[5] Lower levels of government were further stretched for resources. Despite having one of the largest parliaments in the world relative to the size of its population, the Council of States was further expanded to include 18 additional representatives.

The Transitional Constitution permitted the president to remove state governors in the event of insecurity, with the proviso that elections be called within 60 days. Salva, however, repeatedly dismissed state governments where insecurity was not a problem, without elections, and effectively managed the states through the SPLM-state merger that characterized independent South Sudan. Worse, the UN found that the government's system produced 'a pattern of ethnic cleansing and population engineering'.[6]

Southern Sudanese have called for federalism from the eve of Sudan's independence in 1956 until the referendum on secession in 2011, when the SPLM abruptly dropped support for a federal 'New Sudan' and advocated independence. After South Sudan's secession, demands for a genuine devolution of state powers were increasingly made in Equatoria and by the Nuer-inhabited territories of Greater Upper Nile, but a Dinka-dominated government in Juba resisted, fearing that devolution was a stepping stone to the country's dismemberment, a position that mirrored the response of successive governments in Khartoum to southern Sudanese demands. By failing to grant southern Sudanese and other marginalized peoples federalism and undermining the local autonomy agreed upon under the 1972 Addis Ababa Agreement, Khartoum opened the door to secession.

There was a compelling logic for power to be devolved before South Sudan's recent war, and the animosities that have since developed between the country's various ethnic groups make some form of federalism inevitable. There is now a consensus in the country in favour of federalism, but the government's changes had nothing to do with responding to popular and administrative needs. Instead, they were designed to meet its narrow political interests. Moreover, these changes perpetuate the idea that technical approaches to problems of governance can overcome the country's manifold problems. In a paper presented at a conference on federalism at the University of Juba in July 2015 I argued that,

> federalism only provides a *means* to resolve South Sudan's problems and should not be viewed as a short-cut to reforming the SPLA, containing corruption, sharing power, raising living standards, overcoming economic inequities, providing services, or the many other problems that bedevil the country. And crucially no version of federalism can overcome the fundamental problem of a lack of capacity.

With the outbreak of civil war in South Sudan, Riek needed a reform programme that would not only give credence to his revolt but win support beyond his Nuer core. Federalism was key. Riek's proposal involved 21 states modelled after British colonial experience, combining both territorial and ethnic elements, its primary objective being to meet popular demands for service delivery. However, Riek carried out almost no consultations about his proposal and as a result few IO leaders could explain how it would function. Unlike Salva's changes, though, Riek's proposal did not involve a Nuer land grab and the existing power balance between the tribes was retained. The government's opposition to Riek's proposal and all IO demands for federalism during the negotiations put it at odds with the IGAD mediators who acknowledged in ARCSS that 'a Federal system of government is a popular demand of the people of South Sudan' and must be addressed in a constitutional review process.[7] The government calculated that Riek would loudly protest, but having weakened the IO's fighting capacity, he depended on the international community to ensure the implementation of the peace agreement. However much the peace-makers were upset by the establishment of 28 states, they would not let the agreement collapse over the issue.

A few days after Salva's announcement, a debate organized by the Centre for Peace and Development Studies at the University of Juba took place, pitting Dr Lam Akol, leader of the SPLM-Democratic Change Party, against Ambrose Riiny, Chairman of the Jieng Council of Elders, and Lawrence Kirbandy, Presidential Advisor for Legal Affairs. Lam concluded that, 'The president has committed a gross violation of the constitution he has taken a solemn oath to preserve and defend'[8] So devastating was Lam's critique that Ambrose walked out of the debate and went straight to Salva, complaining that Dr Luka Biong, the director of the peace institute and long-time SPLM loyalist, was an opposition agent. The upshot was that Luka was forced to give up his position at the university and flee the country.

SPLM-IO and International Community Respond to the 28-State System

IGAD and the Troika were not short of criticisms of the 28-state system. IGAD concluded that it was, 'Concerned by the recent decision of the Government of South Sudan to implement the October 2, 2015 Presidential Decree on the creation of 28 new states [and] that such action [are] inconsistent with the terms of ARCSS' and then illogically went on to say that the 'Council underlined that this should not delay the formation of the Transitional Government of National Unity … to enable dialogue on this matter'.[9] The Troika concluded, 'this announcement directly contradicts the Government of South Sudan's commitment to implement the peace agreement it signed on August 26' and appealed to President Salva Kiir to 'defer' the order.[10] In response to a question by a journalist about the US response to Salva's imposition of the 28 states 'which is not part of this peace agreement', Susan Rice bizarrely answered, 'both sides are at fault here, and both sides have committed atrocities'.[11] For organizations that had devoted more than two years to reaching a peace agreement and repeatedly complained about the impunity of the belligerents, they gave the government another free pass. Appreciating its victory, the government went on to create 32 states in January 2017 and still more after that. The fact that these states had budgets comparable to districts, and that governors were appointed and removed at the whim of Salva and the Jieng Council of Elders, barely mattered in a context where the entire system of governance had been unceasingly degraded by the SPLM.

Although urged by some IO colleagues to walk away from the peace agreement, given the government's breach of the letter and spirit of it, Riek instead condemned the government's initiative and said that he would take his 21 states proposal to Juba and negotiate with Salva and his 28 states. He was thus complicit in undermining the agreement which called for the ten-state system to be in place until the end of the transitional period, when the constitutional arrangement of the country would be considered. Since Riek did not get to Juba for another seven months, by which time the 28 states system was operational and the peace-makers were not prepared to challenge the government over it, Salva had no need to reach a compromise with Riek.

Almost immediately after Salva's announcement on the 28 states, Riek led a 20-person IO delegation to the US, ostensibly at the invitation of UN Secretary-General Ban Ki-moon, to discuss implementation of the peace agreement. He also visited some of the main Nuer-inhabited states to rally his supporters and spend time with his American wife, Becky, and their daughter. The primary focus of his visit, however, was to win the support of the US government, particularly in his latest tussle over the 28 states. Unlike Salva, Riek was unable to meet President Obama or Susan Rice, apparently because of his reluctance to initial the security arrangements agreement and return to Juba. He did meet John Kerry and Donald Booth on 3 October (together with Vice President James Wani Igga, Deng Alor, Taban Deng, and others) and was urged to go back to Juba.[12] Riek's colleagues claimed Kerry said the establishment of 28 states amounted to an abrogation of the peace agreement and must be reversed, but if that is the case the US did little to force the government to return to the original ten states.

Four days later, on the advice of his national security advisor, Susan Rice, President Obama issued another waiver to the 2008 Child Soldiers Prevention Act, which is meant to block military assistance to countries like South Sudan which recruit children in their armies. Cabinet Affairs Minister Martin Elia Lomuro was quick to say this was 'the right thing to do' and would consolidate 'stability' in the country and strengthen relations with the US.[13] It was also another tacit endorsement of the Juba regime and a means to bring further pressure on Riek.

In addition, John Kerry threatened to have individual sanctions imposed on Riek if he did not set aside his objections to the security arrangements provisions of the peace agreement and return to Juba.[14] Upon leaving the US, Riek toured a number of countries in Africa, including all the IGAD states, except Somalia, requesting 'support of implementation of the agreement, cantonment sites, 28 states declaration, lifting of state of emergency and security violations by the government in Juba ... All responses were go to Juba'.[15] The pressure produced results and on 27 October Riek signed, with reservations, the permanent ceasefire and transitional security arrangements. Following this, the ever optimistic and unrealistic IGAD claimed the war officially ended.

Riek's failure to take a clear stand on the imposition of the 28 states meant that it continued to be a divisive issue in the SPLM-IO. After the IO Advance Mission under Taban Deng went to Juba in early January 2016, as per the peace agreement, Taban asked the government to negotiate with the IO over the issue at an Extraordinary Conference of the SPLM in January (which conformed to the demand by IGAD and the Troika that the belligerents reach an agreement on the matter), but his proposal was rejected. In response, Taban informed the IO Advance Mission at a meeting on 10 January in Juba – to peals of joy – that SPLM reconciliation was a 'non-starter'.[16] Taban quoted an Arab saying that 'the dog keeps barking, but the camel carries on'. In other words, trying to reach a compromise when the government was pursuing Dinka hegemony was a waste of energy.

From that conclusion Taban urged the IO to give up its commitment to ten states and reach agreement with the government on more than 28 states, a position which angered his colleagues. His secret meetings with the government provoked further anger and suspicions that he would defect, and as a result Riek was forced to call an extraordinary meeting of the IO leadership in Pagak to resolve the matter. The leadership rejected Taban's call for agreement with the government on an increase in the number of states, with some demanding he be arrested for opposing IO policy. Riek, however, defended him.

The SPLM-IO's endorsement of the original ten states of the peace agreement had, though, largely become irrelevant given the 28-state system had now taken root and with the international community only opposing it at the rhetorical level, there was little that could be done.

Peace Process Stumbles

The international peace-makers held that the return of the SPLM-IO and Riek to Juba was crucial to the consolidation of the peace agreement. That view was shared by most IO officials, but not Riek. Duabol Lual, IO Head of Protocol and former Under Secretary for Foreign Relations, said Riek spent two days before the Advance Mission left Pagak for Juba trying to convince its members not to go because he had no confidence in Salva's promises, and contended they would merely give him a propaganda victory by demonstrating his supposed commitment to the peace process.[17]

Duabol said that very soon after the Advance Mission arrived in Juba it concluded that peace was not around the corner, jobs were not for the taking, and without an IO army to protect them, or an international community prepared to stand up to the government, they were dangerously exposed. Essentially, Riek's assessment was correct. Frustration led some members of the IO Advance Mission to leave the capital. They were also beginning to overcome the illusion that since the IO was committed to reform (and the government clearly was not) that the US and international community would support them. However, IO members faced a conundrum: while increasingly pessimistic about the prospect for peace, they had no taste for war and were waiting for a signal event to help them decide where to stand. They did not have long to wait.

Meanwhile, Unity state followed its own trajectory. In the wake of the December 2013 Juba killings, Taban joined Riek to form the SPLM-IO and this consolidated the antipathy of the large Bul Nuer clan to the new movement. Meanwhile, Unity state Governor Joseph Manytuil remained loyal to Salva and his brother, Bapiny Manytuil, leader of the SSLA, was appointed lieutenant-general for his support of the government. By the time the peace agreement was signed the SSLA had largely been absorbed into the SPLA.

While Salva had once again proved successful in dividing the Nuer of the state, the peace agreement created new tensions because the state was to pass into IO control under the peace agreement and this meant not only the loss of the governorship, but almost certainly revenge attacks by the non-Bul clans against the Bul. Opposition to the peace agreement drew the Manytuil brothers closer to the government, but Salva's implementation of the 28 states led the Bul to lose territory to the Dinka, thus creating tensions between the two tribes and leading to the defection of Bapiny to the opposition camp.

Government Flouts Security Arrangements

The government's blatant flouting of the peace agreement by establishing 28 states should have signalled its collapse, but more was to come with the failure of the peace-makers to ensure the government implemented the agreement's security arrangements. There were two major problems: first, the presence of government security forces in Juba, and second, the cantonment of non-Nuer IO forces.

Initially, it had been agreed that Juba would be completely de-militarized, but this was opposed by both the government and the SPLM-IO. IGAD and the Troika did not accept parity of forces, apparently because of fear that a large IO army, together with disgruntled Nuer IDPs in the capital, might exact revenge for the civilian killings of December 2013. Eventually it was agreed that the SPLM-IO and government military forces, some 25,000, be redeployed 'outside a radius of 25km from the center of the national capital beginning thirty (30) days after the signing of this Agreement and complete after ninety (90) days',[18] while the demarcation was to be decided upon by a workshop. Not only was the 25-kilometre redeployment outside Juba unlikely to stop the SPLA from quickly moving into the capital if called upon, it also permitted the national army to encircle the capital and block potential escape routes for the IO. In addition, the government was permitted to deploy 5,000 troops in Juba to guard military barracks, bases, and warehouses, and 3,000 more to make up a joint integrated police force that would patrol the capital. Another major flaw in the agreement was its failure to cover the large intelligence forces.

However, early on the government made clear it had no intention of abiding by the conditions of the agreement and hid SPLA soldiers and others belonging to the security forces in the capital. Moreover, SPLA Chief of Staff Paul Malong repeatedly voiced his objection to both the peace agreement and the return of Riek to Juba, and was brazenly bringing militia fighters into Juba from Bahr al Ghazal. Despite widespread awareness of these breaches of the agreement, the threat they posed to the peace process and to the welfare of the people of Juba, and the many unresolved security issues, the US-led peace-makers pressed Riek to return to Juba.

The US pursued its agenda through the UN Security Council (19 April 2016), which urged Riek to return to Juba and form the transitional government, through repeated briefings of the media in which American officials held the IO leader responsible for the failure of the peace agreement to be implemented, and demanded in increasingly harsh language from US Special Envoy Donald Booth that Riek return.[19] According to the US Spokesperson,

> The United States is deeply disappointed by Riek Machar's failure to
> return to South Sudan's capital of Juba today to form the Transitional
> Government of National Unity. His failure to go to Juba despite
> efforts from the international community places the people of South
> Sudan at risk of further conflict and suffering, and undermines the
> peace agreement's reform pillars.[20]

Curiously, no US pressure was exerted on Pagan Amum, General Secretary of the SPLM and leader of the Former Detainees, who was also a signatory of the peace agreement to return to Juba, presumably because by this point his irrelevance was increasingly appreciated.

The lack of a clear understanding of the security arrangements opened the door to disputes over the number of IO soldiers permitted to return to Juba, the kind of weaponry allowed, and the conditions under which Riek would resume his position as first vice president. With US support, Juba contended that the IO could only have light weapons while the SPLA had heavy artillery, tanks, various armoured vehicles, and attack helicopters. Riek also faced opposition to his return from his generals, including IO Chief of Staff, Simon Gatwech, and Johnson Olony, who demanded that he not return until the 28-state system, which had caused outrage among the Shilluk, had been revoked. According to Dr Peter Pham, Director of the Atlantic Council's Africa Center, Riek also had good reason to fear for his own security, since the conflict started not as a civil war, but as an internal political dispute within the ruling SPLA/M ... in which the President, Salva Kiir, tried to settle by force by eliminating his opponents. Where he failed was that Riek Machar and several others got away. In the aftermath of that [Kiir] claimed there was a coup attempt of which US officials and others have always said there was no evidence.[21]

Widespread knowledge that the government was not abiding by the security arrangements provisions begs the question of why Riek returned when he repeatedly said it would be suicidal. The primary reason was pressure by an international community, which Riek was dependent upon for the enforcement of the peace agreement in the absence of a viable IO fighting force. Riek said that people attributed the lack of progress in the peace process to his absence from Juba, while Salva issued repeated ultimatums that if Riek failed to return he would be replaced. Second, in the martial culture of South Sudan, Riek's refusal to return to Juba led to accusations of cowardice, the worst of all epitaphs. Third, as noted, Riek's IO colleagues were anxious to return to Juba. Lastly, Riek has an unwarranted faith in his political skills to overcome obstacles and he hoped to use those skills to divide Salva from the hard-liners in the government. But to the extent that reforms were implemented, important allies of Salva would view them as a conspiracy of the IO and the US to undermine their personal power, as well as to the Dinka tribe and in the state.[22]

Of even more interest than why Riek buckled to US-led pressure to return to Juba was why the US was so insistent he return given its ambassador in Juba, Molly Phee, and many other sources must have made it known to Washington that the government was in multiple breaches of the peace agreement, particularly the security arrangements. While Obama spoke wistfully of a 'Plan B' if the peace process broke down, there was no such plan. The focus from the outset of the peace process had only been on re-establishing the SPLM government on the basis of revised power-sharing arrangements. Everything was directed to that end – threatening to have Salva and Riek removed from the process, organizing IGAD-Plus to bring additional pressure on the parties, threats and applications of sanctions, threats to bring charges against leaders through a US-funded hybrid court, and pressing Riek to return to Juba, when it was widely predicted this would be a stimulus for violence.

Having bent before US demands to return to Juba, Riek had practical problems with organizing his disparate forces and by relying almost exclusively on Nuer troops the perception took hold among many South Sudanese that the peace agreement was a Dinka–Nuer affair. Even while the government was throwing up obstacles to implementing the peace agreement, the US was establishing a narrative which held Riek to be the major problem. On 26 April, in the face of such unrelenting pressures, Riek returned to Juba and was sworn in as first vice president of the TGoNU. The cabinet was sworn in the following week.

Pressuring Riek and his officials and fighters to return to Juba, however, did not serve to overcome differences with the government over federalism, security arrangements, and other issues, while his cabinet appointments created new divisions in the IO. As the deputy leader of the SPLM-IO, Alfred Ladu Gore became minister of interior, but Taban made clear his desire for the lucrative petroleum ministry (with its potential for patronage and corruption) which went to Dak Duop Bishop. Taban, meanwhile, was appointed minister of mining. Almost immediately, rumours circulated that he would defect over the issue. Ezekiel Lol was aggrieved at not being given a ministerial portfolio, instead continuing to serve as Riek's advisor. One of its most respected members, Stephen Parr, was not assigned any official position and he returned to the US.

Meanwhile, Riek tried to broaden his political base. Of the 50 MPs he appointed to the National Assembly 17 were Dinka, 13 Equatorian, 15 Nuer, and 5 from other tribes. Predictably, the relegation of the Nuer to a minority status despite their almost singular war efforts produced grumbling among his Nuer supporters. Riek's priority, however, remained developing a constituency outside his core supporters that could either be used as bargaining leverage within a united SPLM or provide the basis for the formation of a national party. Most of these appointments and the 21 governors under his federal system were young and politically inexperienced, and thus beholden to Riek, unlike old guard politicians who had genuine constituencies. As one of the marginalized old guards noted, 'Riek only wants the cows, not the bulls'.

Equatorians Join the War

While agreement on cantonment of SPLM-IO forces during the transitional period led to an influx of non-Nuer youth to the IO, final resolution of the issue was left to a 'Permanent Ceasefire Arrangements workshop',[23] which held that opposition soldiers fighting at the time the agreement was signed must be placed in cantonment centres. Encouraged by Riek, there had been a massive growth of opposition forces, principally in Greater Equatoria and Western Bahr al Ghazal, and this shocked the government. In response, the government held that cantonment only applied to IO soldiers in Greater Upper Nile, and refused to accept the existence of IO-affiliated soldiers in Western Bahr al Ghazal and Greater Equatoria. While most white army fighters had no desire for cantonment, IO Equatorian rebels and their leaders made it a condition for accepting the peace agreement. For them cantonment was the start to reforming the SPLA, which they viewed as the main instrument of Equatorian oppression, a vehicle for integration into the SPLA, and a means to protect those identified with the SPLM-IO. Government claims that instability in these areas was due to banditry and not political opposition encouraged fighters under the IO banner to increase attacks on government forces, which responded with abuse of civilians. In the event, cantonment centres were not established in Greater Upper Nile or in other parts of the country.

The International Crisis Group claimed that conflict between Equatorians and a Dinka-dominated government was based solely on local-level issues, such as access to grazing lands and the damage done to farms by pastoralists, and that they were not of the same order as those between the Dinka and the Nuer.[24] In fact, the contradiction is greater than between the latter tribes. The biggest structural division in the south is between the modes of production of the largely settled and farming Equatorians and the pastoralist Nilotics, and this intensified because of the greater access to education and modernization of the Equatorians. Moreover, with the Dinka pastoralists supported by the security forces and powerful generals, the conflict increasingly assumed a political form as peasant farmers confronted the Dinka-dominated state. The coming to power of a Dinka-led government under the CPA increased Equatorian subjugation and by the time the December 2013 war broke out many viewed the SPLM government as worse than that of Khartoum.

The civil war brought leaders of local resistance groups to the fore, most of whom affiliated with the SPLM-IO, thus linking local level struggles to the national conflict. The peace process and the resulting agreement of August 2015 was seen in the region as a carve up of the country between the Dinka and Nuer elites, and this served to intensify conflicts in Greater Equatoria and among the Fertit tribes of Western Bahr al Ghazal. In this vortex Dr Riek Machar was held by many Equatorians as a symbol of their aspirations for reform, the means to end Dinka domination, the best prospect to realize their long-supported goal of federalism, and a source of weapons.

A Nuer-Equatorian alliance is viewed as an existential threat to Dinka hegemony, and as a result the government responded partly with carrots, but mostly the stick of widespread repression that in parts of Equatoria bordered on genocide. Instead of dampening resistance to the government, it intensified and further developed in response to the government's refusal to accept cantonment. Meanwhile, Riek saw in aligning with Equatorian resistance a means to strengthen his negotiating position with the government which refused compromise, and the international community, which had concluded the IO had lost the war. As the insurgency declined in Greater Upper Nile it gained momentum in Greater Equatoria.

It is not by chance that the insurgency developed its deepest roots in Western Equatoria, which not only suffered at the hands of Dinka herders, but also the Lord's Resistance Army. The failure of the SPLA to defend the local inhabitants led them to conclude their interests were not represented in the state. They thus felt compelled to protect themselves by establishing an irregular force, the Arrow Boys, so-named because when first organized in 2005 they were only able to fight the marauding LRA with traditional weapons like bows and arrows, and locally made guns.

The lack of government support for the local people when faced with foreign invaders increased alienation and figured in the 2010 election of governor Joseph Bangasi Bakosoro, a former seminarian and SPLA colonel, as independent governor of Western Equatoria. Bakosoro's election was largely due to his aggressive defence of state interests and espousing the cause of the Arrow Boys, including their armament, which was resisted by the SPLA.[25]

Although Bakosoro re-joined the SPLM in 2012, his popularity and positive relations with Vice President Riek Machar caused concern in the government. The outbreak of civil war at the end of 2013 led him to establish a pan-Equatorian reform movement and work with a number of Equatorian dissidents, all of whom were or became senior members of the SPLM-IO, as well as Lieutenant-General Thomas Cirillo, who would defect from the government and form his own rebel group.[26] Bakosoro also developed an alliance with Central Equatoria Governor Clement Wani, who said that Salva was only leader of the Dinka, did not care about the welfare of the rest of the people in the country, and as a result his policies were breeding hatred against the Dinka and support for the IO, which would lead to South Sudan being dividing into three separate states.[27]

In June 2015 Bakosoro said, 'Dinka leaders and their community have failed our country, South Sudan. What's wrong with you people, wherever you go, problems and havoc follows? You ran from danger in your areas and only to come and cause havoc in our state'.[28] Action followed words and fighting broke out in Yambio town between armed youth and the SPLA in late July and early August, which forced thousands to flee to the countryside. Bakosoro so angered the government that he was dismissed as governor and arrested on 16 August 2015. Clement Wani was also dismissed on the same day as governor, but not arrested, presumably because the government feared angering his powerful Mundari militia. Bakosoro was released four days later, but again arrested on 22 December and held until late 2016, after which he fled to the US and formed his own opposition movement.

While non-Dinka have been the primary victims in the war, by the time the peace agreement was signed there was a widespread view among Dinka – and this was cultivated by the government – that their right to rule the country was in danger. The Dinka elder and politician Bona Malwal contends these fears began with the dismal record of a Dinka-led government, but includes the dangers posed by the presence of thousands of angry IDPs in Juba, some of whom were armed and waiting for an opportunity to exact revenge on the government, the arrival of SPLM-IO forces under the terms of the peace agreement, the hatred that most Equatorians in the capital have for the Dinka, and a white army that were it to be armed and organized could reach the capital in two days. Counter-posing Dinka sentiments were fears of Nuer inhabitants of Juba and arriving IO officials and soldiers who retained bitter memories of December 2013 and feared that with their forces considerably outnumbered they could again become victims. The aggressive pursuit of the peace process and demands that Riek and the IO return to Juba created a situation in which the various communities feared for their security.

Despite their victimization in the Juba massacre and a host of other grievances, the Nuer have shown little interest to date in a separate ethnic-based state. This, though, is not the case with the Equatorians, who have long held secession as an option and were suspected of supporting it when they convinced President Nimeiri to re-divide the south in 1983. In a public meeting of Equatorians in Juba in 2010 which I attended, Joseph Lagu, a hero to many for his leading role in the first war, urged Equatorians to consider establishing a separate state if Juba proved unwilling or unable to deliver on a host of demands. Lagu was serving as a presidential advisor at the time, but equally surprising was the almost ecstatic response of the audience. Equatorian disillusionment with the government grew steadily in the intervening period. Equatorian leaders are united in advocating federalism, a term which has a similar meaning to that of the Nuer, namely locally run administrations free of Dinka involvement. Equatorians who support the IO invariably say they are drawn to it because of Riek's espousal of federalism and hold that his support is genuine while Salva's initiatives are not, given his long opposition to federalism.

The growing violence in Greater Equatoria and Western Bahr al Ghazal after the signing of the peace agreement caught the international community off-guard. This anger was due to long-standing grievances, as well as these communities largely being left out of the peace process and failure of the international community to force the government to accept cantonment. Added to that, the SPLA and Mathiang Anyoor carried out a campaign of terror against the local populace suspected of having links with the IO, while the rebels demonstrated a measure of respect for the people that either neutralized or brought many to their side.[29] As the peace agreement was slowly dismantled, the SPLA and Mathiang Anyoor killed thousands of Equatorian civilians and forced hundreds of thousands more to flee for safety in bordering Uganda. Equatorian militias, mostly formally affiliated with the SPLM-IO, in turn killed Dinka civilians living in the region.

Conflicting Visions on the Eve of the Collapse of the Peace Agreement

With the return of Riek to Juba, there were two opposing conceptions of the immediate future. The first group, called here the optimists, contended that government opposition to cantonment of SPLM-IO forces in non-Greater Upper Nile areas would be overcome because the government's position – which held that those fighting in these areas were merely criminals – had been lost intellectually, politically, and in terms of the peace agreement. In the interest of controlling the expanding opposition in these areas, which it could not do militarily, the government would be forced to recognize these forces as part of the SPLM-IO, thus placing them under the security arrangement provisions of the peace agreement and eliminating a major threat to the peace process.

Optimists also argued that since no serious ideological issues divided the belligerents, and given indications that Salva Kiir viewed Paul Malong and the Jieng Council as threats to his presidency, he could make a tactical alliance with Riek to isolate them and build a new and wider coalition to maintain his power. The earlier Salva–Riek power-sharing arrangement broke down and civil war resulted when Riek's ambitions to run for the presidency in the 2015 elections under the SPLM clashed with Salva's belated insistence that he wanted one more term of office. With the assurance under the peace agreement that Salva would hold power for the 30-month transitional period, he could be persuaded to step aside and permit Riek to run uncontested in the next national elections. (Although given US dislike of Riek this would not have been considered a favourable scenario in Washington.) This would both ensure a relatively smooth transitional period and an election that would amount to an exchange of power within the dominant elite, rather than an open contest between SPLM factions, which could lead to a tribal battle between the Dinka and Nuer. Alternatively, some SPLM-IO officials speculated that Salva and Riek could privately agree on extending the transitional period.

The optimists also held that the formation of the TGoNU would bring to the fore groups that had not figured prominently in the civil war and could only advance their interests through political and peaceful means. These groups, and Equatorians figured large here, generally opposed the Salva-led government. However, their alliance with Riek and IO was held to be only tactical and they could align with either party to achieve their ends. The peace process – the optimists contended – would also be kept on track by the important carrots and sticks available to the peace-makers: economic aid to the country, the threat of taking key IO and government leaders, including Salva and Riek, to the hybrid court to bring them into line, and the efforts of JMEC to keep the peace process moving forward.

But JMEC has not lived up to the expectations of the opposition or US Special Envoy Booth, who described it as 'the locus for moving forward the implementation process'.[30] The 'locus' was already spiralling downwards when one of its most experienced officials, Aly Verjee, gained the ire of Information Minister Michael Makuei Lueth, who decided he should be declared persona non-grata and forthwith expelled from South Sudan. Fearing his imminent arrest some diplomats surrounded Verjee, but ultimately it did no good and on 25 April 2016 he left the country. Verjee was variously accused of being an 'intruder', a threat to the security of the country, and being arrogant, but it was widely speculated that Makuei simply wanted to intimidate JMEC and did not want someone with Verjee's experience to be part of JMEC.[31] In that he was successful and Verjee's boss, Festus Mogae, had little to say about the expulsion, and has generally toed the government line.[32] The failure of the international community to stop the government's blatant breaches of the peace agreement convinced Juba that its appeals could be safely ignored, which Bona Malwal and Paul Malong had been saying for years.

In the principle-less world of South Sudanese politics, alliances with the strangest of bed fellows are possible, such as that suggested between Salva and Riek. Such alliances, though, are strictly tactical and subject to quick and destabilizing changes. As a result, a government based on such alliances would always be one step away from collapse and a return to civil war. While Riek does not seem consumed with hatred for Salva, according to one of the president's most trusted advisors Salva loathes Riek and that would have made any cooperation between them very difficult. Even if this personal animosity was overcome it might well produce a military coup.

Collapse of the Peace Agreement

The first and perhaps most telling indication that the return of Riek to Juba was not a harbinger of peace was the refusal of the Juba IDPs to leave the UN Protection of Civilian Camps. After the first cabinet meeting of the TGoNU on 6 May, Riek called for the release of prisoners of war and those arrested in connection with the war, the government to address the issue of the 28 states, cantonment, and the means to achieve security in Juba.[33] These issues were repeatedly brought up in cabinet, only to have them ignored or postponed.

More alarming, the Ceasefire Transitional and Security Arrangements Monitoring Mechanism (CTSAMM, an agency under the auspices of the JMEC responsible for ensuring implementation of the security arrangements as per the peace agreement) reported that government forces were not cooperating with security monitors in implementing security arrangements. The chair of the CTSAMM, Major-General Molla Hailemariam, said he, 'is not in the position to declare completion of transitional security arrangements in Juba, since the government has not declared its forces completely'.[34] The ceasefire panel would continue to report the government's lack of cooperation and its failure to ascertain whether the government was abiding by the provisions of the security arrangements agreement in Juba.

Meanwhile, national and state governments and the SPLA regularly refused to permit UNMISS from carrying out patrols, typically in areas in which the security forces were conducting operations. According to an international investigation, 'UNMISS personnel are regularly attacked, harassed, detained, intimidated and threatened'.[35] UNMISS accepted these constraints even though, under the Status of Forces Agreement with the government, peacekeeping forces have the right to patrol and move throughout the country, as well as use lethal force to protect civilians, regardless of whether they have prior SPLA or government approval. As a result, an independent panel concluded that the 'UN Security Council ... has failed to stand up to the government and impose punitive measures, such as an arms embargo, in response to the Government of South Sudan making a mockery of the SOFA and a Chapter VII mandate'.[36]

Nor did fighting stop between the SPLM-IO and government forces. Within two weeks of Riek's return to Juba there were widespread reports of clashes between the belligerents in various parts of the country.[37] Human Rights Watch released a report based on research carried out in December which found that tens of thousands of Fertit civilians in Western Bahr al Ghazal were forced to flee killings, gang-rapes, torture, and other abuses[38] by the SPLA in attacks against SPLM-IO forces that the government claimed were not operational in the state. After reporting in October the suffocation of more than 60 men and boys in containers in Leer, Unity state, Amnesty International revealed that dozens of detainees were being held in dire conditions in poorly ventilated metal shipping containers 20 kilometres south of Juba, where they were only fed once or twice a week and given insufficient drinking water.[39]

While there was growing concern about the collapsing economy and the failure of the transitional government to address it, Salva appointed ten presidential advisors (all from the SPLM), apparently for no other reason than it was not disallowed under the peace agreement.[40] Nor did the economic crisis stop the government from buying ever more sophisticated weaponry. These problems came to a head on 24 June when three weeks after Salva, Riek, and James Wani Igga had reached a consensus to establish cantonment sites for the SPLM-IO, the president refused to sign the agreement.[41] Salva also failed to agree on the terms of reference for a committee to review the number of states in the country. These two issues, the government's breach of the security arrangements provisions in Juba, and continuing clashes between IO and government forces in the peripheries were further nails in the peace agreement coffin. Even JMEC's Mogae complained about government obstructions to the freedom of movement of the peace monitors to carry out their investigations, some of whom were detained by the SPLA.[42]

In view of what later amounted to an international consensus that both belligerents shared equal responsibility for the collapse of the peace agreement, these events made clear where the brunt of the responsibility lay. It is thus significant that Mogae and other members of the peace-making brigade did not publicly condemn the government given the widespread knowledge – as reported by Human Rights Watch – that by this time between ten and twelve thousand SPLA soldiers were estimated to be hiding in Juba, many in residential areas dressed as civilians.[43] The opposition may also have received reinforcements from various sympathizers and fighters in and around Juba. According to UN officials, under these conditions the two sides effectively began running separate government cabinets in Juba.[44]

Instead of organizing a joint police force for Juba as required by the peace agreement, the government police set up roadblocks around the city. These had the stated objective of maintaining security but involved harassing and detaining IO fighters. On 2 July, two IO soldiers were killed, including Lieutenant-Colonel George Gismalah, who was accused by the SPLA of being a spy. To improve relations between the president and his first vice president, Riek was given the honour of handing over Salva's daughter in marriage on 7 July. On the same day, a group of SPLM-IO soldiers bringing food to fellow soldiers at the first vice president's office were stopped at a checkpoint in the Gudele area of Juba by government security forces. A fire-fight ensued in which two IO soldiers were wounded and five SPLA soldiers were killed, including the brother of Nihal Deng (the government's chief negotiator), probably in anger at the killing of George.

In that context, the head of UNESCO South Sudan, Salah Khaled, was shot near the Egyptian embassy in Juba on 7 July. On the same day, the SPLA fired between 50 and 100 rounds at two armoured SUVs from the US embassy as they passed the presidential palace. The SUVs contained seven officials, including James Donegan, the second-highest ranking US official in South Sudan.[45] None of the US diplomats, who were eventually rescued by US Marines, were hurt or killed in the attack. While US outrage would have been expected and justified, Washington and its Juba embassy played down the incident and held ill-disciplined troops and not Salva responsible. The next morning the potential for violence was so great that the UN ordered its employees to return home at mid-day.[46]

In response to the deteriorating situation JMEC chairman Festus Mogae arranged for Salva, Riek, and James to meet at the presidential palace (J1) on 8 July. Riek arrived just as US ambassador Molly Phee left from her own meeting with Salva, thus leading to IO accusations that the US was complicit in what followed. Questioned about the officer responsible for the death of the five SPLA soldiers in Gudele, Riek said he had been arrested, but he was subsequently identified as part of Riek's guards and shot by the SPLA outside the presidential palace while the presidential party met, thus providing the stimulus for widespread fighting. The personal body guards of the three members of the presidency kept close to their charges and although fighting quickly spread through Juba there was no fighting in the room. During a lull in the fighting, Riek was escorted back to his base.

There were conflicting accounts of what happened and why it happened. Some on the government side claimed, as they did in December 2013, that Riek had tried to launch a coup, while Salva said Riek had tried to kill him. In view of the small number of IO troops in the city, neither of those claims seem credible. Conversely, IO supporters alleged that, as was the case in December 2013, the government tried to assassinate Riek, but this also cannot be confirmed. International opinion was mixed, with most observers holding that the fighting was the product of growing tensions between the belligerents and not planned. The government and military, though, used it as a pretext for attempting to deliver a fatal blow to the IO.[47] While Riek may not have been the target of an organized assassination attempt at the presidential palace, his compound and house quickly became the focus of attacks by artillery, tanks, and helicopter gunships. Moreover, the US would justify its efforts to subsequently bring sanctions in the Security Council against SPLA Chief of Staff Paul Malong by accusing him of being responsible for trying to kill Riek.[48]

Although Riek and the IO were the focus of SPLA attacks, soldiers also murdered, robbed, and raped Juba civilians, most of whom were Nuer, and looted the main warehouses of the World Food Programme of $30 million worth of supplies, equipment, and vehicles.[49] As was the case in Malakal, SPLA soldiers had few compunctions about targeting people in the Juba UN POCs, where more than 30 IDPs were killed.[50] Humanitarian and UN officials reported that SPLA soldiers blocked civilians accessing safe places and sometimes fired upon those trying to enter UN bases. In the wake of the SPLA attack an estimated 300 people were killed and 60,000 Juba citizens fled the country.

While the POCs became a magnet for terrified civilians, there were also reports of IDPs leaving the sites to fight the SPLA and after being wounded or sensing defeat, leaving their weapons and uniforms outside and resuming civilian status in the UN sites. One UN official said, 'Because of the IO movement back and forth it was completely predictable ... that the SPLA would want to dominate the [POC site] perimeter'.[51]

As well as not protecting South Sudanese nationals, UN peacekeepers also failed to protect international aid workers who were robbed, beaten, raped, and suffered mock executions by SPLA soldiers (many wearing the Tiger insignia of Salva's Presidential Guard) on 11 July at the Terrain hotel complex only minutes away from a UN compound. This despite repeated appeals for help over many hours.[52] Americans, whose government had demonstrated remarkable tolerance for the Salva regime, were singled out for abuse. Again, the US government response was muted.

The SPLA restricted UNMISS peacekeepers to their bases during the fighting, even though the government had no legal right to interfere with their activities. After a ceasefire was declared, UN peacekeepers still did not leave their bases to protect civilians under imminent threat, and Human Rights Watch reported that on 17 July peacekeepers guarding a POC site did not intervene when SPLA soldiers abducted a woman only metres away,[53] and long after IO forces had fled the city. The agency went on to recommend that, 'Malong, as well as Kiir and Machar, who formally are the commanders-in-chief of their respective forces, should be among those investigated for their role in these abuses', although nowhere in the report is there any evidence of abuses by forces under the command of Riek. Instead the report concludes, 'Soldiers, operating under the formal command of General Paul Malong and President Kiir committed most of the crimes'.[54]

Conclusion

Although some internationals, including the JMEC chairman, would claim for the next year that the peace process was badly damaged, but still alive, most disinterested observers concluded that the July fighting signified its collapse. The international community was quick to express its despair and disgust with the belligerents, and there is no denying their collective guilt, but the prevailing narrative condemned both parties when all the evidence pointed to the overwhelming responsibility of the government for the July 2016 violence and collapse of the peace process. The contention of an equally shared responsibility has been a constant theme since the conflict began with SPLA and Dinka militia attack on Nuer civilians in Juba in 2013.

While the UN made a less than thorough assessment of its failings, IGAD, the Troika, and the US government refused to acknowledge any failings. This despite the fact that some US diplomats (how many is not known) had from the beginning been opposed to open-ended US support of the regime. But as the authors and backers of the peace agreement and organizations which pressured Riek and the IO to return to Juba – despite their being good reason to suspect the kind of breakdown and violence which occurred – their collective responsibility is clear. Moreover, the unwillingness of the US to critically assess the failure of its peace-making efforts meant that the ground was being laid for shifting from the position in this period of 'giving Salva a chance' to 'giving war a chance' in the post-peace agreement period.

7 | COMING OUT OF THE SHADOWS

Introduction

Although disappointed at its failure to kill Dr Riek Machar and defeat the SPLM-IO military mission in Juba in July 2016, the government had high hopes that he would be killed during the retreat to the Congo while under attack by ground forces and helicopter gunships. Meanwhile, Taban used the opportunity to cobble together a group of disgruntled IO officials who 'elected' him as their new leader, after which he was appointed first vice president by President Salva Kiir. The US officially recognized the appointment and urged Riek not to return to Juba, thus undermining a key element of the peace agreement which it had worked two years to achieve and another year to implement. It then pressed its peace partners to endorse Taban's appointment and for Sudan and Ethiopia not to host Riek. In the event, he ended up under house arrest in South Africa.

With Riek apparently marginalized and Taban endeavouring to divide the mainstream SPLM-IO, the Juba government was convinced it could ignore its commitments under the peace agreement without cost and win a convincing military victory over the opposition. The US also believed that the Salva–Taban team was the best means to bring peace to the country. However, to pursue this policy it had to twist the facts and contend that Riek, and not the government, was the principal obstacle to achieving sustainable peace. Although American diplomats and those of its Western and African allies never tired of repeating the formula that there was no military solution to the conflict in South Sudan, the actions of the US suggested otherwise. There was no more talk about peace processes and while the Juba government went about its brutal business Washington was largely silent.

To be sure, there was no formal US commitment to war and the defeat of Riek and the IO. But through a whole series of decisions that began with pressuring Riek to return to a Juba through to the US endorsement of Taban Deng as first vice president, a policy took form which had this effect. Whether it was a case of 'give Salva and Taban a chance' or supporting the war option the result was the same, and amounted to giving the government a free reign to achieve its ends by military means.

But the South Sudanese government over-played its hand: Taban proved unsuccessful in dividing the mainstream IO and Riek retained the loyalty of most of the IO military forces. Moreover, the forced departure of Riek for the Congo provided the stimulus for the war to take root in parts of the country that had largely escaped violence and for new rebel leaders and forces to challenge the government, thus deepening the humanitarian crisis and making the conflict more difficult to resolve. Making clear its profound aversion for Riek, the US government attempted (and failed) to bring sanctions against him in the Security Council for war-mongering.

President Obama had congratulated the US for its role in reaching the CPA and overseeing the secession of South Sudan, but he left office with the collapse of the peace agreement and the US-led international community increasingly being looked upon with disdain by war weary and frustrated South Sudanese. After setting the pace for political change for almost two decades in southern and South Sudan, the US was reduced to placing its hope in the military defeat of the SPLM-IO. When that failed, it had no other options.

Taban Deng: Saving the Government and Rescuing the Peace Process?

The appointment of Taban Deng as first vice president was made possible because it was endorsed by the US, which concluded that he would help bring stability to the country. Belatedly appreciating the intentions of Taban, Riek dismissed him from the SPLM-IO on 22 July.[1] But that mattered little and Taban cobbled together a group made up of the elderly Alfred Ladu and Richard Mulla, both too infirm to join the IO retreating forces, Dhieu Mathock, traumatized after being severely beaten by government security forces, Ezekiel Lol, another job-seeker, and Hussein Mar, upset – like Taban – at not being appointed to the lucrative petroleum ministry. Together with a few others they held a meeting on 23 July of what they claimed to be the

SPLM-IO and 'elected' Taban, number four in the party's hierarchy, as chairman and commander-in-chief of an army that did not exist.[2]

To smooth over the illegal appointment, those attending the meeting insisted that Taban would step down when Riek returned to Juba, a position he would repeat for a few weeks before insisting, along with Salva, that Riek could not return. Meanwhile, after going through the charade of appealing to Riek to return to Juba during his flight to the Congo, Salva claimed Riek to be in dereliction of duty and under the authority of the peace agreement appointed Taban as first vice president on 26 July 2016. On 15 March 2017, Salva appointed more members of Taban's group to his cabinet and replaced Riek's appointees to the National Assemblies with Taban's people. Although disingenuous, the appointments allowed the government to claim that it was continuing to implement the August 2015 peace agreement.

Meanwhile, Riek and approximately 1,000 SPLM-IO soldiers, politicians, and civilians were involved in a desperate 30-day trek under constant SPLA ground and air attack to reach the Democratic Republic of the Congo (DRC) and safety.[3] There was every expectation he would be killed, a consideration that undoubtedly figured in Taban's appointment. Sixty-eight, overweight, and not in the best of health, Riek was carried part of the way, but many members of the fleeing IO group died en route, including the veteran fighter Major-General Martin Kenyi. Even after getting to Garamba Park in the DRC on 14 August, the IO contingent was attacked by SPLA helicopter gunships. Those IO members who survived the trek, though, began receiving food and medical attention from the United Nations Organization Stabilization Mission in the DRC. Riek and a few close colleagues and family members were flown to Khartoum in what the Sudanese government emphasized was a humanitarian gesture. On 24 August, 139 more senior and ill SPLM-IO members were evacuated to Khartoum, but dozens more still died from the severity of their march. Nine months later there were still 631 SPLM-IO fighters in the DRC and only eight had accepted an amnesty offer by the Juba government.[4]

While the Congo drama was unfolding the international community was determining the legitimacy of Taban's appointment as first vice president. After evacuating Juba at the start of fighting, the JMEC chairman said on 24 July from Nairobi, 'We recognize First Vice

President Riek Machar as the legitimate leader of the SPLM-IO'. Then, demonstrating his characteristic indecisiveness, he added, 'A change to the leadership depends on the IO itself and we are not here to speculate as to any change of leadership'.[5] The same indecisiveness was evident in a UN-issued statement three days later. After warning President Salva that Taban's appointment as first vice president constituted a violation of the peace agreement, Ban Ki-moon said that the UN would continue to work with the TGoNU to ensure the implementation of the peace agreement.[6] The response of the IGAD Heads of State Summit of 5 August was equally unclear, but like the UN and JMEC the regional leaders did not endorse Taban as first vice president.

> [IGAD] Encourages H.E. Dr Riek Machar to rejoin the peace process and for H.E. President Salva Kiir Mayardit and the people of South Sudan to embrace a return to the spirit of long lasting peace in their country. In this regard, [it] welcomes the gesture of H.E. General Taban Deng Ghai to step down with a view of returning to the status quo ante in line with the ARCSS.[7]

The AU's Peace and Security Council echoed the call that Taban step down so that Riek could be reinstated.[8] Despite these statements challenging the legitimacy of Taban's appointment as first vice president, the US was notably silent.

But just as a consensus quickly emerged endorsing Riek as first vice president, it changed to endorsing Taban. On 22 August US Secretary of State John Kerry said:

> [I]t's quite clear that legally, under the agreement, there is allowance for the replacement, in a transition of personnel, and that has been effected with the appointment of a new vice president. With respect to Machar, it's not up to the United States; it's up to the leaders of South Sudan and the people of South Sudan and the political parties and the political process, and their neighbors, to weigh in on what is best or not best with respect to Machar.[9]

Six days later the JMEC's Mogae said that diplomats 'don't have an option' in endorsing Taban, and his appointment 'adds weight to efforts to realize peace in the country' because, 'potentially you have two SPLM-IOs: one which will enter negotiations, and another in the bush and fighting'.[10] The IGAD Heads of States Summit fell in line with the US on 5 September, pledging to abide by the South Sudan government's decision to appoint Taban as first vice president. Firming up the new international consensus, US Special Envoy Booth told the US Congress on 7 September that Riek should not return to the post of first vice president.[11]

Former Sudan and South Sudan Special Envoy Princeton Lyman was one of the few American officials to publicly challenge a policy that wrote off Riek, threw its weight behind Taban, and brought the region and the broader international community in line with its views. Speaking to the House of Representatives Foreign Affairs Africa Subcommittee, Lyman said that trying to cut off Riek from the government was an 'illusion' and that, 'Taban Deng does not command the loyalty of all those forces that have been fighting the government of Salva Kiir. Without broad-based participation in a transitional government, conflict will surely continue. Indeed, conflict continued in several parts of the country'.[12] His words proved prophetic but were ignored.

Marginalizing Riek

Using resources from a near bankrupt government, Taban set about trying to win over the Nuer by bribery and appointments. While a handful came to his side he never gained the allegiance of Nuer either in South Sudan or abroad, where he had been hated before his appointment as first vice president and was subsequently reviled. He achieved few of his stated objectives and what successes he did claim can largely be attributed to the US. He failed to bring over more than a handful of IO soldiers to the government, establish cantonment centres, change the Dinka-favoured decentralized state system, significantly divide and undermine the SPLM-IO,[13] or construct a viable alternative organization. His one uncontested success came in May 2017, when he convinced CTSAMM to replace the SPLM-IO representatives with his representatives, thus fatally undermining the organization. Taban played a supportive role to the US in isolating Riek in the region, but had little currency in Khartoum because of his long support for the northern rebels when governor of Unity state.

Although first vice president, he proved unable to stop the SPLA from continuing to support northern rebels. Most importantly, instead of bringing stability to the country, the war deepened and spread during the first year he held office.

The US government could do little to win Taban support among his fellow Nuer, but – through Ambassador Molly Phee in Juba, Susan Rice with her two-decade long opposition to Riek, together with John Kerry and Donald Booth – it pursued a policy to marginalize Riek, providing political cover for the Salva regime to ignore the peace agreement and instead focus on war. Thus, the US refused to condemn the regime's flagrant use of violence in Juba against the SPLM-IO, Nuer citizens of the capital, and – paralleling its attempt to play down the SPLA attack on the vehicles of the deputy US ambassador on the eve of the 8 July conflagration – it had little to say about the SPLA attack on its own nationals at the Terrain Hotel or the anti-American sentiments expressed by the SPLA perpetuators of the crime. Nor did the US condemn the ground and air attacks on the IO forces retreating to the Congo or support Riek's appeals during that period for a ceasefire. The US also did little to overcome government objections to the deployment of the Regional Protection Force to Juba to stabilize the situation, and made no attempt to resurrect the peace process.

The JMEC's Festus Mogae also lobbied throughout the region and internationally to isolate Riek and the senior IO leadership. His partisanship was not surprising in view of his claim that the government violence of July 2016 that brought about the collapse of the peace agreement was merely a 'regrettable confrontation'.[14] Like CTSAMM, Mogae proved too weak to stand up to the political pressures, became a virtual representative of the Juba government, and lost all credibility early on in the peace process. When Mogae met Riek in Pretoria he urged him to denounce violence, declare a unilateral ceasefire, and participate in the national dialogue, even though Salva had already rejected Riek's participation.

Crucial to garnering support for Riek's marginalization was to present him as an obstacle to peace. Both the US and Taban used the SPLM-IO Politburo meeting in Khartoum on 20–23 September 2016 to make their case. According to the IO Politburo statement, the peace agreement and the TGoNU had collapsed and the Juba regime was a 'rogue government'. It requested that IGAD rapidly deploy the Regional Protection Force in Juba, and cantonment centres be established throughout the country. The IO made clear it remained 'committed to peaceful resuscitation of the peace agreement and reinstitution and reconstitution of the TGoNU' and the implementation of the various peace agreement provisions.[15] But in apparent contradiction – and these were the words emphasized by the Americans – it called for the 'reorganization of the SPLA (IO) so that it can wage a popular armed resistance against the authoritarian and fascist regime of Salva Kiir in order to bring peace, freedom, democracy, and the rule of law to the country'. This contradiction stemmed from the Politburo's efforts to square the circle of supporting a peaceful end to the conflict while responding to the anger of its supporters after the government disregarded the peace agreement and attempted to kill the party's leader.

While there were complaints from at least one Politburo member that Riek had in fact watered down the IO's commitment to armed struggle in the statement, the US used the Politburo statement to launch a personal attack on him as a war monger. This contention was also used to try and bring sanctions against him in the Security Council. Secretary of State Spokesperson, John Kirby, 'strongly condemned' what he called Riek's statements (but were in fact the collectively expressed views of the IO's Politburo) and said, 'We find it inexcusable that he would continue to promote armed resistance'.[16] Riek and the IO were slow to appreciate that the US position was not due to a misunderstanding, but by the conviction that peace depended on his removal. As a result, Riek's subsequent attempt to emphasize his commitment to peace, risks he had taken to achieve it, and peacemaking proposals were ignored and, in the circumstances, irrelevant.

What was not known at the time was that Khartoum and Washington were carrying out sensitive negotiations over the removal of presidential sanctions against Sudan.[17] Obama's timing was, firstly, due to his imminent departure from office, which would mean he would not have to face the expected outrage by the Sudan lobby. Second, although the sanctions were imposed because of Khartoum's supposed support for terrorism, the US wanted to use the promise of their removal to pressure the Sudan government not to provide assistance to the SPLM-IO, or host Riek.

While there was grumbling among Sudanese Islamists at this infringement of the country's sovereignty, President Bashir had been working to improve relations with Washington for many years. Despite residual sympathy for the SPLM-IO among the country's rulers, Bashir was not going to rock the boat when victory, or at least a major concession, was in sight. Indeed, the author's meetings in Khartoum in May 2017 with government officials made clear their awareness that US support for Taban and efforts to marginalize Riek would be unsuccessful. However, fearing any action that they might take would be misinterpreted and undermine their diplomatic offensive with Washington, the government was only prepared to work through established organizations, like the increasingly dysfunctional IGAD.

Having pressured Khartoum not to support the IO or host Riek, the US turned its attention to Addis Ababa, the only other capital in the region that had demonstrated any balanced approach to the IO. Ethiopia had hosted Riek during the IGAD negotiations, and – it was assumed – feared upsetting the Nuer majority in Gambella, most of whom supported the IO and Riek. But the Ethiopia of Prime Minister Haile Mariam Desalign was not like that of the late Meles Zenawi, who had led an earlier Sudan peace process and would not have been so easily manipulated by the US. Ethiopia was now beset by political instability in the wake of a civil disobedience campaign by the Oromo. It feared that Eritrea and particularly Egypt would use these circumstances to further destabilize the country through support for the rebel Oromo Liberation Front and other Asmara-based dissident groups, because of its objections to the construction of the Renaissance Dam, or that Cairo might strengthen its relations with Juba, which it was already supplying with weapons.

According to diplomatic sources in Addis Ababa, these concerns were supplemented with an aggressive campaign by John Kerry and Susan Rice directed at Prime Minister Haile Mariam and Foreign Minister Workneh Gebeyehu to keep Riek out of the country. As a result, the government opposed the presence of Riek in Ethiopia even though Dr Lam Akol and Lieutenant-General Thomas Cirillo, leaders respectively of the National Democratic Movement and National Salvation Front, which were committed to the overthrow of the Juba government, were permitted to live unhindered in the country. Whether domestic considerations, US diplomatic pressures, or the desire to maintain a fragile regional unity on South Sudan proved paramount, both SPLM-IO officials and those from Taban's organization in Addis Ababa reported that by late 2016 what had been a general government openness to the IO had turned to opposition and a desire to instead improve relations with Juba.

The other IGAD countries – Uganda, Kenya, and Djibouti – hosted American military bases and could not be expected to oppose the will of the US. Uganda was the primary backer of the Juba regime, while the Kenyan government had made clear its sentiments by arresting and turning over the IO's spokesperson, James Gadet, to the Juba government. The Kenyan government was almost certainly complicit in the disappearance in Nairobi in January 2016 of two other IO officials, human rights lawyer Dong Samuel Luak and Aggrey Idri Ezbon, and in December 2017 of SPLM-IO Governor of Kapoeta Eastern Equatoria, Marko Likidor. All three are thought to be held by South Sudan's national security, or may have been killed.

The biggest achievement of the US campaign to isolate Riek, or at least so it seemed, was having him placed under house arrest in Pretoria. How this came about remains unclear even to Riek, but what is known is that after going to South Africa for follow-up treatment related to an outstanding eye problem and complications from his march to the Congo, in November 2016 he was taken to a house outside Pretoria, placed under guard, and detained without charges. Riek concluded that he had been 'set up' by the Americans, who wanted him killed.[18] Questions have periodically been raised in the South African parliament about Riek's status in the country, the government's response ranging from claiming he is a 'guest', alleging he was replaced as SPLM-IO leader (although that does not explain why he is being held), and sometimes acknowledging that he is being held against his will, but that it is in the interest of preserving peace, although no peace is being preserved.

Riek is convinced that the US is paying for his detention ($500,000 a month he said in a telephone call) through the auspices of the South Sudan government, a claim that has been widely reported in the South African and South Sudanese media. That may be true and is consistent with US efforts to marginalize him, but Riek is also not liked by Deputy President and President Jacob Zuma's Special Envoy to South Sudan, Cyril Ramaphosa (subsequently appointed president), who holds him responsible for the division in the SPLM and has been sympathetic to the Juba government. Meanwhile, Paul R. Sutphin, Acting Director in the Office of US Special Envoy for Sudan and South Sudan, told a group of SPLM-IO officials in Addis Ababa that the US would stop any attempt by Riek to return to the region before a peace agreement took hold.[19] While encouraging the IO to engage the Juba government in peace-making, Sutphin said that Riek would not be permitted to play any role as a peace-maker, a claim that led one IO official to ask him whether it was US policy to encourage a coup against Riek? Sutphin denied the suggestion, but in effect that is precisely what he was proposing and is consistent with the broad parameters of US policy.

In a further effort to marginalize Riek and present him as a war monger, US Representative to the UN, Samantha Power, introduced a resolution in the Security Council calling for an arms embargo against the belligerents and personal sanctions against Michael Makuei Lueth, Paul Malong (for among other things being 'responsible for efforts to kill opposition leader Riek Machar'), and Riek Machar.[20] Riek was accused of supporting Equatorian rebels that attacked government forces in late 2015 and early 2016, and once again was personally quoted for a statement issued by the SPLM-IO Politburo in Khartoum in September 2016 calling for war against the government. Consistent with the refusal of the US to condemn the government for the July 2016 fighting, the resolution refers simply to 'fierce fighting that broke out in Juba'. Power's resolution failed to gain a majority in the Security Council.

In a classic case of blow-back, however, not only did the detention of Riek not isolate him from the IO and the broader international community, it provided him a secure environment, something of critical importance after the Juba government repeatedly tried to kill him. While Riek was stopped from having face-to-face meetings with all but a few senior diplomats, his South African guards did not stop him from being in almost constant communication with a wide range of people globally. As a result, he had only marginally less control over the SPLM-IO than before, laying down political and military policies, appointing and dismissing officials, and consulting his chief of staff, Simon Gatwech, almost every day.[21] And by going over the top of the various organization heads, he micro-managed and disrupted the orderly functioning of the IO, just as he had done previously from his headquarters in Addis Ababa. There is reason to believe that through the increasing use by the IO of social media, WhatsApp in particular, and the establishment of various IO-related forums in which he participates, Riek has developed stronger links to his supporters than he had previously. Indicative of this, on 24 May 2017, Riek used a WhatsApp link to speak to 700 supporters gathered at the Presbyterian Church in Khartoum to pray for his release.

Regional Protection Force: Another Failed International Initiative

When the peace process did not proceed as desired the peace-makers threatened to first sanction and then have Salva and Riek removed. When those threats failed, a 'forced agreement' was imposed. With the collapse of that agreement, the AU approved the establishment of an RPF made up of soldiers from Ethiopia, Kenya, Rwanda, Uganda, and Sudan.[22] Although IGAD had originally approved the RPF in 2014, it was not until September 2016 that the UN Security Council adopted resolution 2304 authorizing the establishment of a 4,000-member RPF, in addition to the existing 12,000 members of the UNMISS peacekeeping force. The RPF mandate would facilitate safe movement in and out of Juba, protect the airport and key facilities in Juba, and engage any force preparing for or engaging in attacks against civilians, humanitarian actors, or UN personnel and premises.

However, there were problems with the project from the outset. Although designated as a regional protection force, Rwanda is not a member of IGAD and Uganda and Sudan excused themselves because they were interested parties to the conflict. Protection of the airport and key facilities suggested an alliance with the government against attack by rebel forces, while the government contended this involved a breach of national sovereignty. It was also hard to believe that a 4,000-member force would be any more effective defending civilians than the existing 12,000-member UN force, the more so because the RPF was to include some of the same forces that made up UNMISS. Also lost on Security Council members was the irony of a UN force operating in the centre of the national capital, protecting citizens from their own government. And if the non-Dinka citizens of Juba were at risk the Security Council refused to impose an arms embargo against the government. Nor did the Security Council have any plan to link concern with civilian protection with the broader objective of advancing the peace process, or even stabilizing the rapidly deteriorating situation in the country outside of Juba. As the former acting chief of staff of JMEC acknowledged, the RPF was 'largely a solution of soldiers without a strategy'.[23]

The biggest problem faced by the peace-makers, however, was the opposition of the government. At various times, the government rejected the RPF in its entirety, claiming that it undermined South Sudan's sovereignty and saying it would fight the RPF if it attempted to enter South Sudan.[24] The government would then be persuaded that it could not go against the will of the entire international community. It would, though, insist the RPF forces must come entirely from the region, contested the numbers proposed, challenged the objectives of the force, and raised concerns about its weaponry. This led to a merry-go-round of negotiations and announcements of the imminent arrival of the forces, only for the government to raise more objections, a process which went on for ten months from the time the proposal was originally made until the advanced force arrived in May 2016, after which the government threw up additional obstacles that necessitated more delays. In the interim, more people died and an increasingly discredited international community lost further legitimacy.

Despite a Security Council resolution threatening the government with sanctions if it obstructed UNMISS in the performance of its mandate, and overwhelming evidence that it did just that, no sanctions were levied. This was due to the objections of Russia and China, who were sceptical as a result of previously having been on the receiving end of US-orchestrated sanctions. The government continued to carry out military offensives throughout the country, harass the non-Dinka citizens of Juba without interference, and obstruct the peace agreement and UNMISS monitoring mechanisms. By so doing, the message was conveyed that the international community was a paper tiger that could largely be ignored.

SPLM-IO: Post 8 July 2016

The implications of the Juba battles of 8–10 July 2016 between the SPLM-IO on the one side and the SPLA, Dinka militias, and Ugandan army on the other, continued to reverberate. But the widely held conclusion that the fighting represented a disaster for the IO and a victory for the government has not been borne out. Riek, and to a lesser extent the IO, have been marginalized in the IGAD region, Africa, and internationally, but within South Sudan in the year since 8 July, Riek's authority has probably grown, the rebellion has spread, the US government policy of trying to marginalize him has increasingly been recognized as a failure, and both internationally and within the country it is the government that has become isolated, even while they continue to hold a dominate position militarily.

To be sure, the US blackmail of Sudan appears to have stopped its limited supply of weapons and logistics to the IO, and in the absence of other potential sources the rebels have been hard-pressed to confront government advances, take their own initiatives, and for Riek to buy support through the provision of weapons. This has reduced Riek's authority over field commanders and encouraged the decentralization of conflict, but he has other tools. First, Nuer soldiers constituted the majority of the SPLA when it disintegrated in the wake of the December 2013 Juba massacre. They went in various directions, but a crucial handful, including senior officers, defected to rebel forces fighting the government in the Equatorias and Western Bahr al Ghazal. More joined the Equatorian rebel forces after the July 2016 fighting with heavy artillery. Second, while government policies continue to drive non-Dinka politicians and generals to defect, and in this light former Western Equatorian Governor Joseph Bakosoro and former SPLA Deputy Chief of Staff, Thomas Cirillo loom large, they suffer from joining the fray two or three years after the IO went to ground and like Riek they do not have a ready access to weapons. As a result, Riek retains considerable popularity among Equatorians, who view him as the leader in the war against the Dinka government and a consistent spokesperson for federalism.

One of the biggest obstacles to an SPLM-IO success is Riek. Riek is a rebel, but he is not a revolutionary, and consistent with the SPLM tradition from which he has spent almost his entire political life he has no transformative vision. Like Garang he aspires to individual control, opposes institutions and sharing power with his colleagues, even though he has repeatedly been willing to serve as Salva's junior partner in a Dinka-led government. From the outset of the conflict in December

2013 the SPLM-IO, which in practice meant Riek as the all-powerful leader, has consistently failed to produce a coherent political and military strategy, much less a realistic vision of an alternatively structured South Sudan. In the absence of ideological convictions upon which to construct such strategies, Riek falls back on a grab-bag of liberal clichés. These might pass muster in the developed West, but not in South Sudan, where the state is merely a brutal security agency writ large, directed to extracting resource surpluses and keeping rebellions in check. In any case, with IO policy directed to resurrecting ARCSS, Riek would only be first vice president to Salva or another SPLM candidate who would be unlikely to endorse his reform proposals.

Riek constructed a post-8 July 2016 SPLM-IO that includes all the weaknesses of its earlier version. In appearance, the new version suggested rich institutional arrangements, but in practice Riek monopolized the reigns of power and the only individuals, not positions, of influence were Taban Deng and Angelina Teny. With Taban's defection, only Angelina has real influence over Riek and that is widely resented in the IO and by the international diplomats, who dislike her almost as much as Riek. Protective of Riek, she played a crucial role in his appointment of Dak Duop Bishop as minister of petroleum over Taban Deng and Hussein Mar, who both wanted the position, because she reckoned he was more loyal. The contrary view is that Angelina wanted the position, arguing that she had the most experience based on her position as state minister in the Government of National Unity and further that Dak would be easier to control than Taban or Hussein. She continues to serve as the secretary of the IO's Security Committee despite her lack of military experience.

In the wake of the defection of the deputy leader and general secretary of the IO, Riek appointed Henry Odwar and Tinto Peter, respectively. From Equatoria and Western Bahr el Ghazal they emphasized the national character of the party. But with limited constituencies, lacking charisma, and having no military backgrounds, they were ill-placed to challenge Riek's leadership. There were fears in the SPLM-IO that by inviting Henry Odwar to lead SPLM-IO delegations or attend conferences without going through Riek, some in the international community were trying to ween him away from Riek. There is no indication, though, that Henry would be susceptible to such appeals. Even if successful, it would have the effect of creating yet another opposition group and further complicating the peace process. The problem was that like his predecessor, Ladu Gore, it was not clear whether Henry had genuine power or was just an agent of Riek, and that Angelina was the real second in command.

Henry and Tinto have wanted to play an important role in building an alternative party, but Riek has not made clear whether he accepts the judgement of his party members who want to end all attachments to the SPLM, while the poor state of the IO's organization and his reluctance to provide funds and appoint people to the party's secretariat suggest a leader who fears institutionalization. The other potential restraint on Riek's unbridled power was the widely attended party conferences in Pagak, but through controlling the agenda, using his personal prestige, and assuming responsibility for writing up the motions approved he only had to make minor concessions to the popular will. Now, with the US-led effort to keep him out of the region, such conferences are no longer possible. Instead, as confirmed by Angelina Teny, the primary foreign policy concern of the SPLM-IO since Riek's house arrest has been his release,[25] which undermines other objectives. Moreover, Angelina acknowledged she has no idea of where he could safely go if released. She said that the most convincing argument she has made to other opposition politicians in order to encourage them to also call for Riek's release (and it has generally been successful) is that they too could be arrested at the instigation of the US.

Riek oversaw the departure of the former SSDF generals in 2015 and the Taban-led politicians in the wake of the 8 July fighting, but unhappiness with his leadership in the military and political spheres of IO remains. Some of the dissenters look to Chief of Staff, Simon Gatwech, as a potential replacement or interim leader because of the respect with which he is held in the IO, but he is exhausted and does not harbour any political ambitions. There is, however, a younger – albeit now middle-aged – generation of Nuer leaders who could replace Riek. It is they who are raising the most complaints about his leadership.

Ironically, US efforts to marginalize Riek has made challenges to his leadership and the demand for accountability more difficult because he cannot be directly confronted and anyone advocating his replacement can be accused of being an American agent. Also protecting Riek is the continuing desire of the Nuer to maintain unity and not engage in a leadership struggle at this critical juncture. In addition, there is no reason to assume that his strong support base among the Nuer tribal leadership and masses has been seriously eroded. Meanwhile, non-Nuer IO members consider Riek less tribally oriented than other potential Nuer leaders, and a symbol of their revolt against the Dinka dominated Juba government. Riek has frequently failed the Nuer and the South Sudanese, but by handing over power to the SPLM in which he was the vice president, giving him sole power to represent the opposition in the civil war negotiations, and finally trying and failing to isolate him, the US-led international community has repeatedly, if inadvertently, reinforced his authority.

Another element in the changing power configuration of the SPLM-IO is the rising significance of the Equatorians, who now constitute a bigger group than the Nuer on the Politburo, which not only makes the IO a more ethnically representative party than the ruling SPLM, but also means that a non-Nuer leader of the party is becoming a possibility. To be sure, most IO fighters, the white army, and senior officers continue to be Nuer, and without a change in that balance it would be difficult for a non-Nuer to assume overall leadership of the party, but as the war has advanced, Greater Equatoria is replacing Greater Upper Nile as the focal point of the struggle against the government and that means its military officers and politicians are assuming central stage. Moreover, unlike Greater Upper Nile, where Riek has relied on an old guard and marginalized the intellectuals to ensure he is not challenged, in Greater Equatoria intellectuals and the community assume a much more active role that is giving a more progressive character to the struggle.

While Riek deserves credit for giving the SPLM-IO a strong national character, he has been less successful in reconciling with dissident members of his own Nuer. Peter Gadet has repeatedly urged reconciliation in the interests of Nuer solidarity, but Riek appears content to be rid of the dissenting former SSDF generals who challenged his leadership, even if their departure seriously undermined the fighting capacity of the SPLM-IO.[26] Unlike Gathoth Gatkouth, who joined Taban in the Salva government and lost considerable legitimacy, Gadet remained on the sidelines in Khartoum and is recapturing his former status among the Nuer because his opposition to peace-making with Salva is now seen by many as correct.

The SPLM-IO continues to suffer from Riek's misplaced faith in the peace process and the international community's commitment to implementing the peace agreement, as well as a reluctance to fully commit to war, despite efforts by his enemies to present him as a war-monger. Indeed, there is a virtual consensus among the IO Nuer that Riek has never been committed to armed struggle. However, in the wake of the collapse of the peace process and efforts to marginalize him he has little option but to turn to military means to achieve the IO's ends, including the oil fields,[27] long the most significant strategic target. This presents a challenge, however, because to attack the oil fields runs the risk of upsetting Sudan, the US, and China, as well as damaging some of the country's most valuable assets. To date the IO has not had the capacity to attack Juba, but the growing support of Equatorians for the IO and their alienation from the government, com-bined with the disaffection of Equatorian SPLA fighters and irregular salaries, make that increasingly possible.

Meanwhile, IO efforts to surround the northern Upper Nile oil fields began in late 2016 under James Koang but made little pro-gress in the dry season. Instead, between January and May 2017 the SPLA and allied militias recaptured much of Jonglei and Upper Nile, carrying out one of the most destructive campaigns of the war and leading to the displacement of almost the entire Shilluk tribe.[28] Even those victories, however, were largely reversed by the IO in a series of attacks on government positions in May and June, made possible by the start of the rains which limited the capacity of the SPLA to use its heavy equipment and provided an environment in which the rebel soldiers could get water and food. Moreover, with the SPLM-North in disarray it was not able to offer assistance to its southern comrades. But it is a mistake to over-emphasize the changing military fortunes of the government and the SPLM-IO. Instead, the govern-ment's military victories have limited worth when the rebels cannot be conclusively defeated, the SPLA is weak in the countryside, and in the face of growing opposition it cannot achieve its political ends. Moreover, international support is not sustainable when the govern-ment must assume the primary responsibility for the UN declaration of famine in parts of Unity state and the flight of almost 4 million South Sudanese from their homes, half internally displaced and half refugees in neighbouring countries.[29]

SPLM-IO and the Broader Opposition

Although appointed minister of agriculture in TGoNU, in the wake of the breakdown of the peace process in July 2016 Dr Lam Akol resigned that position, as well as chairman of his Democratic Change party. He then established the National Democratic Movement in the hope that it would provide an umbrella for the various groups outside South Sudan opposed to the Juba government. Although the IO's Dr Peter Adwok attended a founding meeting and there were hopes that it could develop conciliatory relations with the IO, those hopes broke down for two reasons. First, efforts to establish a front based on a common set of principles and objectives was premature given the fluidity of the political and military situation. Second, Riek feared losing control of the IO to the wily Lam and endeavoured to bring all the opposition groups under the IO. Hopes for the front ended after two of Lam's generals, Gabriel Tang Ginya and Yohanis Okiech, were killed in a fight with the IO forces of Johnson Olony in Upper Nile in early January 2017.[30]

For a number of reasons – the stalemate in the war and the peace process, the opposition's need to improve its domestic and international image, the growing appreciation of the political weakness of the government, and in some cases the desire of marginal groups to opportunistically link with the more powerful IO – the desire for opposition cooperation and coordination has grown. Apart from Lam's organization, these efforts include the South Sudan National Movement for Change of former Western Equatoria Governor Joseph Bakosoro, the National Salvation Front of former Deputy SPLA Chief of Staff Thomas Cirillo, the Federal Democratic Party of Gabriel Changeson, the People's Democratic Movement of Dr Hakim Dario, and the Pagan Amum-led Former Detainees, although with two ministers in the government their claim to opposition status is questionable. Lam, Cirillo, and Changeson claim to have armed wings, but apart from the widely reported fighting between Lam's organization and the SPLM-IO in Upper Nile, there have been few confirmed reports of clashes between these forces and those of the government in the year since the collapse of the peace agreement. The military weakness of the opposition means that, according to Riek, the issue of military cooperation is not an issue.[31] In the non-military sphere, however, there have been a number of jointly issued statements and on 7 May 2017 seven opposition groups, including the SPLM-IO, committed to work closely to oust President Salva Kiir's government.[32]

Given his past opposition to collaboration with Lam, the commitment of Riek to this process will determine its success, the more so because the SPLM-IO is by far the biggest opposition group. But apart from Riek's fears of others dominating the process, a major obstacle to opposition cooperation is his failure to clearly break from the SPLM. This despite both his own party membership as well as all the opposition parties, with the exception of the Former Detainees, being firm in struggling not only to overthrow the government, but also to permanently remove the SPLM.

Conclusion

US frustration with the South Sudan conflict and its leadership came to the fore with the collapse of ARCSS in July 2016, even if Washington claimed that, although threatened, the peace process continued. However, US support for Taban Deng as first vice president, efforts to marginalize Riek, and the free reign it gave to the government over the next year made clear that Washington was pursuing what constituted a policy, even if there was no clear profession of it by either the politicians or the diplomats. But 'policy' can be defined as 'a definite course of action adopted for the sake of expediency, facility',[33] and thus the collected actions pursued by Washington during this period can be said to constitute a policy that involved undermining the SPLM-IO and making it more vulnerable to military defeat by the government.

This policy had been anticipated by US insistence that Riek return to Juba and take up his position as first vice president, even though it was widely known that government breaches of the security arrangements agreement placed not only him, but the citizens of Juba, in grave danger. The US-led international community did little while the government repeatedly violated the peace agreement and launched military campaigns. The SPLM-IO was not innocent of crimes, but most of the breaches of the peace agreement were carried out by the government and that continued to be the case in the year after the break-down of the peace agreement, as documented by UNMISS.[34] Those facts would never be known, however, by the statements made by the US government, which endeavoured to establish a narrative in which the main obstacle to the peace process was Riek Machar.

That the US government would put its faith in the likes of Salva, Taban, Malong, and the Jieng Council of Elders to bring peace to South Sudan speaks to the extent to which reason had been replaced by ignorance, frustration, and a blind hatred of Riek. The result has been a political disaster and a peace process impasse because Riek has not been marginalized, Taban has not gained the expected national legitimacy, the war has spread, and the humanitarian crisis has deepened. Obama came to the presidency claiming credit for Bush's achievement of the independence of South Sudan and left office with the country near collapse because of the misjudgements of his and previous administrations.

The period under examination in this chapter corresponds with the US coming out of the shadows and taking overt control of what was still called the peace process. Thus, it must assume considerable responsibility for the resulting disaster. However, the other participants in the peace process – the Troika, IGAD, and JMEC, with the AU and the UN in the wings – have also distinguished themselves by contributing to the problem, not its resolution. By the end of this period the US was complaining – albeit disingenuously – about IGAD, while the other Troika members were privately alleging that American leadership, or lack of, had produced a political impasse. But the US did not have to press hard to gain the support of its peace partners for tacitly supporting the government's war policy – all of them had lost faith in the peace process, accepted that Riek was a major obstacle to achieving peace, were left to hope that the marriage of Salva and Taban would be the key to stability, and accepted American leadership.

8 | CONCLUSION

Collapse of an Illusion

The SPLA imagined by its foreign backers was always an illusion, along with the hopes that it would be the instrument to construct a liberal democratic state on the harsh grounds of southern Sudan. Such hopes collapsed on 15 December 2013, although even after four years of failed peace processes and countless corpses this illusion has not always been recognized. US policy proceeded from its role as the global hegemon with important interests and regional allies in the Horn of Africa. But the extent of the engagement in South Sudan and the importance attached to a country of no strategic value make little sense, and owe much to lobbyists operating within an ideological framework shaped by notions like the US as the indispensable nation and R2P. The lobbyists propagated the view – against overwhelming evidence to the contrary – that the SPLM was a democratic movement with national support, a worthy ally for the US in the region, and a counterpoint to the Khartoum Islamists.

The US and its allies then oversaw the construction of a South Sudan state complete with a gender ministry, human rights commission, anti-corruption commission, a 25 per cent female quota in the National Assembly, and many other features that befit a liberal Western society. The surprise is not that these Western-designed institutions, policies, and values have not flourished in South Sudan. Rather, it is that such a thing could be expected to develop roots in an illiberal and pre-modern South Sudan under the authoritarian SPLM. Almost as surprising is that lobbyists, academics, journalists, and others who claimed expert knowledge on Sudan and South Sudan based their assessments on emotional responses, ignoring the brutal facts about the SPLM. While the SPLM repeatedly gave rhetorical support to democracy and liberal values, in practice this only served as window-dressing to satisfy their American and Western supporters.

The US did not make any assessment of its policy failures, and never questioned whether it was wise to support the SPLM and the independence of South Sudan. Instead, it quickly assumed the leading role in the peace process to end the country's civil war. The failure of the US to achieve its objectives in a region largely made up of client states, a South Sudan it midwifed, acceptance by IGAD, the Troika, the AU, and the UN of its leadership, together with the expenditure of enormous financial and political resources, emphasizes the extent of the failure of its policies.

From the outset of the peace process, the US brought its heavy baggage to bear, including support for the SPLM, particularly the Former Detainees, a visceral hatred of Riek Machar, and reliance on Ugandan President Yoweri Museveni. Rather like the US-Israeli relationship, that between the US and Museveni's Uganda leaves one wondering which party is leading the other. Both, however, had an interest in ensuring that the Salva regime did not fall under the sway of Khartoum. Taking a feather from the West, Museveni justified sending his army into South Sudan on humanitarian grounds when – just like the West – other strategic interests were uppermost. And with his army and air force crucial to the defence of the regime he also used his considerable political skills to defend the regime in the IGAD and Arusha peace processes. It often appeared that Museveni was the effective president of South Sudan, an astonishing achievement, even if in the end it proved to be another defeat in victory.

While post-Meles Ethiopia could not bring to bear its considerable political weight even when formally leading the IGAD peace process, Museveni's Uganda has punched far above its regional weight and that makes any settlement of the conflict in South Sudan without its sign-off difficult to imagine. Although also allied with Kenya and Ethiopia, the US has relied on Uganda, and Museveni is not a character that can be taken for granted. With the lack of interest shown by the Trump administration in this part of the world (one US diplomat noted that it had 'zero sentimental or any other connection to South Sudan'), powerful local actors like Museveni are likely to be even more influential in the region.

To return to a central theme in this book, the US-led international community failed to ensure the implementation of their own peace agreement. And after the July 2016 fighting in Juba it recognized

Taban Deng as first vice president of South Sudan in breach of the peace agreement, attempted to marginalize Riek Machar despite having no legal basis to do so, blackmailed Sudan not to host Riek after a timely recognition that Sudan was no longer a sponsor of terrorism, and gave the Salva regime full reign to pursue a war agenda. US leadership was confirmed by the quick endorsement of these initiatives by IGAD, the Troika, AU, and the UN, all in the misplaced belief that they would bring peace to the country.

The Obama administration policies and omissions served to bring about the collapse of the peace agreement, intensify the conflict, convince the Juba government that it could operate with impunity, make the conflict more difficult to resolve, and deepen the humanitarian crisis. Since the US government was informed that Taban had little prospect of replacing Riek as the leader of the Nuer or the SPLM-IO, and there was extensive evidence that the government was committed to war and not implementing the peace process, its approach can only be understood as the result of cynicism, arrogance, and the legacy of two decades of misunderstanding Sudan and South Sudan. The failure of the Obama administration policy was evident long before it left office, but an in-coming Trump administration, pre-occupied with crisis management in Washington, did not have the ability or interest to change gears. With the international community dependent on US leadership, the policy has continued.

The CPA was held to not only affirm the virtue of the US in supporting southern Sudanese in their quest for self-determination, but also a foreign policy success, all the greater when set against its failures in the greater Middle East. However, the CPA was based on a profound misunderstanding of conditions in South Sudan and of the capacity and character of the SPLM. Thus, it served as a crucial step on the road to the country's civil war. It speaks to how poorly the US understood conditions in South Sudan that up until the eve of the civil war it continued to view the secession of the country as a major foreign policy achievement and the SPLM as a well-meaning government. That level of misunderstanding cannot be attributed simply to a lack of knowledge, but to policy misinformed and distorted by ideological convictions and a personalization of the conflict. President Ronald Reagan considered the Afghan mujahedeen as equivalent to the founding fathers and through most of the presidencies of William Clinton,

George W. Bush, and Barak Obama, the US viewed the SPLM in a similar light. Just as it was woefully wrong about the mujahedeen, the US was equally mistaken about the SPLM; indeed, the US played a crucial role in giving legitimacy and handing over power to a monster.

Mahmood Mamdani's finding that US policy on Darfur proceeded from the assumption that it was 'a place without history and without politics'[1] applies in spades to the conflict in South Sudan. Indeed, the narrative had been shaped earlier by the Friends of South Sudan and a host of American Christian, black, and human rights groups. This narrative produced an African hero in the form of John Garang, and those who opposed him and his political project were defined as enemies, including Dr Riek Machar. As with the Save Darfur Coalition, these lobbyists made a political and military struggle into a moral crusade which the US as the exceptional country must take up, aligning with the good and coming down hard on the evil. But as de Waal pithily said, 'philanthropic imperialism is imperialism nonetheless'.[2]

Mamdani also argued that the simplification of the Darfur conflict facilitated the objectives of the campaigners by encompassing a wide ideological and religious spectrum. Unlike the case of Darfur, the South Sudan lobby went through stages in which the largely secular liberal interventionist Friends came to the fore under the Clinton administration, while the Christian and conservative campaigners gained ascendancy under George Bush. Neither group had close relations with the Obama administration, although Susan Rice was still there pressing the same views as she did under Clinton. By then her perspective on Sudan and South Sudan had become mainstream, and however misguided, would not be challenged by a cautious leader like Obama. Those same misunderstandings and convictions ensured that the US would be an obstacle, and not the indispensable nation, to achieving a peaceful end to South Sudan's civil war.

Trump's rejection of the notion that the US was the exceptional nation[3] needed in the resolution of conflicts, condemnation of the over-reach of US foreign and military policy, support for improved relations with Russia, and lack of interest in Africa during the 2016 presidential election campaign all suggested a more balanced approach towards US foreign policy globally, and this had implications for South Sudan. Under sustained assault from a foreign policy establishment committed to a globalist agenda, however, Trump stacked his government with a similar mix of generals and bankers as made up previous administrations, and has been increasingly unwilling to challenge critical beliefs that have underpinned US foreign policy for decades. However, his slowness to appoint officials responsible for Africa and South Sudan make it unlikely that the Trump administration will devote the political and financial capital to the country as that of his three predecessors.

Into that void various proposals are being circulated. Joshua Meservey from the Heritage Foundation has argued that US failure in South Sudan is due to its unwillingness to fully exert its power. He proposes that the US give up on negotiations and instead apply rigorous sanctions, break relations with Juba, prosecute belligerents in the hybrid courts, confiscate government financial assets in the US, and go after those responsible for violence against Americans, etc.[4] While Meservey acknowledges that the US has suffered a marked decline in credibility which undermines its authority, he attributes this to its weak approach to the belligerents. He concludes, 'The U.S. government needs to determine what went wrong with its South Sudan policy to ensure it does not repeat the mistakes, and to be accountable to taxpayers for the billions of dollars it spent with no return'.[5] This proposal follows the disastrous logic of US peace-making: come up with technocratic solutions, ignore politics, disregard history, and only afterwards, if at all, ask what is the problem.

Equally out of touch is John Prendergast, of Friends of South Sudan and Enough fame, with his grab-bag of techno-fixes to the problem of South Sudan. These include a focus on corruption, a broadened mediation, smart sanctions, and banning arms deliveries to the war zones.[6] What any of this could do to rectify the governance and accountability deficits in South Sudan and bring sustainable peace to the country is anyone's guess. Unsurprisingly, Prendergast has little to say about the SPLM, since that would put the spotlight on his own role in bringing to power the group which is the biggest obstacle to peace in the country. Presumably out of recognition that he will not find the same level of sympathy with the Trump administration as he did with Obama, Prendergast has directed his appeal to South Sudan's neighbouring states, the African Union, the United Nations, and interested governments like the United Kingdom.

Meanwhile, and pursuing its own track in the face of the collapse of the peace agreement, the Ethiopian government has attempted to restart the IGAD peace process. However, the peace-makers are caught by their own conundrum: not holding another round of negotiations makes them appear unconcerned with the humanitarian disaster, while holding negotiations when there is little reason to think they will make any progress threatens to further undermine their authority. Moreover, any negotiations will invariably bring to the fore the illegal house arrest of Riek, as well as the illegal appointment of Taban Deng as first vice president. Another round of peace-making would have to deal with those political and military organizations that have joined the opposition to the government, but not the SPLM-IO. Lastly, it would again bring to the fore IGAD with its now well-documented record of failures and divisions. That record is leading some to look to the AU, but like IGAD it has played follow-the-US-leader and there is no indication it would inaugurate a different approach to peace-making. And while the election of Donald Trump and his policy of America First led Europeans to call for an independent European Union foreign policy, they took no initiatives following the collapse of the South Sudan peace agreement in July 2016.

Moreover, the scope of peace-making has always been restricted to achieving a negative peace of the 'absence of conflict, absence of war' and focused on re-ordering the SPLM elites in government and returning the country to the pre-December 2013 period. As this study has stressed, however, the pathology of South Sudan was evident long before that. Instead, there is a need to move beyond this limitation and recognize that, 'Peace is more than the cessation of military hostilities, more than simple political stability. Peace is the presence of justice and peace-building entails addressing all factors and forces that stand as impediments to the realization of all human rights for all human beings'.[7]

Out of fear that IGAD would resurrect its peace process and end Riek's marginalization, and to ensure the maintenance of the status quo, the Juba government announced a national dialogue which began in May 2017. But the government's refusal to permit Riek and the other armed combatants to participate in the process, the lack of basic freedoms in South Sudan, coupled with the government's obvious insincerity, means that it was just another diversion and has gained little traction. Meanwhile, the Juba government's principal backer, President Museveni, tried to resurrect the Arusha process and reunite the SPLM factions, despite the opposition of many South Sudanese to again having the SPLM foisted on them by the international community, and the refusal of Riek and the SPLM-IO to participate in the process.

The proposal that both Riek and Salva step down remains popular, particularly with the Former Detainees and the US government. Deng Alor, who was both the Juba government foreign minister (albeit with little power) and a Former Detainee, supported the call for his own president to step down. Not surprisingly, he was accused of being a traitor in the South Sudan Council of Ministers, but he explained to Salva that this was the best means to ultimately prevent him from being sent to prison. It was left to Bona Malwal, however, to reject the proposal and insist that a Dinka must hold the reigns of power if the tribe was not to be threatened. To the extent that this contention is correct, it speaks powerfully to the disaster produced by the Dinka-led government. What Bona advocated, effectively, was that this disaster continue.

The popularizers of the proposal to remove both Salva and Riek have never explained how it could be carried out or why their successors would necessarily be more amenable to reaching (and implementing) a peace agreement. Also not explained is why Riek has been singled out when he has been amenable to peace and was the victim of the government's abrogation of ARCSS, as well as how any replacement leaders could resolve fundamental structural problems in South Sudan, including a governance deficit. What is also disturbing is to equate Salva and the SPLA with Riek and the IO when their levels of responsibility for the conflict, continuation of the conflict, and support for the peace process are not comparable.

There are two other approaches to the South Sudan crisis which represent a challenge to past policies – giving war a chance and the imposition of an international trusteeship for the country. The US and its ally Kampala foreclosed the possibility of an early military resolution of the conflict by coming to the assistance of the Juba government after it engineered the mass murder of the capital's Nuer civilians and attempted to assassinate Riek. The rationale for Ugandan military intervention was couched in humanitarian terms, namely fear that an aroused Nuer white army would wreak havoc on Juba's Dinka inhabitants. But there is no way of knowing if the Nuer forces would have defeated the SPLA and Dinka militias in Juba, carried out atrocities, been defeated, or just possibly created the conditions under which a genuine reconciliation could take place. All that can be known is that by stopping the internal dynamics the war continued and produced a greater humanitarian disaster. Even after the Ugandan army had supposedly withdrawn after the signing of the August 2015 peace agreement, it rescued the government during the July 2016 Juba fighting, when the SPLA again carried out atrocities against the Nuer civilian population and attempted to assassinate Riek.

In the wake of this fighting the US gave tacit support to the Salva government, setting aside its commitments to the peace agreement and focusing on militarily defeating the SPLM-IO. But instead of staying above the fray as advocated by Edward Luttwak in his 'give war a chance' thesis,[8] the US supported the government and worked to marginalize Riek and the IO. Luttwak does not support war as an end in itself but as a better means than formal peace processes to achieve sustainable peace, and experience in the Horn of Africa backs him up. While international peace-making in Sudan and South Sudan has repeatedly failed over two decades, conflicts in Eritrea, Ethiopia, and Uganda were conclusively ended by military means and with little or no international involvement. Luttwak also warned that intervention often exacerbated conflicts. This was clearly the case with US support of the Juba government, which has also led to the loss of US prestige in the region.

Were the US and its allies willing to stand back and give war a chance, the hope is that a coalition of the opposition would achieve a convincing victory, since it comes closer than the government to representing the will of the people of South Sudan in all their diversity. It is also the leading force in opposing Dinka hegemony, which has been a perennial source of instability. But the armed opposition is weak and even achieving unity has thus far been beyond the ability of its politicians. Moreover, although most of the people of South Sudan oppose the SPLM government, the IO's isolation in the region and the continuing military support of the government by Museveni make a clear-cut victory difficult unless he changes his views.

This is compounded by the fact Riek Machar is not by choice a military leader. The conflict was thrust upon him, he has no taste for war, and attempts by the Juba government and others to present him as a militarist are little more than propaganda. After the signing of the CPA I met Riek in his role as an SPLA commander in Upper Nile and asked him if he would remain in the SPLA. He replied that he would never again wear a military uniform. Given an option, Riek would opt for a political solution over a military solution to the conflict and his performance, dismissal of the former SSDF generals, and repeatedly over-ruling his supporters and party in favour of peace-making, rather than war, makes that clear. It has been the mistake of the peace-makers to not give him a realistic political option and instead to support the war-obsessed Juba government. Given his distaste for war, though, Riek is not the person to lead opposition forces to a military victory and he will likely grasp at the first genuine compromise on offer, which might well preserve a regime and ruling party whose departure is long over-due.

For the IO to give reason for hope that it could successfully confront the manifold problems of the country it would have to irrevocably break from the SPLA and its modus operandi and instead develop an accountable institutional-based leadership, commit to a national democratic revolution, and carry out reforms beyond Riek's limited conceptions. It is noteworthy that in the Horn, revolutionary groups of a leftist character have come to power in Eritrea, Ethiopia, and Uganda, and even the Islamist NCP made no secret of its adoption of organization and mobilization techniques derived from the Sudan Communist Party. Riek, though, has repeatedly made clear his distaste for leftist politics. The SPLM-IO would have to focus on the concerns and needs of its grassroots and not the elites, deepen its embrace of all the people of South Sudan, develop collaborative relations with other opposition groups, and establish governance structures that correspond with conditions in the country, not those of the West. Lastly, while appreciating the tribal character of South Sudan, the IO would have to emphasize the class contradiction between the elites who have brought the country to the verge of collapse, and the marginalized masses from all the tribes who have a common interest in dispensing with these elites.

Even in a broad-based coalition, however, the SPLM-IO may not be capable of militarily defeating the government. Its leadership and membership are ideologically weak, there is an almost complete absence of political education, and under Riek it will likely grasp at the first credible political opening, providing another opportunity for the international community to affirm in power the elites that destroyed South Sudan. Indeed, in the run up to the signing of ARCSS and even after its collapse in July 2016, the IO aspired to no more than the first vice presidency and was prepared to again accept Salva as president. A party with such limited objectives is unlikely to provide the kind of structural changes desperately needed in South Sudan, nor can the demand for the vice presidency inspire its followers.

There is also the legitimate fear that no South Sudanese government, no matter how it is constructed, can administer a country that should not have been created in the first place. The tragedy of southern Sudan began with its exploitation under the Ottoman empire and its limited incorporation and development under the Mahdist regime, the failure of British colonialism to develop the south and then turning the unprepared southerners over to post-colonial Khartoum-centred governments more interested in the Islamization and Arabization of the people than development and genuine nation building. Added to that the people have suffered because of the failures of two international-led peace processes and their collapsed agreements – the CPA and ARCSS. The South Sudanese are so disillusioned that some are even entertaining the idea of reuniting their country with Sudan, but that is neither realistic nor offers the prospect of escaping their dilemma. It emphasizes, though, the need for serious, critical, and outside-the-box thinking if there is to be any hope that the present tragedy is to be overcome.

It is against that background that consideration of an international trusteeship must be entertained. Trusteeship is a notion that has been on the margins of African politics since the 1990s. In response to state failures in Africa during the 1990s, Stephen Ellis wrote, 'This idea [of trusteeship], anathema since the end of colonialism, deserves rehabilitation'.[9] The issue of principle has not changed since then, with trusteeship advocates considering it a means to end wars and respond to state collapse, while their opponents raise the banner of national sovereignty and claim it represents the return of white colonialism.

A trusteeship has been considered by a variety of actors for South Sudan since the outbreak of the civil war. Meanwhile, almost without exception there were concerns by both leaders of the government and Riek about the loss of sovereignty it would entail. However, South Sudan only gained independence because of international support and appeals to national sovereignty by SPLM politicians who for 20 years have benefited from the support they have received from the international community reek of hypocrisy. Moreover, as Dr Laku Jada Kwajok, who supports a UN trusteeship, has argued, 'a failed state has no sovereignty' and from a citizen's perspective sovereignty 'has no value when the state fails to deliver essential services, uphold the rule of law and promote peace and harmony between its communities'.[10]

Former US Assistant Secretary of State for Africa, Dr Herman Cohen, and Dr Peter Adwok, soon to join the SPLM-IO, called for a UN trusteeship for South Sudan shortly after civil war broke out, after concluding that the SPLM did not have the ability to govern the country.[11] A number of leaders of South Sudanese political parties have told the author they support an international trusteeship, but because of fear of being labelled traitors they do not want to be publicly identified, which suggests there might be a broader basis of support in favour a trusteeship among the political class than is imagined. Meanwhile, Pagan Amum, former Secretary-General of the SPLM and leader of the Former Detainees, initially endorsed an international trusteeship before supporting the views of his colleagues and calling for an interim government of technocrats.[12] Speaking from the US liberal interventionist wing, Professor G. Pascal Zachary quoted Colin Powell that, 'you break it, you own it' to contend that the US created the problem of South Sudan and therefore the country should be placed under a US trusteeship.[13]

However, the proposal for an international trusteeship for South Sudan was first interjected into the South Sudan peace process by Professor Mahmood Mamdani in his separate submission to the AU Commission of Inquiry.[14] He argued that South Sudan only gained independence because of the US-led Troika, which handed over power to the criminal SPLA that lacked capacity, the country never had genuine sovereignty and called for a trusteeship under the AU to ensure African sovereignty. He subsequently proposed that former South African President Thabo Mbeki should chair an AU High Panel to carry out this task.

While Mamdani's assessment of the artificiality of South Sudan and of the disastrous error of the US and its allies in turning over power to the SPLM is supported by the analysis above, his contention that the best means to rectify the problem and ensure African sovereignty is to delegate the task to the AU under Mbeki is questionable. The AU has rarely been a defender of African sovereignty, its role in the South Sudan peace process has not set itself apart from the failed efforts of IGAD, and with the Western-led overthrow of el-Qaddafi the AU's capacity to stand up to the West has been further reduced. As president of South Africa, Mbeki closely followed Western neo-liberal policies and oversaw growing inequality and foreign control of the national economy, while in Africa he is best known for his espousal of NEPAD (New Partnership for African Development) in the late 1990s and early 2000s, which endorsed the link between development and security, the need for regional security organizations dependent on the West, and Africa's role as a provider of raw materials. On balance, the UN Security Council would seem a better defender of African sovereignty, because unlike the AU it has members who oppose Western-led nation and state building.

While Mamdani's proposal for a trusteeship was made before the full extent of the failure of the US-led peace process became apparent, Kate Almquist Knopf's advocacy of it came after the collapse of the peace agreement in July 2016. Given her status as a former USAID official in the Horn of Africa and director of the US Africa Center for Strategic Studies at the National Defense University, her call and that of Princeton Lyman, former Sudan and South Sudan Special Envoy, for an international trusteeship for South Sudan carries weight in Washington.[15] Knopf drew attention to the humanitarian crisis in the country, which she contended is not dissimilar in scale to that of Syria, even though it has largely been ignored by the international media. She expressed fear of genocide and that given endemic insecurity and numerous examples of South Sudan's conflicts destabilizing neighbouring states, more outside military interventions could be expected. This in turn could lead to the country being carved up. Knopf noted that as a result of economic collapse, the people of South Sudan are entirely dependent on the international community for the provision of services. She reported that between 2005 and 2016 the US spent an astounding $11 billion in the country and concluded that 'US taxpayers deserve a better return on their investment than the humanitarian and security catastrophes we see today', a statement with which President Trump would agree. Against that background she makes the case for a trusteeship by arguing, 'It is past time to abandon several myths regarding South Sudan's political culture, the capacity of its leaders, and the potential impact of technical interventions – from development assistance to peacekeeping – in a country that has for all intents and purposes had no meaningful experience with governance'.

While Knopf charts new ground in her analysis, she reverts to the long-held US view that the removal of Salva and Riek would 'defuse much of the impetus to continue the war', only later acknowledging, 'there is no evidence to suggest that the replacement of Riek Machar with Taban Deng Gai will result in the Kiir regime voluntarily changing course to act in the interests of its people rather than against them'. Demonizing some and glorifying others instead of carrying out system-level analysis has been the starting point of many US foreign policy failures. The notion is also dangerous because it assumes that Riek and Salva are holding back the emergence of a class of peace-making politicians, and there is no evidence of that.

Knopf emphasized the efforts the international community have made to achieve peace in South Sudan. She failed, however, to appreciate that all that involvement has produced is a litany of failures that have not gone unnoticed by the citizens of the country. Knopf is right to note how ill prepared South Sudan was for independence, but that speaks to the errors of the international community, and especially the US, which championed the country's independence and turned over power to the SPLM.

Knopf's strongest argument in favour of a trusteeship for South Sudan is that resorting to technical solutions like power-sharing to solve problems of a structural nature have been a failure, and there is no reason to think that present technical proposals will be any different. That includes US proposals to remove Salva and Riek, the post-8 July marginalization of Riek, and the organization of a regional armed force in Juba.

Meanwhile, Knopf's proposed international trusteeship for South Sudan is informed by the assumption that the US would be the driving force behind the trusteeship, which again draws on notions like the US as the indispensable nation to any sustainable solution, something which has been discredited many times over in the past two decades.

More alarming, in neither the Mamdani nor Knopf proposals is there any attempt to consider the sentiments of the South Sudanese. As a result, they resemble the all too familiar top-down approach of failed peace-making in Sudan and South Sudan.

Having little faith in liberal peacemaking given its failures during the process leading to the CPA (see my *The Fate of Sudan*), I was not optimistic when the international community rolled out the same model to confront South Sudan's civil war. As a result, I have regularly questioned eastern Nuer (to whom I have had the most access) about their attitude to the imposition of an international trusteeship, and for much of the conflict a large majority supported the proposal. Even when it was emphasized that a trusteeship would remove all politicians, including Riek, from the political arena, they still supported the notion, contending that their main concern was to eliminate Salva, the killer of their people, and a trusteeship would accomplish that. But in December 2016 when I carried out interviews of South Sudanese Nuer, mostly from the white army and elders, in Gambella, Ethiopia, their attitude had dramatically changed.

Only a few among the white army held that the removal of all the leaders, including Riek, would facilitate peace. Some held that if the Dinka and Nuer failed to resolve their problems that another tribe should assume the leadership, and only if that failed should the UN take control of the country. More focused on the issue of justice and noted that the actions of Salva caused the war, and there could be no peace unless he and those Dinka leaders close to him were removed, and thus there was no reason to sideline Riek. Some contended that the 'white man's peace process' had failed and the trusteeship represented a response to the failure, but the white man could no longer be trusted. One fighter said that the white men had failed in Iraq, Libya, and Syria and they should not be permitted to carry out another failed programme in South Sudan. The South Sudanese, he argued, should look after their own affairs. Another interviewee considered the UN a branch of the US, while his friend said that with the return to war, the US now wanted a 'mandate to rule the country'.

The Nuer elders interviewed were united in their opposition to a trusteeship. William Deng, a Jikany elder from Olang County visiting Gambella to have an eye operation, said that the peace process granted South Sudan an independent state and a trusteeship amounted to taking that state away and would be resisted. A couple of other respondents made similar comments. Another group of Jikan elders opposed any notion of a trusteeship because they had lost faith in the international community after the collapse of the peace agreement on 8 July 2016. They noted the failure of the international community to condemn the killing of Nuer civilians in December 2013 and again in July 2016. Another three elders said that President Obama and Secretary of State John Kerry supported the Salva government, were not impartial in the resolution of the conflict, and could not be trusted to oversee any international intervention. The elders contended that since 'the man of the US Salva', could not survive the opposition of almost the entire country, the Americans now wanted to rescue him through the imposition of a trusteeship. Two other elders said that the white men had badly messed up the peace process in South Sudan and now wanted to extradite themselves by forcing an international trusteeship on the country. Another elder shared these sentiments, but raised the question of what power was going to disarm the SPLA and SPLA-IO? Suggestions on my part that the trusteeship could be administered by the AU to ensure that Africans were in control led to the same response as the white army fighters, namely that the AU was also controlled by the US or white men. After initially supporting a UN trusteeship, Peter Adwok also changed his views: 'UN Trusteeship would be another attempt to freeze this crisis and prevent its resolution to the satisfaction of the people of South Sudan'.[16]

While not claiming to be representative, this sampling nonetheless suggests that ordinary Nuer are surprisingly well-informed, frequently have insightful views, and are thoroughly disillusioned with the international community, particularly the US. Just as the US was almost universally admired for its critical role in the creation of South Sudan, it is now singled out for the failure of the peace process and that makes the imposition of a trusteeship problematic. Both the Sudan and South Sudan peace processes were explicitly designed to side-line the people and focus on the interests of the elites, an approach increasingly consistent with Western practices of governance, but they have repeatedly failed. Democratic transformation must be at the centre of an agenda of change, but it is doubtful that a West enthralled by neo-liberalism could be the agent of that process.

None of the proposals for a reinvigorated US-led peace process, SPLM reconciliation, national dialogue, giving war a chance, or an international trusteeship, provide a convincing way out of the impasse US and IGAD policies have produced, although some are clearly better than others. Nor, based on their records in South Sudan, do the actors proposed to lead these initiatives inspire confidence. The US saw in its support for southern and then South Sudan a means to affirm its role as a peace-maker, and to oversee the emergence of a new state committed to democracy, free enterprise, and the support of its regional interests. But a new regime in Washington abandoned the state its predecessors midwifed and its officials were reduced to hoping the war would stop so commentators would not link the pictures of famine victims on their television screens with another US foreign policy failure.

What is needed is an approach to peace-making that is rooted in the values of the indigenous communities in conflict and not the imposition of foreign Western values and institutions. International-led peace-making re-affirmed the perspective of modernization theory that the obstacles to development are entirely indigenous, ignoring the international dimensions and causes of conflict. By holding local actors wholly responsible for wars and ignoring the role of the international community in sometimes causing the conflicts, invariably exacerbating and shaping them, and giving legitimacy to favoured elites, international actors absolved themselves of responsibility, placed it entirely on local actors, and made the resolution of these conflicts considerably more difficult. The decline of modernization theory with its overt ethnocentrism corresponded with the end of the Cold War and the rise of neo-liberalism, which is also Western-centric.

Conflicts in peripheral states are typically viewed as unjustified, meaningless, non-political, and a result of violent pathologies which frequently target civilians, women, and children. Alternatively, they are due to individual greed and naked political ambitions. These themes were endlessly repeated to justify Western interventions and figured prominently in the Western presentation of the conflicts in Sudan and South Sudan. By way of contrast Western-led wars are held to be rational, use smart bombs and the like to minimize civilian casualties, and are fought for, and shaped by, principles, most often humanitarian. Against this background, Western-led peace-making is assumed to be disinterested, non-political, and designed to help Africans in a context where weak or criminal states prey on their citizens who are incapable of helping themselves. The prevailing view is that 'the West has no responsibility for conflict or violence in Africa, it is only an observer, and it is only out of charity that the West intervenes to stop violence that, it is assumed, is fated to erupt without international intervention'.[17]

The ideological nature of post-Cold War peace-making was further emphasized when it became increasingly concerned with 'state failure', after states in conflict were held to pose a security threat to the Western-dominated international state system. This position was first highlighted in Somalia but was later put forward as a rationale for US and Western military interventions in Afghanistan, Iraq, Libya, and for peace-making in Sudan. It was formalized in the wake of 9/11 with US policy which held that, 'poverty, weak institutions, and corruption can make weak states vulnerable to terrorist networks and drug cartels within their borders'.[18] This new thinking replaced notions of deterrence which dominated defence policies during the Cold War years in favour of a pre-emptive strategy against hostile states and terrorist groups. It also led the US to expand development assistance, encourage free trade, promote democracy, conflict resolution, and commit to a neo-liberal project of nation-building. This same thinking figured in the promotion and financial support for regional security, assistance to the SPLA, the establishment of a culturally inappropriate liberal democratic form of government and constitution in South Sudan, and the leading role the US assumed in the peace process to end the December 2013 South Sudan civil war. But it has all been a massive failure.

To be sure, destructive Western intervention in peripheral states like South Sudan could only be accomplished by the cooperation of indigenous elites, who invariably have supped deeply on Western doctrines and values and or see their self-interest best pursued by supporting these efforts. Indeed, in Sudan and South Sudan the monopoly of the peace processes by the international community meant that failure to win the support of the West led to marginalization. In neither the Sudan nor the South Sudan peace processes were there any mechanisms in place to ensure public validation. For both the CPA and ARCSS, they were specifically rejected.

When South Sudan's civil war broke out, the West and its regional allies would have better served the South Sudanese by letting the conflict be resolved by traditional means. Instead of rushing in with a peace process based on notions that never had any resonance with South Sudanese and which demeaned the politicians who attempted to maximize their gains on the backs of the slaughtered Juba Nuer civilians, it would have been better for these professed leaders of their people to raise the singular question asked by all the Nuer – why did the government kill our innocent people? That was the burning issue, one that has never been addressed and thus remains an open sore, and one that traditional society is better equipped to resolving than a neo-liberal-packaged Western peace process which wanted to bury collective pain under political formulas.

The failed peace agreement and the undoubted peace processes that will follow will not address the killing of the Nuer and all the killings that have subsequently followed, and which have now reached into every community in this tortured country. The Nilotic Nuer and Dinka have a long history of reconciling after committing crimes against others within their own tribe or against other tribes. But for reconciliation to proceed there is a need for the abusers to acknowledge their crime. The peace processes that have been rolled out since December 2013 have all worked to obscure this original crime, as well as providing mechanisms for which its acknowledgement can be avoided. If there is any hope to overcoming the present impasse and the illusions of Western peace-makers, it must start by demonstrating some humility in light of the litany of their failed efforts, drop their foreign superiority, and allow the affected societies to look within their own cultures for means to resolve the conflicts.

POSTSCRIPT

The enormous financial and political resources devoted to southern and then South Sudan by successive US administrations was never based on genuine strategic concerns or – as claimed – national security. It proceeded from liberal interventionism and the false portrayal of the SPLA and the conflict advanced by lobbyists, their friends in the media, and government shills led by Susan Rice. But their message and links with the Democratic Party had no resonance with the incoming President Donald Trump, while his commitment to 'America First' and rejection of policies associated with his predecessor (and George Bush) led to a marked decline in human and financial resources to Africa in general and South Sudan in particular.

But corresponding to a decline in resources devoted to South Sudan has been the formulation of a more reasoned US policy. While the Obama Administration backed the Juba government, even though it was the primary instigator of the war and most frequently in breach of the 2015 peace agreement, the Trump Administration imposed an arms embargo against the regime in February 2018, sanctioned people close to Salva considered corrupt and leading officials in the oil industry, and in July sponsored a successful Security Council resolution imposing an arms embargo against Juba and a travel ban and asset freezes on selected individuals. The Juba government's biggest backer, Museveni, however, continues to receive US military aid and has repeatedly said he would not abide by any embargo against South Sudan and thus the impact of such measures is limited, but they go far beyond what was possible during the Obama era.

Militarily the Juba government continued to dominate the conflict, remained in control of the capitals of the now 32 states, and captured the SPLM-IO administrative and military headquarters in Pagak. But the rebels controlled much of rural Greater Upper Nile, Western and

Central Equatoria, and parts of Western Bahr al-Ghazal and there was little sign they could be militarily defeated.

Meanwhile, Salva dismissed his SPLA Chief of Staff, Paul Malong, in May 2017 and 11 months later Malong formed an armed opposition group, the South Sudan United Front. The military potential of this group remains in doubt, but it makes clear the divisions within the Dinka.

Despite no change in the negotiating position of the belligerents, IGAD hosted consultations with the government, SPLM-IO, and eight other rebel groups in Addis Ababa in February 2018. Bringing the other opposition groups into the process reflected the widening hostility to the regime even if they were not militarily significant. But the absence of a workable negotiating strategy and adherence to the same failed model of peace-making left most of the delegates interviewed on site by the author confused as to why they had been brought to Addis Ababa. Although little was accomplished in the negotiations, on the sidelines the non-IO opposition groups, including the Former Detainees, formed the South Sudan Opposition Alliance (SSOA) which negotiated with the government under Gabriel Changeson. While the SSOA appealed for unity with the IO, Riek made that impossible by continuing to insist from exile in South Africa that he alone lead the opposition.

With the imminent collapse of the negotiations, Riek – who had been told by the US and IGAD that he would not be allowed to participate in the negotiations – was brought out of house arrest in South Africa at the instigation of the new Ethiopian prime minister, Abiy Ahmed, and held face-to-face meetings with Salva in Addis Ababa. But there was no progress, and with Salva insisting that Riek had no place in the government of South Sudan, it looked like he would again be returned to South Africa.

However, in the wake of this failure and four and an half years of botched IGAD and Troika led peace-making, conditions were falling in place for a Sudan led peace initiative. First, although the Trump Administration would not conduct its own peace process and the other Troika partners depend on American leadership, IGAD was under increasing pressure from the UN to come up with a workable agreement or face the prospect that its monopoly of the peace process would end and be transferred to the African Union.

Second, as long as the Obama Administration held sway the best Sudan could do was follow IGAD's lead, but with the coming to power of Trump, Khartoum had more room to manoeuvre. Meanwhile, Ethiopia's incoming Prime Minister Abiy Ahmed was pre-occupied with his own peace-making in Eritrea while Kenya's Uhuru Kenyatta does not have the ability or power. The other key regional actor, Yoweri Museveni, had been Bashir's most bitter enemy in the region, but considerable effort had gone into building trust between the leaders over the previous two years. Moreover, Museveni needed peace to regenerate South Sudan's economy upon which Uganda's own economy had become closely linked. And while he dominated Salva, he had little influence over the opposition and Uganda was far from the income generating oil fields on Sudan's border.

Third, Bashir and his security apparatus had the strongest ties and best intelligence on the leading political and military actors in South Sudan. The new initiative was orchestrated by Bashir but led by his recently appointed foreign minister, Dirdiery Ahmed, an astute lawyer who had served as the Sudan government legal advisor during the Navaisha peace negotiations. Moreover, most of the opposition leaders were based in Khartoum and while the Sudanese military only provided them with minimal support, they maintained close relations and there was nowhere else in the region they could live.

Lastly and most importantly, Sudan was facing an economic crisis which threatened to bring about the collapse of Bashir's regime and to overcome it he had broken relations with Iran and provided troops for the Saudi and Emirates' war against the Houthis in Yemen, and while this resulted in increased Gulf financial support, Sudan's economic ills continued. Moreover, after closely cooperating with US security agencies in the GWOT, making major changes to Sudan's foreign policy, and not supporting the South Sudanese opposition the US ended its sanctions (although it continued to designate Sudan as a 'state sponsor of terrorism' and maintained targeted sanctions against individuals) the international community remained reluctant to invest in the country. Against that background and Sudan's recent experience of long queues at gasoline filling stations, bringing peace to South Sudan was considered crucial to both regenerating that country's oil industry and overcoming Sudan's predicament. Improving the economy would also strengthen Bashir's position going into the 2020 national elections, even though under the CPA provided Interim National Constitution he could not legally run. Finally, assuming a leading role in the peace process would help to resolve the outstanding border demarcation issue to Sudan's advantage.

The Sudanese mediation largely relied on pressuring the opposition to accept Juba's positions and was mostly pursued without face-to-face meetings between the parties, which does not bode well for their future relations in the anticipated transitional government. On 27 June 2018 the Khartoum Declaration, a document of intent, was signed by Salva and Riek, and after some revisions they initialed the agreement on 25 July and on 5 August signed it, although many outstanding issues remained to be resolved. The agreement made no attempt to confront the structural issues that had made South Sudan ungovernable even before the outbreak of war in December 2013 and it followed the established pattern of elite accommodation.

With Salva serving as president, the agreement provided for five vice-presidents: as well as Riek being reappointed as first vice president, two would be nominated by the transitional government (the existing vice-presidents, Taban Deng and James Wani Igga), another nominated by SSOA who was to be a woman, and a final vice president nominated by the Former Detainees, with no hierarchy among them except that of the first vice president.[1] There would be 35 ministers, with the transitional government appointing 20, SPLM-IO nine, SSOA three, Former Detainees two and Other Political Parties one. The agreement also provided for ten deputy ministers, of whom five would come from the transitional government, three from the IO, and one each from the SSOA and Other Political Parties. The Transitional National Legislature would be expanded to 550 members, of whom 332 would come from the government, 128 from the IO, 50 from the SSOA, 30 from Other Political Parties, and ten from the Former Detainees. The agreement also stipulated that 35% of the executive positions be women. Even Salva acknowledged that the country could not afford this vast expansion in government.

While the enormous extension of government and the patronage network was accepted by the belligerents, controversy focused on the means to address the government's increase in the number of states to 32 from the ten stipulated by the CPA, the transitional constitution, and ARCSS. The opposition saw this expansion as a critical means by which the government institutionalized Dinka domination, the take-over of land of displaced people, and held that it would produce instability. The Khartoum proposals involved the government retaining 55% of the power in all the states with 27% for the IO, 10% for the SSOA, and 8% for Other Political Parties.

The Sudan-led peace initiative had little concern with democracy, largely ignored civil society, and although the SSOA could not be excluded, the focus was on reaching an agreement between Salva and Riek. Reforms to the system were either ignored or – in the case of the number of states – would be resolved by a Boundaries Commission or failing that an AU supervised referendum. Questions of whether leaders fully controlled their armed forces or if a peace process could continue with the conflict ongoing were simply ignored when the cease-fire agreement broke down within hours of it going into effect on 30 June and fighting continued throughout the negotiations. These same forces, which could number 100,000, are to be held in cantonment centres for the eight months of the pre-transitional period, during which part of them will be integrated with an equal number from the SPLA into the national army. The pre-transitional period is scheduled to last eight months and the transitional government 36 months followed by a national election.

Although the ceasefire is to be monitored by the belligerents with African forces invited to 'supervise' it, a primary thrust of the agreement is to regenerate the economy through rehabilitating and securing the oil industry in Unity state in which Sudan would work 'in collaboration and coordination' with South Sudan. Even before the peace agreement Khartoum and Juba agreed in June 2018 to repair oil infrastructure facilities destroyed by the war within three months to increase production and to establish a joint force to protect the oilfields from attacks by rebel forces. A peace agreement with both the government and the SPLM-IO (which alone in the opposition posed a threat to the oil fields) would further ensure the security of the oil fields. This provision took place in the context of Trump's threat to launch a war against Iran, which was producing higher oil prices given the expected shortfalls. Moreover, according to Dirdiery, Sudan is to play the lead role in supervising the formation of one army in South Sudan, which is to be completed within 12 months of the signing of the agreement.[2]

The question is why the belligerents endorsed the agreement? Riek was clearly influenced by the fact that to openly reject the agreement would likely mean a quick return to house arrest in South Africa and the expulsion of the SPLM-IO leadership from Khartoum. So anxious was he to reclaim his previous position as first vice president that he bent to Salva's demands to accept 32 states and two vice-presidents loyal to the president. He could count on the support of the SPLM-IO leadership since they were hand-picked by him, even though they were not as keen to return to Juba as they were after signing ARCSS. Additionally – as noted above – Riek has an unrealistic assessment of his political abilities and he assured his colleagues the IO would win the struggle over the number of states (i.e. his proposal for 21 states) and the national elections. Since neither South Sudan nor Sudan has had anything approaching a free and fair election since that of 1986 (and southern Sudan was largely excluded because of insecurity) that is at best naïve. Moreover, Riek would be a fool not to worry that after twice trying to kill him Salva would not make a third and successful attempt. Indeed, the UN Special Envoy for South Sudan said neither the region nor the existing Regional Protection Force could ensure protection for opposition leaders in Juba.[3]

Riek's core constituency, the Nuer, are again being asked to endorse as president the man who killed their tribe members in December 2013 and for Riek to serve as his deputy. Moreover, since the minority position of the IO (and the rest of the opposition) in the transitional government will preclude structural changes that challenge Dinka dominance, the Nuer, Shilluk, Equatorians, Fertit, and others whose communities have suffered the most from the war are only promised reforms after the IO wins the election. Although the government has become increasingly isolated since the signing of ARCSS, the mediators have based their power-sharing arrangements – the core of the agreement – solely on military control and as a result the IO presence in the government has declined.

Salva signed on to the Sudanese initiative because it is difficult for him to refuse Bashir whom he views as a sort of uncle, while his major benefactor, Museveni, also pressed him to agree and along with Sudan, Uganda is a guarantor of the agreement. Unlike under Obama, Salva can no longer count on US support and he and his government could not indefinitely test the patience of the international community.

Moreover, hanging over both Salva and Riek was the threat that refusal to end the conflict could lead to an international effort to have them both ostracized and/or face charges by the International Criminal Court. The prospect of increased oil revenues and new money for patronage is attractive for Salva while the rehabilitation of the oil industry would be welcomed by China, which would add to the pressure on Juba. Unable to defeat the armed opposition, the regime had been attempting to rehabilitate the oil industry, but with oil production on the Sudanese border and dependent on a pipeline to Port Sudan, Juba was in a weak position to challenge Khartoum. Lastly, while no intellectual, Salva has gained the grudging respect of even his enemies as a survivor who has repeatedly got away with challenging the international community and has regularly bested Riek, and he has reason to think he will continue to do so.

However, Salva leads a Dinka regime and the Dinka are hated and divided and that could leave them dangerously exposed under the agreement, not just to genocidal attacks, but, with Salva in poor health and an election at the end of the process, the Dinka face the threat of being dethroned. Bashir acknowledged that he was approached by Dinka elders (known to be Bona Malwal and Francis Deng) who appealed to him to go further than providing security in the oil fields and ensure that the Dinka are protected. Bashir rejected these appeals and his position was shared by his government who want to control South Sudan's oil production but oppose getting involved in the country's many internal conflicts, although whether that position can be maintained in practice remains to be seen.

The SSOA was highly critical of the proposed peace agreement. Having little military capacity and largely marginalized in a peace process that focused on Salva and Riek, SSOA accused the mediators of ignoring the core issues and only bargaining between the warring parties over the allocation of cabinet and parliamentary seats. The opposition alliance was particularly upset at the agreement's continuation of 32 states, doubted that a referendum would be fair, and was anxious to ensure that seized land the Dinka would be returned to their rightful owners. Unity in their ranks was, however, undermined when Alliance member, Peter Gadet, who was financed by Khartoum and had forces on the border of South Sudan, supported the peace agreement. It was speculated that these forces would be used to provide security for the Bentiu oil fields, his home area, a task he had previously successfully carried out for Khartoum. Despite their concerns Bashir convinced SSOA to initial the agreement in Khartoum on 5 August with the understanding that the details regarding the number states and their boundaries would be resolved in a further round of negotiations. Two of the SSOA parties, however, Thomas Cirillo's National Salvation Front and the People's Democratic Movement of Hakim Dario, refused to sign because of the lack of commitment to federalism.

Before the agreement was finalized the US concluded, 'A narrow agreement between elites will not solve the problems plaguing South Sudan. In fact, such an agreement may sow the seeds of another cycle of conflict.'[4] The statement went on to demand inclusivity, implementation of the ceasefire, condemned the South Sudan's Legislative Assembly decision to extend Salva's term of office to three years, and threatened more sanctions. The statement concluded that the 'United States will not be a guarantor of any agreement and will not fund – or call for additional United Nations resources to support – the transitional government, in the absence of a sustained, demonstrated commitment to peace, inclusivity, financial accountability and good governance'.[5] For more than two decades the US government misunderstood the SPLA and claimed a major political victory in overseeing the secession of South Sudan when it was another step on the road to disaster. But the Trump administration has thrown away the blinkers that have blinded three previous presidencies, even if this knowledge came too late in the day to have much influence on the shape of the peace agreement. The EU followed the US in voicing its scepticism about the agreement.

The critical role Khartoum is expected to play in policing the peace process and having its hands on the economic destiny of South Sudan seriously compromises its sovereignty. It also casts in doubt the enormous efforts by the US led international community to achieve the CPA which provided the basis for the secession of South Sudan. Moreover, Riek who broke with the SPLA in 1991 over the demand for the right of southern Sudan to self-determination gushed, 'this agreement will normalize the relations between the two Sudans which means our people will live happily ... It is going to be an agreement that will *integrate* us'[6] (italics added).

On 30 August 2018 Riek Machar, on behalf of the SPLM-IO and Gabriel Changeson from the SSOA, initialed the Revitalized Agreement on the Resolution of the Conflict in South Sudan but listed points of disagreement – the number of states, cabinet quorum and parliament meetings, and the constitution-making process. In addition, they asked that Ethiopia and Kenya join Sudan and Uganda as guarantors of the agreement, deploy forces within UNMISS, and that Bashir ensure their concerns are addressed by a forthcoming summit of the IGAD Heads of State.

If this or a similar agreement is formally agreed to by the principle belligerents it will almost certainly break down, but Khartoum will continue to provide security for the oil fields which will ensure both Sudan's revenue stream and that of the Salva government to fight the rebels. Indeed, the critical logic of the peace initiative and why it gained the support of IGAD was that unlike the Congo where neighbouring countries participated in a free-for-all looting spree of the country's resources, in South Sudan the region has agreed upon an orderly means by which the rush for spoils can be pursued and the threat of conflict between neighbouring states reduced.

Like ARCSS, this agreement claims to solve the problem of war, but has not considered its causes and has focused on gaining the support of a tiny discredited SPLM elite. Like the other peace processes, the latest effort is designed to return South Sudan to the status quo before the outbreak of war, but this period was characterized by endemic insecurity, kleptocracy, and mal-governance which produced the war. Such approaches to peace-making will not work and as a result IGAD's monopoly of the peace process will likely end, but there is no reason to think that either the AU or the UN, which operate from similar misplaced assumptions, would prove more successful at achieving a sustainable peace in South Sudan. As a result, sooner or later consideration for an international trusteeship for the country will again come to the fore.

John Young
4 September 2018

NOTES

Preface

1 See John Young, (2012), *The Fate of Sudan: Origins and Consequences of a Flawed Peace Process*, Zed Books.

Chapter 1

1 See John Markakis, Guenther Schlee, and John Young, (forthcoming, 2018), *The Nation-State: A Wrong Model for the Horn of Africa*.
2 Richard Williamson, (2009), 'Sudan and the Implications for the Responsibility to Protect,' Stanley Foundation, October, p. 7.
3 Author interview with Salva Kiir, (2009), Yei, 14 May.
4 John Young, (2012), *The Fate of Sudan*.
5 Author interview with Sudan Communist Party Politburo member, Siddig Yousif, (2017), Khartoum, 24 May.
6 John Young, (2012), *The Fate of Sudan*.
7 During the election for the governor, a group of Angelina's supporters visited the Carter Center in Khartoum, which was officially observing the election, and laid before the author hundreds of ballots marked for their candidate which had been discarded and not counted.
8 Alex Perry, (2014), 'George Clooney, South Sudan, and How the World's Newest Nation Imploded,' *Newsweek*, 2 October.
9 Alex de Waal, (2016), 'Introduction: Making Sense of South Sudan,' *African Affairs*, 14 November, p. 4.
10 John Young, (2007), 'Sudan People's Liberation Army: Disarmament in Jonglei and Its Implications,' Occasional Paper No. 137, Institute of Security Studies, Pretoria, April.
11 Ibid.
12 Author interview with General Peter Gadet, (2016), Khartoum, 14 June.
13 Author interview with Lt.-General retired Joseph Lagu, (2011), Juba, 12 April.
14 Government of Republic of South Sudan Ministry of Finance, (2015), 'Approved Budget Tables Financial Year 2014/15,' August.
15 Enough, (2017), 'Weapons of Mass Corruption: How Corruption in South Sudan's Military Undermines the World's Newest Country,' January.
16 As witnessed by the author in Juba.
17 SPLM supporters in the Nuba Mountains apparently came to the same conclusion in May 2017 and have dissociated themselves with the Malik Agar leadership and demand self-determination for their territory.
18 Alan Boswell, (2012), 'American Expelled from South Sudan for Anti-Corruption Work,' McClatchy Newspapers, 20 August.
19 Chairman and Commander-in-Chief, SPLM-IO, (2016), 'Policy Recommendations for Ending the Civil War,' Pretoria, South Africa, 25 November.

20 African Union, (2014), 'Final Report of the African Union Commission of Inquiry on South Sudan,' Addis Ababa, 15 October, www.peaceau.org/uploads/auciss.final.report.pdf.

21 Alex de Waal, (2012), 'South Sudan's Doomsday Machine,' *New York Times*, op-ed, 24 January.

22 African Union, (2014), 'Final Report of the African Union Commission of Inquiry on South Sudan.'

23 John Young, (2012), *The Fate of Sudan*.

Chapter 2

1 American exceptionalism had its origins during the American Revolution and its profession of individualism, republicanism, democracy, and laissez-faire economics. From that developed the notion that the US had a unique mission in the world and the country's history made it superior to other nations. As the exceptional country, rules of accountability for international conduct do not apply as with other countries. American exceptionalism also goes along with the notion of the US as the 'indispensable nation' or sometimes the 'indispensable power', a term frequently used by Obama, but first coined by Bill Clinton's Secretary of State, Madeleine Albright in 1998. In justifying the US attack on Iraq, she said that, 'if we have to use force, it is because we are America; we are the indispensable nation. We stand tall and see further than other countries into the future, and we see the danger here to all of us'. See Madeline Albright, (1998), stated on NBC's *Today Show*, 19 February. Both terms suggest that the US must be the leader in promoting a rules-based world order centred on free markets, democracy, and human rights. An early proponent of the R2P was Dr Francis Deng, Sudan's best-known intellectual who argued that just as governments had certain sovereign rights, they also had responsibilities to protect their citizens from calamities. States no longer had an automatic right to sovereignty and if governments failed to protect their people their sovereignty could be withdrawn. However, when Francis served as UN Representative for the government of South Sudan he markedly changed his tune and opposed any interventionist measures by the international community that were justified in terms of human rights. See Francis Deng et al., (1996), *Sovereignty as Responsibility: Conflict Management in Africa*, Brookings Institution Press. The doctrine was officially endorsed by the AU in 2002 and by the UN in 2006. However, the then president of the UN General Assembly, Reverend Miguel d'Escoto Brockmann, more accurately called R2P 'redecorated colonialism' and that a more precise name for R2P would be 'the right to intervene'. See Rev. Miquel D'Escoto Brockman, (2009), Remarks at the Opening of the Thematic Dialogue of the General Assembly on the Responsibility to Protect, UN Headquarters, New York, 23 July.

2 By 2013 the US had military stations in 49 out of 55 countries in Africa. See Nick Turse, (2013), 'The Pivot to Africa,' *TomDispatch.com*, 5 September.

3 The political significance of this project to the US is made clear by the fact that $300 million was raised for 'Operation Moses' in 1984 to transport 8000 Falashas to Israel while only $30 million was spent to service 600,000 refugees in Eastern Sudan. See Africa Rights, (1997), *Food and Power in Sudan: A Critique of Humanitarianism*, London, p. 35.

4   Veronica Nmoma, (2006), 'The Shift in United States–Sudan Relations,' *The Journal of Conflict Studies*, 26(2).

5   Donald Petterson, (1999), *Inside Sudan: Political Islam, Conflict, and Catastrophe*, Westview Press, p. 9.

6   Africa Rights, (1997), *Food and Power in Sudan*.

7   CIA, (2012), 'Sudan: The Costs of Nonalignment. An Intelligence Assessment,' 15 October. Then Assistant Secretary of State for African Affairs, Herman Cohen, subsequently made clear US support for the coup. See Herman Cohen, (2000), *Intervening in Africa: Superpower Peacemaking in a Troubled Continent*, St Martin's Press.

8   D. Petterson, (1999), *Inside Sudan*, p. 47.

9   Ibid., p. 88.

10 Ibid., p. 178.

11 Ibid., p. 69.

12 US Department of State, (2003), www.UStreas.gov/ofac/legal/sudan.html.

13 Thomson Financial Publishing, (1997), 'The US Imposes New Sanctions on Sudan,' 4 November, www.tfp.com/news/USSudan.htm.

14 Ted Dagne, (2002), 'Sudan: Humanitarian Crisis, Peace Talks, Terrorism, and U.S. Policy,' Washington DC; Congressional Research Service, (1992), The Library of Congress, 11 December.

15 United States Institute of Peace, (1997), 'Religion, Nationalism and Peace in Sudan,' Washington DC, 17 December.

16 Alex de Waal, (2016), 'Writing Human Rights and Getting It Wrong,' *Boston Globe*, 6 June.

17 United States Congress, (1999), S.1453, 106th Congress, 1st Session, 19 November.

18 Alex de Waal, (2002), 'Sudan: Social Engineering, Slavery and War,' *Covert Action Quarterly*, Spring; and *The Irish Times*, (2002), 'The Great Slave Scam,' 23 February.

19 'Slave Redemption,' (2002), Email message from Rev. Cal Bombay to the European-Sudanese Public Affairs Council, 8 April.

20 Timothy Carney, (2002), 'Intelligence Failure? Let's Go Back to Sudan,' *The Washington Post*, 30 June.

21 Mansoor Ijaz, (2001), 'Clinton Let Bin Laden Slip Away and Metastasize,' *Los Angeles Times*, 5 December.

22 Center for African Development Policy Research, (2011), 'US Policy towards the Horn of Africa,' Kalamazoo, Michigan, 30 September.

23 *New York Times*, (1998), 'Decision to Strike Factory in Sudan Based on Surmise Inferred from Evidence,' 21 September.

24 United States Congress, (1999), S. Res. 109, 106th Congress, 1st Session, 1 July.

25 House of Lords, (1998), *Official Report*, cols. 818–820, 19 March.

26 Reuters, (1999), 'US Adds Religious Freedom to Old Sanctions,' 23 December.

27 Reuters, (1998), 'White House Says No Sign Iraq Exported Arms,' 17 February.

28 Veronica Nmoma, (2006), 'The Shift in United States–Sudan Relations.'

29 Royal Ministry of Foreign Affairs, (1997), 'Evaluation of Norwegian Humanitarian Assistance to the Sudan,' Oslo, November.

30 *The Washington Times*, (1997), 'Ex-President Opposes Policy of Aiding Khartoum's Foes,' 25 September.

31 *New York Times*, (1999), 'Misguided Relief to Sudan,' 6 December.

32 See for example, Africa Watch, (1989), *Denying the Honor of Living: Sudan a Human Rights Disaster*, London; Amnesty International, (1993), *Sudan: The Ravages of War: Political Killings and Humanitarian Disaster*, London, 29 September; Amnesty International, (1994), *Amnesty International Report 1994*, London; Africa Rights, (1997), *Food and Power in Sudan*; etc. Even the USG's own State Department's Country Reports recorded numerous examples of human rights abuses by the SPLA – United States Department of State, (1997), *Sudan Country Reports on Human Rights Practices for 1996*, Bureau of Democracy, Human Rights and Labor, 30 January.

33 Human Rights Watch, (1999), 'Open Letter to US Secretary of State, Madeleine Albright,' 13 December.

34 Alex de Waal, (2009), *Famine Crimes: Politics and the Disaster Relief Industry in Africa*, Indiana University Press.

35 Rebecca Hamilton, (2012), 'Special Report: The Wonks Who Sold Washington on South Sudan,' *Reuters*, 11 July.

36 Roger Winter, (2009), Testimony before the Subcommittee on Africa and Global Health, Committee on Foreign Affairs, House of Representatives, 111th Congress, Sudan: U.S. Policy and Implementation of the Comprehensive Peace Agreement, 29 July.

37 Enough, (2011), 'United States Should Provide Air Defense Capabilities to Protect Civilians in Sudan,' 16 June.

38 Alan Boswell, (2012), 'The Failed State Lobby,' *Foreign Policy*, 10 July.

39 For an amusing but insightful consideration of Clooney's political activism, see Ken Silverstein, (2015), 'Why Is South Sudan a Hellhole? Blame George Clooney,' *Gawker*, 2 June.

40 Satellite Sentinel Project, sentinel.org/our story.

41 The Sentry, the sentry.org.

42 Rebecca Hamilton, (2012). 'Special Report.'

43 Princeton Lyman, (2013), US Special Envoy to Sudan and South Sudan 2011–2013, Council of American Ambassadors, Fall.

44 Mahmood Mamdani, (2009), *Saviors and Survivors: Darfur, Politics, and the War on Terror*, Doubleday.

45 Princeton Lyman, (2013), Council of American Ambassadors, Fall.

46 Center for Public Integrity, (2016), 'The Misinformation Ministry: Rape, Murder, Famine – and $2.1 Million for K Street PR,' 14 July.

47 John Ryle and Philip Winter at the Rift Valley Institute, who have since left the organization, Douglas Johnson, the independent researcher based in Oxford and his now retired wife from Oxford, Professor Wendy James, and Gillian Lusk, formerly at *Africa Confidential* stand out in this respect. They effectively served as 'gate keepers', ensuring a positive portrayal of the SPLM and opposing negative and alternative perspectives on the organization and its leadership. Similar to the Friends of South Sudan they had close relations with the Garangist leadership of the SPLA and with the Dinka elite, had limited links with the Nuer and their leaders, and generally supported southern secession. But unlike the Friends they largely worked in academia and research and at best were able to influence the British government, very much a junior partner to the US in determining the future of South Sudan.

48 Asteris Huliaras, (2006), 'Evangelists, Oil Companies, and Terrorists: The Bush Administration's Policy towards Sudan,' Foreign Policy Research Institute, 1 October.

49 R. Brown, (2003), *American Foreign Policy toward the Sudan: From Isolation to Engagement*, National Defense University.

50 J. Merritt, (2015), 'Franklin Graham's Turn towards Intolerance,' *The Atlantic*, 19 July.

51 CBC, (2006), 'Evangelist's Views on Islam Draw Critics in Winnipeg,' 22 October, www.cbc.ca/news/canada/evangelist-s-views-on-islam-draw-critics-in-winnipeg-1.589396.

52 *New York Times*. (2009), 'Put Peace before Justice,' 2 March.

53 Huliaras, (2006), 'Evangelists, Oil Companies, and Terrorists'.

54 Ibid.

55 Center for Strategic and International Studies, (2001), 'US Policy to End Sudan's War,' Washington DC; International Crisis Group, (2002), 'Sudan's Best Chance for Peace: How Not to Lose It,' Brussels, 17 September; and United States Institute of Peace, (1999), 'New Approach to Peace in Sudan,' Washington DC.

56 John Danforth, (2002), 'Report to the President of the United States on the Outlook for Peace in Sudan,' Washington DC, 26 April.

57 www.iri.org.

58 DynCorp International was awarded a five-year contract on 23 January 2003, to provide peacekeeping-related services to African countries. In South Sudan it was tasked with the transition of the Sudan People's Liberation Army into a professional force for which funding of $40 million was budgeted, but it requested $52.8 million, thus leading to an audit. See United States Government, (2010), Office of Audits, 'Audit of Allegations Pertaining to Contract with DynCorp International for the Security Sector Transformation Project in South Sudan,' Report No. AUD/SI-10-23, Africa, August. Blackwater repeatedly attempted to sign security contracts with the Salva Kiir government, including when southern Sudan was still part of Sudan and covered under US sanctions. There are also widespread, but unconfirmed, reports that Blackwater is providing security in the northern Upper Nile oil fields.

59 United States Department of State, (2007), 'Sudan Peace Act,' Fact Sheet, 21 October.

60 Ibid.

61 David Shinn, (2011), 'U.S. Policy Toward the Horn of Africa,' *International Policy Digest*, 13 October.

62 US Department of State, (2005), 'Roger P. Winter Appointed Special Representative for Sudan,' 26 July.

63 Ken Silverstein, (2005), 'Official Pariah Sudan Valuable to America's War on Terrorism,' *Los Angeles Times*, 29 April.

64 Richard Williamson, (2010), Former US Special Envoy on Sudan, 'How Obama Betrayed Sudan,' *Foreign Policy Magazine*, op-ed, November–December.

65 Susan Rice, (2007), 'Dithering on Darfur: U.S. Inaction in the Face of Genocide,' Foreign Relations Committee, United States Senate, Washington DC, 11 April.

66 Enough, (2009), 'Sudan Advocacy Groups React to General Gration's Statements to The Washington Post,' 28 September. www.enoughproject.org/news/sudan-advocacy-groups.

67 *Time*, (2012), 'Rocky Road from Air Force to Ambassador,' 14 August.

68 Open letter to President Barack Obama signed by 29 international and South Sudanese NGOs calling for US support for a Security Council resolution in favour of an arms embargo against both belligerents, (2015), 7 January.

69 Colum Lynch, (2015), 'Inside the White House Fight Over the Slaughter in South Sudan,' *Foreign Policy*, 26 January.

70 Intercept, (2016), 'Long War: Hillary Clinton's State Department Gave South Sudan's Military a Pass for Its Child Soldiers,' 9 June.

71 Ibid.

72 United States Department of State, (2011), 'Country Reports on Human Rights Practices for 2011,' www.state.govdocuments/organization/18790.pdf.

73 United Nations, (2016), Office of the Special Representative of the Secretary-General for Children and Armed Conflict, South Sudan, 20 April.

74 United States Department of State, (2011), 'Country Reports.'

75 United States Government, (2017), ForeignAssistance.gov, South Sudan.

76 Nick Turse, (2015), 'The United States Is Supporting an Army That Is Recruiting Child Soldiers,' The Nation, 18 May.

77 Intercept, (2016), 'Long War'.

78 Alan Boswell, (2012), 'The Failed State Lobby.'

79 John Gay, (2013), 'How Susan Rice Bungled Sudan,' The National Interest, 6 June.

80 Chester Crocker, (2016), 'Consider the Transitional International Administration of South Sudan,' in OPENCANADA.ORG, 'Six Urgent Ways to Give Peace a Better Chance in South Sudan,' 26 August.

81 South Sudan News Agency, (2013), 'Friends of South Sudan Warned of Serious Consequences if Serious Changes and Reform Are Not Made,' Washington DC, 8 July.

Chapter 3

1 Guardian, (2013), 'South Sudan Fighting Forces Civilians to Seek Refuge at UN Bases,' 17 December.

2 Foreign Policy, (2013), 'Drill Down: Energy Is Supposed to Be Africa's Future. But When Violence Erupts in South Sudan and Elsewhere, the Pipelines Can Quickly Run Dry,' 23 December, www.foreignpolicy.com/articles/2013/12/23/south_sudan_violence_oil#sthash.hYuv7uGi.Q4YUVbSr.dpuf.

3 The Washington Post, (2013), 'South Sudan's Growing Conflict Reflects Rivalry between President and His Former Deputy,' 23 December.

4 Sudan Tribune, (2013), 'Riek Machar's End-Game: What Is It?' 29 December.

5 Daily Beast. (2014). 'Can the US Stop Civil War in South Sudan?' 4 January.

6 African Union, (2014), 'Final Report of the African Union Commission of Inquiry on South Sudan.'

7 Ibid., p. 130.

8 Author interview with General Peter Gadet, (2014), Addis Ababa, 14 November.

9 UN Mission in South Sudan, (2014), 'Human Rights Crisis in South Sudan, Report Coverage 15 December 2013 – 31 January 2014,' Human Rights Division, 21 February.

10 African Union, (2014), 'Final Report of the African Union Commission of Inquiry on South Sudan.'

11 Author interview with Lieutenant-General James Hoth, (2016), Juba, 11 April.

12 Mahmood Mamdani, (2014), Separate submission to the AU Commission of Inquiry on South Sudan.

13 African Union, (2014), 'Final Report of the African Union Commission of Inquiry on South Sudan.'

14 Radio Tamazuj. (2015). 'Generals Say Juba Massacres Done by Private Militias, Not SPLA,' 9 March.

15 Ibid.

16 African Union, (2014), 'Final Report of the African Union Commission of Inquiry on South Sudan.'

17 Mahmood Mamdani, (2016), 'Who's to Blame in South Sudan?' *Boston Review*, 4 July, www.gurtong.net/ECM/Editorial/tabid/124/ctl/ArticleView/mid/519/articleId/24/Whos-To-Blame-In-South-Sudan.aspx.

18 Human Rights Watch, (2014), 'South Sudan's New Civil War: Abuses by Government and Opposition Forces,' 7 August.

19 African Union, (2014), 'Final Report of the African Union Commission of Inquiry on South Sudan.'

20 Author interview with former Governor of Central Equatoria, Clement Wani, (2016), Juba, 10 April.

21 African Union, (2014), 'Final Report of the African Union Commission of Inquiry on South Sudan.'

22 IRIN, (2016), 'Should the UN Surrender over Peacekeeping?' 23 August.

23 Human Rights Watch, (2014), 'South Sudan's New Civil War.'

24 Mahmood Mamdani, (2016), 'Who's to Blame in South Sudan?'

25 Mahmood Mamdani, (2014), Separate submission to the AU Commission of Inquiry on South Sudan.

26 African Union, (2014), 'Final Report of the African Union Commission of Inquiry on South Sudan.'

27 Hilde Johnson, (2016), *South Sudan: The Untold Story from Independence to Civil War*, I.B. Tauris. Johnson refers to the SPLM and SPLA leaders as 'comrades', 'freedom fighters', and 'cadres'.

28 Nuer Council of Elders.

29 International Crisis Group, (2014), 'South Sudan: A Civil War by Any Other Name,' Crisis Group Africa Report No. 217, 10 April, p. 11.

30 African Union, (2014), 'Final Report of the African Union Commission of Inquiry on South Sudan.'

31 John Young, (2016), 'Popular Struggles and Elite Cooptation: The Nuer White Army in South Sudan's Civil War,' *Small Arms Survey*, Graduate Institute of International Studies, Geneva.

32 Author interview with Governor Duir Tut Duir, (2014), Addis Ababa, 8 October.

33 African Union, (2014), 'Final Report of the African Union Commission of Inquiry on South Sudan,' p. 153.

34 John Young, (2007), 'Sudan People's Liberation Army'; and John Young, (2016), 'Popular Struggles and Elite Cooptation.'

35 Author interview with General Peter Gadet, (2014), Addis Ababa, 14 November.

36 John Young, (2016), 'Popular Struggles and Elite Cooptation.'

37 Ibid.

38 Ibid.

Chapter 4

1 African Union, (2014), 'Final Report of the African Union Commission of Inquiry on South Sudan.'

2 Author interview with Major-General Simon Gatwech, (2013), Juba, 8 December.

3 Human Security Baseline Assessment, (2015), 'Conflict in Unity State: Describing Events through 29 January 2015,' *Small Arms Survey*, University of Geneva.

4 According to ICG, the Chinese reached an agreement with the SPLM-IO leadership that it would not attack the oil fields. See International Crisis Group, (2017), 'China's Foreign Policy Experiment in South Sudan,' Report No. 288, 10 July.

5 Author interview with Gabriel Changeson, (2016), Nairobi, 6 April.

6 Email from Dr Lam Akol, (2017), 15 February.

7 SPLM/SPLA Consultative Conference, (2014), 'Resolutions,' Nasir, Upper Nile State, April.

8 Author interview with Major-General Gathoth Gatkouth, (2015), Addis Ababa, 13 June.

9 Ibid.

10 SPLM/A, Military Governor's Office, (2014), 'Resolutions by the Upper Nile Peace and Consultative Meeting,' Pagak, Upper Nile state, 28 November.

11 John Young, (2015), 'A Fractious Rebellion: Inside the SPLM-IO,' *Small Arms Survey*, Graduate Institute of International Studies, Geneva.

12 General Headquarters, (2014), Sudan People's Liberation Movement, Communiqué, Pagak, 12 December.

13 SPLM/A Chairman and Commander-in-Chief, (2014), 'Establishment of General Staff Command for SPLA,' 21 December.

14 General Peter Gadet told the author that the sanctions had no impact upon him, that he has no financial holdings in any of the countries that have sanctioned him, and has no intention to travel to them. Author interview with Peter Gadet, (2018), Addis Ababa, 6 February.

15 SPLA Chief of General Staffs, (2015), Letter signed by SPLA-IO Chief of Staff, Simon Gatwech, to President Omar Bashir, Pagak, 7 July.

16 Author interview by telephone with Major-General Gathoth Gatkouth, (2015), 18 September.

17 Author interview with Gabriel Changeson, (2016), Nairobi, 18 June.

Chapter 5

1 Author interview with General Salim Salih, (2015), Kampala, Uganda, 13 October.

2 There have long been rumours along these lines, but they gained more credibility after Yoweri Museveni and Egyptian President Abdel Fattah el-Sisi met in December 2016 in Kampala, unconfirmed reports of Egyptian weapon supplies to the SPLA, and widespread reports of an Antonov bombing of an IO base in Kaka Upper Nile that was held by the IO to have been carried out by the Egyptian air force since South Sudan does not have Antonovs. See South Sudan News Agency, (2017), 'Egyptian Air Force Bombs South Sudanese Rebels in Upper Nile,' 3 February.

3 *Sudan Tribune*, (2017), 'Egypt Provides South Sudan with Arms and Ammunition: al-Bashir,' Khartoum, 22 February.

4 Payton Knopf, (2017), Coordinator, South Sudan Senior Working Group United States Institute of Peace, 'Testimony before the Senate Foreign Relations Subcommittee on Africa and Global Health Policy,' 26 July.

5 John Young, (2012), *The Fate of Sudan*.

6   Riek Machar, (2014), as related during a speech in Pagak before the SPLM-IO, 12 December.

7   African Union, (2014), 'Final Report of the African Union Commission of Inquiry on South Sudan.'

8   Author interview with Gabriel Tang, (2014), Pagak, 12 December.

9   Author interview with Dr Riek Machar, (2014), Addis Ababa, 9 November.

10 Peace and Security Council of the African Union (AU) on developments on the situation on South Sudan, (2014), Communiqué, 22 May.

11 United States Department of State, (2014), Remarks by John Kerry, South Sudan Embassy, Juba, 2 May.

12 Riek Machar, (2015), Chairman and Commander-in-Chief SPLM/A, 'Failures of IGAD Plus Proposed Agreement,' 11 June.

13 H. E. Salva Kiir Mayardit, Dr Riek Machar Teny, and Mr Deng Alor Kuol, (2015), 'Agreement on the Reunification of the SPLM,' Arusha, 21 January.

14 Author interview with Ezekiel Lol, (2015), Addis Ababa, 2 June.

15 Author interview with Dr Riek Machar, (2015), Addis Ababa, 9 June.

16 Author interview with Major-General Martin Kenyi, (2016), Juba, 11 April.

17 The international community also extolled the Garang-Ali Osman private negotiations, but that turned out badly when Garang died and Ali Osman was not the power in Khartoum that the diplomats assumed.

18 Author interview with Dr Lam Akol, (2016), Juba, 18 August.

19 Author interview with Sudan Ambassador, Gamal Elsheikh Ahmed, (2016), Juba, 20 August.

20 IGAD, (2015), ARCSS, Addis Ababa, 17 August, Art. 1.6.

21 Senate Committee on Foreign Relations, (2015), Testimony of Special Envoy for Sudan and South Sudan Donald Booth, 'Independent South Sudan: A Failure of Leadership,' 10 December.

22 Alex de Waal, (2015), Executive Director of the World Peace Foundation at Tufts University, *International Business Times*, 9 October.

23 African Union, (2014), 'Final Report of the African Union Commission of Inquiry on South Sudan.'

Chapter 6

1   Aecom, (2015), Maps of ten states, Riek's proposed 21 states, and the 28 states of the Salva-led government, 5 October.

2   Ibid.

3   Transitional Constitution of South Sudan, (2011), Juba, 23 April.

4   Center for Civilians in Conflict, (2016), 'Under Fire: The July 2016 Violence in Juba and UN Response,' USA; and VOANEWS, (2016), 'UN Peacekeepers Accept Responsibility for Massacre at Malakal,' 24 June.

5   African Union, (2014), 'Final Report of the African Union Commission of Inquiry on South Sudan.'

6   United Nations, (2017), 'Speech of the Chair of the Commission on Human Rights in South Sudan to the Human Rights Council,' 14 March, www.ohchr.org/EN/NewsEvents/Pages/DisplayNews.aspx?NewsID=21374&LangID=E#sthash.CS7aHIRP.dpuf.

7   ARCSS, (2016), Preamble.

8   Lam Akol, (2015), Public lecture, University of Juba, 8 October.

9   IGAD, (2016), Communiqué of the 55th Extra-Ordinary Session of the IGAD Council of Ministers, Addis Ababa, 30–31 January.

10 Troika, (2015), Press release on South Sudan, London, 6 October.

11 National Public Radio, (2016), 'Both Sides Are at Fault: Susan Rice on South Sudan's Civil War,' 9 March.

12 Riek Machar, (2017), email to author, 4 February.

13 *Sudan Tribune*, (2016), 'South Sudan welcomes U.S. Extension of Military Aid,' Juba, 8 October. The Obama administration's justification for its repeated overrule of the CPSA was that the list of barred countries was created before South Sudan came into existence.

14 Eye Radio, (2016), 'Kiir and Machar Face Individual Sanctions – Kerry,' Juba, 25 February.

15 Riek Machar, (2017), email to author, 4 February.

16 Author phone interview with Bol Gatkouth, (2016), member of the SPLM-IO Advance Team, Juba, 11 January.

17 Author phone interview with Duabol Lual, (2016), Juba, 9 January, and subsequent meetings with him in Addis Ababa 17–20 February 2016 after he gave up on the Advance Mission.

18 ARCSS, Transitional Arrangements, 5.1.

19 Riek Machar, (2016), email to author, 4 February.

20 *Africa Review*, (2016), 'Meeting to Discuss the Failed Machar Return (South Sudan),' 21 April.

21 Ashish Kumar Sen, (2016), 'South Sudan: Paging Dr. Riek,' an interview with Dr Peter Pham, *Atlantic Council*, 20 April.

22 Author interview with Bona Malwal, (2016), Juba, 8 April.

23 ARCSS, (2016), Chapter II on the Permanent Ceasefire and Transitional Security Arrangements Section 2.2.

24 International Crisis Group, (2016), 'Conflict in the Equatorias,' 25 May.

25 Author interview with Lieutenant-General James Hoth, (2016), Juba, 11 April.

26 Author interview with Adel Sandrai, (2016), Bakosoro's former campaign manager and subsequent SPLM-IO official, Juba, 14 April.

27 Author interview with Clement Wani, (2016), Juba, 10 April.

28 *Wangdunkon Media*, (2015), 'The Cool War between Governor Bakasoro and Dinka Council Elders,' 25 June.

29 Jason Patinkin and Simona Foltyn, (2017), 'The War in Equatoria: A Special Report,' IRIN, Kajo Keji, 12 July.

30 *Africa Newswire*, (2015), 'Conflict in South Sudan,' New York, 1 October.

31 *Sudan Tribune*, (2016), 'South Sudan Defends Expulsion of Peace Monitor,' 28 April.

32 Vergee was to subsequently say, 'JMEC has failed to live up to expectations. It has not moved quickly enough to take corrective action at moments of acute crisis, and not held the parties to account when they dishonored their obligations.' Aly Vergee, (2017), Testimony before the Senate Foreign Relations Subcommittee on Africa and Global Health Policy, United States Institute of Peace, 26 July.

33 *Sudan Tribune*, (2016), 'South Sudan Convenes First Cabinet Meeting after Forming Unity Government,' Juba, 6 May.

34 Voice of America, (2016), 'South Sudan Cease-Fire Panel Accuses President's Forces of Violations,' Juba, 12 May.

35 United Nations. (2015). 'Final Report of the Panel of Experts on South Sudan Established Pursuant to Security Council resolution 2206,' UN SC Doc. S/2016/70, para. 142, 22 January.

36 Center for Civilians in Conflict, (2016), 'Under Fire,' p. 32.

37 *Sudan Tribune*, (2016), 'South Sudan Armed Men Clash with Sudanese Rebels in Bahr el Ghazal,' Juba, 18 May.

38 *World News*, (2016), 'South Sudanese Army "Getting Away with Murder" as Thousands Flee Abuses: Rights Group,' London, 24 May.

39 Amnesty International, (2016), 'South Sudan: Dozens of Detainees at Risk of Death in Shipping Containers,' 27 May.

40 *Sudan Tribune*, (2016), 'South Sudan Presidency Defends Appointment of Advisors,' 7 June.

41 *Sudan Tribune*, (2016), 'S. Sudan President Rejects Consensus to Establish Cantonment Areas for SPLA-IO,' 25 June.

42 Ibid.

43 Human Rights Watch, (2016), 'South Sudan: Killings, Rapes, Looting in Juba,' 15 August.

44 Center for Civilians in Conflict, (2016), 'Under Fire.'

45 *Foreign Policy*, (2016), 'Dinner, Drinks, and a Near Fatal Ambush for U.S. Diplomats,' 6 September.

46 Center for Civilians in Conflict, (2016), 'Under Fire.'

47 Ibid.

48 United Nations Security Council, (2016), 'United States of America Draft Resolution,' 23 December, www.securitycouncilreport.org/atf/cf/%7B65BFCF9B-6D27-4E9C-8CD3-CF6E4FF96FF9%7D/s_2016_1085.pdf.

49 United Nations, (2016), 'WFP Condemns Looting of Food Warehouse in Juba, Still Assists Thousands Affected by Fighting,' World Food Programme, 14 July, www.wfp.org/news/news-release/wfp-condemns-looting-food-warehouse-juba-still-manages-assist-thousands-affected-f.

50 Center for Civilians in Conflict, (2016), 'Under Fire,' p. 19.

51 Ibid.

52 *The Washington Free Beacon*, (2016), 'US, UN Stood By While South Sudan Troops Raped, Beat Aid Workers,' 15 August.

53 Human Rights Watch. (2016). 'South Sudan.'

54 Ibid.

Chapter 7

1 *Sudan Tribune*, (2016), 'South Sudan's FVP Machar Fires Taban Deng,' 23 July.

2 Joshua Craze and Jerome Tubiana with Claudio Gramizzi, (2016), 'A State of Disunity: Conflict Dynamics in Unity State, South Sudan 2013–15,' *Small Arms Survey*, December.

3 *Small Arms Survey*, (2017), 'Spreading Fallout: The Collapse of the ARCSS and New Conflict along the Equatorias–DRC Border,' May.

4 Author phone interview with Lieutenant-General Dheling Chuol, senior SPLM-IO commander in DRC, (2017), 20 May.

5   Ethiopian Broadcasting Corporation, (2016), 'JMEC Recognizes First VP Machar as "Legitimate Leader of the SPLM-IO,"' 24 July.

6   *Sudan Tribune*, (2016), 'UN Warns Over Replacement of Machar as First Vice President,' 27 July.

7   IGAD, (2016), Communiqué of the Second IGAD Plus Extraordinary Summit of the Situation in the Republic of South Sudan, Addis Ababa, 5 August.

8   *Sudan Tribune*, (2016), 'African Union Tells South Sudan to Sack New Vice President Taban Deng,' 12 August.

9   *Daily Nation*. (2016). 'IGAD Accepts Riek Machar's Ouster as South Sudan's Vice President,'26 August.

10 Associated Press, (2016), 'Top Diplomat Backs New South Sudan Vice President,' 28 August.

11 *Africa Review*, (2016), 'US Envoy Opposes Machar's Return to Office, Faults Kiir's Actions,' 8 September.

12 Reuters, (2016), 'U.S. Diplomats on South Sudan Conflict Over Machar's Fate,' 8 September.

13 Dr Juk Madut, from the Western-supported and supposedly impartial Sudd Institute spoke of a best-case scenario in which Taban would build a constituency among the opposition that bleeds support away from Machar. See IRIN, (2016), 'South Sudan's Never Ending War,' Nairobi, 12 October.

14 Statement by H. E. Festus G. Mogae, Chairperson of JMEC, to the IGAD Heads of State and Government Summit on the Status of the Implementation of the Agreement on the Resolution of the Conflict in the Republic of South Sudan, (2016), Addis Ababa, 16 July.

15 SPLM-IO, (2016), 'The Political Military Situation Following the Eruption of Violence in July 2016 and the Future of the Agreement,' Khartoum, 27 November.

16 Reuters, (2016), 'U.S. Condemns South Sudan Opposition Leader's Call for Renewed War,' 28 September.

17 *The Washington Post*, (2016), 'Obama Administration to Lift Some Sanctions against Sudan,' 13 January. Obama said the permanent lifting of sanctions would be based on an assessment of five tracks agreed by the two countries in July: cooperation on counter-terrorism, addressing the LRA threat, ending hostilities in the Two Areas and Darfur, improving humanitarian access, and ending negative interference in South Sudan, which was understood to mean not providing assistance to the SPLM-IO or other rebel groups and not hosting Riek. Not surprisingly this initiative was opposed by the Enough Project, which issued a report titled, 'The July Deadline Won't Work: Why the U.S. Needs to Delay the Decision on Sudan Sanctions.' See *Sudan Tribune*, (2017), 'U.S. Needs a New Track for Peace before It Discards Sudan's Sanctions: Expert,' 24 June.

18 Author phone interview with Dr Riek Machar, (2016), 8 November.

19 Author interview with SPLM-IO Ethiopia officials who reported on their meeting with a US delegation led by Paul R. Sutphin, (2017), Acting Director in the Office of US Special Envoy for Sudan and South Sudan, and showed the author notes of the meeting, Addis Ababa, 12 May.

20 United Nations Security Council, (2016), 'United States of America Draft Resolution,' 23 December 2016, www.securitycouncilreport.org/atf/cf/%7B65BFCF9B-6D27-4E9C-8CD3-CF6E4FF96FF9%7D/s_2016_1085.pdf.

21 Author phone interview with Dr Riek Machar, (2017), 15 May.

22 BBC, (2016), 'South Sudan Conflict: African Union Approves Regional Force,' 19 July.

23 Aly Verjee, (2016), 'The Future of South Sudan and the Peace Agreement,' Chatham House, Africa Programme Transcript, 26 October.

24 *Aljazeera*, (2017), 'South Sudan Rejects 4,000 Additional UN Peacekeepers,' 11 January, www.aljazeera.com/news/2017/01/south-sudan-rejects-4000-additional-peacekeepers-170111151623667.html.

25 Author interview with Angelina Teny, (2018), Addis Ababa, 6 February.

26 Author interview with Lieutenant-General Peter Gadet, (2017), Khartoum, 20 May.

27 Author phone interview with Dr Riek Machar, (2016), 8 December.

28 Amnesty International, (2017), 'South Sudan: Killings, Mass Displacement and Systematic Looting as Government Forces Purge Civilians from Upper Nile,' 21 June.

29 United Nations, (2017), 'Report of the Secretary-General on South Sudan (Covering the Period from 2 March to 1 June 2017,' 15 June.

30 Radio Tamazuj, (2017), 'Top Rebel Commander Killed in Clashes in Upper Nile,' 6 January.

31 Author phone interview with Dr Riek Machar, (2017), 15 May.

32 The Political Opposition Forces, (2017), 'Communiqué,' 11 May.

33 www.dictionary.com/browse/policy.

34 United Nations, (2017), 'Report of the Secretary-General on South Sudan (covering the period from 2 March to 1 June 2017,' 15 June. The UN Secretary-General found that, 'Although both Government and opposition forces were responsible for human rights violations and breaches, SPLA was responsible for the majority of cases documented by UNMISS'.

Conclusion

1 Mahmood Mamdani, (2009), *Saviors and Survivors*.

2 Alex de Waal, (2007), 'No Such Thing as Humanitarian Intervention: Why We Need to Rethink How to Realize the "Responsibility to Protect" in Wartime,' *Harvard International Review*, 21 March.

3 In response to *Fox News* anchor Bill O'Reilly calling Russian president Vladimir Putin 'a killer', in-coming President Donald Trump responded by saying, 'There are a lot of killers. We have a lot of killers. You think our country is so innocent?'

4 Joshua Meservey, (2017), 'South Sudan: Time for the U.S. to Hold the Combatants Accountable,' The Heritage Foundation, 28 April. See also his testimony to the US Senate, (2017), South Sudan's Conflict and Famine Testimony before the Subcommittee on Africa and Global Health Policy, United States Senate, 26 July.

5 Joshua Meservey, (2017), 'South Sudan: Time for the U.S. to Hold the Combatants Accountable.'

6 John Prendergast, (2017), Opinion Contributor, *U.S. News*, 27 June.

7 Alejandro Bendana, (2003), 'What Kind of Peace Is Being Built? Critical Assessments from the South. A Discussion Paper,' Prepared on the occasion of the tenth anniversary of An Agenda for Peace for the International Development Research Centre (IDRC), Ottawa, Canada, January.

8 Edward Luttwak, (1999), 'Give War a Chance,' *Foreign Affairs*, 78(4): 36–44.

9   Stephen Ellis, (2005), 'How to Rebuild Africa,' *Foreign Affairs*, September/October, www.foreignaffairs.com/articles/61028/stephen-ellis/how-to-rebuild-africa.

10 Lako Jada Kwajok, (2016), 'United Nations Trusteeship Is the Best Option to Resolve the Crisis in South Sudan,' *South Sudan Nation*, 16 July.

11 Herman Cohen, (2014), 'South Sudan: UN Should Rule Juba, Says Ex-U.S. Official,' *African Arguments*, 6 January; and Peter Adwork, (2014), 'The Political Significance of Cessation of Hostilities Agreement,' *South Sudan Nation*, 25 January.

12 Radio Tamazuj, (2015), 'Pagan Amum Calls for S. Sudan International Trusteeship if Peace Talks Fail,' 23 December. And in the wake of the July fighting in Juba, Pagan again called for international intervention in the country and the formation of a government of technocrats. See *Sudan Tribune*, (2016), 'Former Minister Wants S. Sudan under UN Administration,' 3 August.

13 *New York Times*, (2014), 'South Sudan Needs to Be Placed Under a U.S.-Led Trusteeship,' 7 January.

14 Mahmood Mamdani, (2015), Statement to the Peace and Security Commission, AUC, Addis Ababa, 24 July.

15 Princeton Lyman and Kate Almquest Knopf, (2016), 'To Save South Sudan, Put It on Life Support,' *Financial Times*, 20 July; and Kate Almquest Knopf, (2016), 'Ending South Sudan's Civil War,' Council on Foreign Relations, Special Report No. 77, November.

16 Peter Adwok, (2016), letter to the author, 23 October.

17 Adam Branch, (2013), *Displacing Human Rights: War and Intervention in Northern Uganda*, Makerere Institute of Social Research, Kampala, p. 20.

18 United States Government, (2002), *National Security Strategy Paper*, September.

Postscript

1   'Agreement on Outstanding Issues of Governance 25th July 2018,' *Sudan Tribune*, 25 July.

2   Sudan Tribune (2018), www.sudantribune.com/spip.php?article66156.

3   Sudan Tribune (2018), www.sudantribune.com/spip.php?article66102.

4   US State Department (2018), 'Statement by the Press Secretary on the South Sudan Peace Process,' Washington, 22 July.

5   Ibid.

6   Roger Alfred Yoron Modi (2018), 'Normalize Sudan South Sudan Relations,' *Sudan Tribune*, 9 July, https://sudantribune.com/spip.php?article65824.

REFERENCES

Adwork, Peter. (2014). 'The Political Significance of Cessation of Hostilities Agreement.' *South Sudan Nation*. 25 January.

Aecom. (2015). Maps of ten states, Riek's proposed 21 states, and the 28 states of the Salva-led government. 5 October.

Africa Newswire. (2015). 'Conflict in South Sudan.' New York. 1 October.

Africa Review. (2016). 'Meeting to Discuss the Failed Machar Return (South Sudan).' 21 April.

Africa Review. (2016). 'US Envoy Opposes Machar's Return to Office, Faults Kiir's Actions.' 8 September.

Africa Rights. (1997). *Food and Power in Sudan: A Critique of Humanitarianism*. London.

Africa Watch. (1989). *Denying the Honor of Living: Sudan a Human Rights Disaster*. London.

African Union. (2014). 'Final Report of the African Union Commission of Inquiry on South Sudan.' Addis Ababa. 15 October. www.peaceau.org/uploads/auciss.final.report.pdf.

Aljazeera. (2017). 'South Sudan Rejects 4,000 Additional UN Peacekeepers.' 11 January. www.aljazeera.com/news/2017/01/south-sudan-rejects-4000-additional-peacekeepers-17011151623667.html.

Amnesty International. (1993). *Sudan: The Ravages of War: Political Killings and Humanitarian Disaster*. London. 29 September.

Amnesty International. (1994). *Amnesty International Report 1994*. London.

Amnesty International. (2016). 'South Sudan: Dozens of Detainees at Risk of Death in Shipping Containers.' 27 May.

Amnesty International. (2017). 'South Sudan: Killings, Mass Displacement and Systematic Looting as Government Forces Purge Civilians from Upper Nile.' 21 June.

ARCSS. (2016). Chapter II on the Permanent Ceasefire and Transitional Security Arrangements Section 2.2.

Associated Press. (2016). 'Top Diplomat Backs New South Sudan Vice President.' 28 August.

BBC. (2016). 'South Sudan Conflict: African Union Approves Regional Force.' 19 July.

Bendana, Alejandro. (2003). 'What Kind of Peace Is Being Built? Critical Assessments from the South. A Discussion Paper.' Prepared on the occasion of the tenth anniversary of An Agenda for Peace for the International Development Research Centre (IDRC). Ottawa. Canada. January.

Boswell, Alan. (2012). 'American Expelled from South Sudan for Anti-Corruption Work.' McClatchy Newspapers. 20 August.

Boswell, Alan. (2012). 'The Failed State Lobby.' *Foreign Policy*. 10 July.

Branch, Adam. (2013). *Displacing Human Rights: War and Intervention in Northern Uganda*. Makerere Institute of Social Research. Kampala.

Brockman, Rev. Miquel D'Escoto. (2009). Remarks at the Opening of the Thematic Dialogue of the General Assembly on the Responsibility to Protect. UN Headquarters. New York. 23 July.

Brown, R. (2003). *American Foreign Policy toward the Sudan: From Isolation to Engagement.* National Defense University.

Carney, Timothy. (2002). 'Intelligence Failure? Let's Go Back to Sudan.' *The Washington Post.* 30 June.

CBC. (2006). 'Evangelist's Views on Islam Draw Critics in Winnipeg,' 22 October. www.cbc.ca/news/canada/evangelist-s-views-on-islam-draw-critics-in-winnipeg-1.589396.

Center for African Development Policy Research. (2011). 'US Policy towards the Horn of Africa.' Kalamazoo. Michigan. 30 September.

Center for Civilians in Conflict. (2016). 'Under Fire: The July 2016 Violence in Juba and UN Response.' USA.

Center for Public Integrity. (2016). 'The Misinformation Ministry: Rape, Murder, Famine – and $2.1 Million for K Street PR.' 14 July.

Center for Strategic and International Studies. (2001). 'US Policy to End Sudan's War.' Washington DC.

Chairman and Commander-in-Chief. SPLM-IO. (2016). 'Policy Recommendations for Ending the Civil War.' Pretoria. South Africa. 25 November.

CIA. (2012). 'Sudan: The Costs of Nonalignment. An Intelligence Assessment.' 15 October.

Cohen, Herman. (2000). *Intervening in Africa: Superpower Peacemaking in a Troubled Continent.* St Martin's Press.

Cohen, Herman. (2014). 'South Sudan: UN Should Rule Juba, Says Ex-U.S. Official.' *African Arguments.* 6 January.

Congressional Research Service. (1992). The Library of Congress. 11 December.

Craze, Joshua and Tubiana, Jerome with Gramizzi, Claudio. (2016). 'A State of Disunity: Conflict Dynamics in Unity State, South Sudan 2013–15.' *Small Arms Survey.* December.

Crocker, Chester. (2016). 'Consider the Transitional International Administration of South Sudan.' In OPENCANADA.ORG. 'Six Urgent Ways to Give Peace a Better Chance in South Sudan.' 26 August.

Dagne, Ted. (2002). 'Sudan: Humanitarian Crisis, Peace Talks, Terrorism, and U.S. Policy.' Washington DC.

Daily Beast. (2014). 'Can the US Stop Civil War in South Sudan?' 4 January.

Daily Nation. (2016). 'IGAD Accepts Riek Machar's Ouster as South Sudan's Vice President.' 26 August.

Danforth, John. (2002). 'Report to the President of the United States on the Outlook for Peace in Sudan.' Washington DC. 26 April.

De Waal, Alex. (2002). 'Sudan: Social Engineering, Slavery and War.' *Covert Action Quarterly.* Spring.

De Waal, Alex. (2007). 'No Such Thing as Humanitarian Intervention: Why We Need to Rethink How to Realize the "Responsibility to Protect" in Wartime.' *Harvard International Review.* 21 March.

De Waal, Alex. (2009). *Famine Crimes: Politics and the Disaster Relief Industry in Africa.* Indiana University Press.

De Waal, Alex. (2012). 'South Sudan's Doomsday Machine.' *New York Times.* Op-ed. 24 January.

De Waal, Alex. (2015). Executive Director of the World Peace Foundation at Tufts University. *International Business Times.* 9 October.

De Waal, Alex. (2016). 'Introduction: Making Sense of South Sudan.' *African Affairs.* 14 November.

De Waal, Alex. (2016). 'Writing Human Rights and Getting it Wrong.' *Boston Globe.* 6 June.

Deng, Francis et al. (1996). *Sovereignty as Responsibility: Conflict Management in Africa.* Brookings Institution Press.

Ellis, Stephen. (2005). 'How to Rebuild Africa.' *Foreign Affairs.* September/October. www.foreignaffairs.com/articles/61028/stephen-ellis/how-to-rebuild-africa.

Enough. (2009). 'Sudan Advocacy Groups React to General Gration's Statements to The Washington Post.' 28 September. www.enoughproject.org/news/sudan-advocacy-groups.

Enough. (2011). 'United States Should Provide Air Defense Capabilities to Protect Civilians in Sudan.' 16 June.

Enough. (2017). 'Weapons of Mass Corruption: How Corruption in South Sudan's Military Undermines the World's Newest Country.' January.

Ethiopian Broadcasting Corporation. (2016). 'JMEC Recognizes First VP Machar as "Legitimate Leader of the SPLM-IO."' 24 July.

Eye Radio. (2016). 'Kiir and Machar Face Individual Sanctions – Kerry.' *Juba.* 25 February.

Foreign Policy. (2013). 'Drill Down: Energy Is Supposed to Be Africa's Future. But When Violence Erupts in South Sudan and Elsewhere, the Pipelines Can Quickly Run Dry.' 23 December. www.foreignpolicy.com/articles/2013/12/23/south_sudan_violence_oil#sthash.hYuv7uGi.Q4YUVbSr.dpf.

Foreign Policy. (2016). 'Dinner, Drinks, and a Near Fatal Ambush for U.S. Diplomats.' 6 September.

Gay, John. (2013). 'How Susan Rice Bungled Sudan.' *The National Interest.* 6 June.

General Headquarters. (2014). Sudan People's Liberation Movement. Communiqué. Pagak. 12 December.

Government of Republic of South Sudan Ministry of Finance. (2015). 'Approved Budget Tables Financial Year 2014/15.' August.

Guardian. (2013). 'South Sudan Fighting Forces Civilians to Seek Refuge at UN Bases.' 17 December.

Hamilton, Rebecca. (2012). 'Special Report: The Wonks Who Sold Washington on South Sudan.' *Reuters.* 11 July.

House of Lords. (1998). *Official Report.* cols. 818–820. 19 March.

Huliaras, Asteris. (2006). 'Evangelists, Oil Companies, and Terrorists: The Bush Administration's Policy towards Sudan.' Foreign Policy Research Institute. 1 October.

Human Rights Watch. (1999). 'Open Letter to US Secretary of State, Madeleine Albright.' 13 December.

Human Rights Watch. (2014). 'South Sudan's New Civil War: Abuses by Government and Opposition Forces.' 7 August.

Human Rights Watch. (2016). 'South Sudan: Killings, Rapes, Looting in Juba.' 15 August.

Human Security Baseline Assessment. (2015). 'Conflict in Unity State: Describing Events through 29 January 2015.' *Small Arms Survey.* University of Geneva.

IGAD. (2015). ARCSS. Addis Ababa. 17 August.

IGAD. (2016). Communiqué of the 55th Extra-Ordinary Session of the IGAD Council of Ministers. Addis Ababa. 30–31 January.

IGAD. (2016). Communiqué of the Second IGAD Plus Extraordinary Summit on the Situation in the Republic of South Sudan. *Addis Ababa.* 5 August.

Ijaz, Mansoor. (2001). 'Clinton Let Bin Laden Slip Away and Metastasize.' *Los Angeles Times.* 5 December.

Intercept. (2016). 'Long War: Hillary Clinton's State Department Gave South Sudan's Military a Pass for Its Child Soldiers.' 9 June.

International Crisis Group. (2002). 'Sudan's Best Chance for Peace: How Not to Lose It.' 17 September.

International Crisis Group. (2014). 'South Sudan: A Civil War by Any Other Name.' Crisis Group Africa Report No. 217. 10 April

International Crisis Group. (2016). 'Conflict in the Equatorias.' 25 May.

International Crisis Group. (2017). 'China's Foreign Policy Experiment in South Sudan.' Report No. 288. 10 July.

IRIN. (2016). 'Should the UN Surrender over Peacekeeping?' 23 August.

IRIN. (2016). 'South Sudan's Never Ending War.' Nairobi. 12 October.

Johnson, Hilde. (2016). *South Sudan: The Untold Story from Independence to Civil War.* I.B. Tauris.

Knopf, Kate Almquest. (2016). 'Ending South Sudan's Civil War.' Council on Foreign Relations. Special Report No. 77. November.

Knopf, Payton. (2017). Coordinator, South Sudan Senior Working Group United States Institute of Peace. 'Testimony before the Senate Foreign Relations Subcommittee on Africa and Global Health Policy.' 26 July.

Kwajok, Lako Jada. (2016). 'United Nations Trusteeship Is the Best Option to Resolve the Crisis in South Sudan.' *South Sudan Nation.* 16 July.

Luttwak, Edward. (1999). 'Give War a Chance.' *Foreign Affairs.* 78(4): 36–44.

Lyman, Princeton. (2013). US Special Envoy to Sudan and South Sudan 2011–2013. Council of American Ambassadors. Fall.

Lyman, Princeton and Knopf, Kate. (2016). 'To Save South Sudan, Put It on Life Support.' *Financial Times.* 20 July.

Lynch, Colum. (2015). 'Inside the White House Fight Over the Slaughter in South Sudan.' *Foreign Policy.* 26 January.

Machar, Riek. (2015). Chairman and Commander-in-Chief SPLM/A. 'Failures of IGAD Plus Proposed Agreement.' 11 June.

Mamdani, Mahmood. (2009). *Saviors and Survivors: Darfur, Politics, and the War on Terror.* Doubleday.

Mamdani, Mahmood. (2014). Separate submission to the AU Commission of Inquiry on South Sudan.

Mamdani, Mahmood. (2015). Statement to the Peace and Security Commission, AUC. Addis Ababa. 24 July.

Mamdani, Mahmood. (2016). 'Who's to Blame in South Sudan?' *Boston Review.* 4 July. www.gurtong.net/ECM/Editorial/tabid/124/ctl/ArticleView/mid/519/articleId/24/Whos-To-Blame-In-South-Sudan.aspx.

Markakis, John, Schlee, Guenther and Young, John. (Forthcoming). *The Nation-State: A Wrong Model for the Horn of Africa.*

Mayardit, Salva Kiir, Teny, Riek Machar and Kuol, Deng Alor. (2015). 'Agreement on the Reunification of the SPLM.' Arusha. 21 January.

Merritt, J. (2015). 'Franklin Graham's Turn towards Intolerance.' *The Atlantic.* 19 July.

Meservey, Joshua. (2017). 'South Sudan: Time for the U.S. to Hold the Combatants Accountable.' The Heritage Foundation. 28 April.

Meservey, Joshua. (2017). South Sudan's Conflict and Famine Testimony before the Subcommittee on Africa and Global Health Policy. United States Senate. 26 July.

Mogae, Festus. (2016). Chairperson of JMEC. Statement to the IGAD Heads of State and Government Summit on the Status of the Implementation of the Agreement on the Resolution of the Conflict in the Republic of South Sudan. Addis Ababa. 16 July.

National Public Radio. (2016). 'Both Sides Are at Fault: Susan Rice on South Sudan's Civil War.' 9 March.

New York Times. (1998). 'Decision to Strike Factory in Sudan Based on Surmise Inferred from Evidence.' 21 September.

New York Times. (1999). 'Misguided Relief to Sudan.' 6 December.

New York Times. (2009). 'Put Peace before Justice.' 2 March.

New York Times. (2014). 'South Sudan Needs to Be Placed Under a U.S.-Led Trusteeship.' 7 January.

Nmoma, Veronica. (2006). 'The Shift in United States–Sudan Relations: A Troubled Relationship and the Need for Mutual Cooperation.' *The Journal of Conflict Studies*. 26(2).

Open letter to President Barack Obama signed by 29 international and South Sudanese NGOs calling for US support for a Security Council resolution in favor of an arms embargo against both belligerents. (2015). 7 January.

Patinkin, Jason and Foltyn, Simona. (2017). 'The War in Equatoria: A Special Report.' IRIN. Kajo Keji. 12 July.

Peace and Security Council of the African Union on developments on the situation on South Sudan. (2014). Communiqué. 22 May.

Perry, Alex. (2014). 'George Clooney, South Sudan, and How the World's Newest Nation Imploded.' *Newsweek*. 2 October.

Petterson, Donald. (1999). *Inside Sudan: Political Islam, Conflict, and Catastrophe*. Westview Press.

Prendergast, John. (2017). Opinion Contributor. *U.S. News*. 27 June.

Radio Tamazuj. (2015). 'Generals Say Juba Massacres Done by Private Militias, Not SPLA.' 9 March.

Radio Tamazuj. (2015). 'Pagan Amum Calls for S. Sudan International Trusteeship if Peace Talks Fail.' 23 December.

Radio Tamazuj. (2017). 'Top Rebel Commander Killed in Clashes in Upper Nile.' 6 January.

Reuters. (1998). 'White House Says No Sign Iraq Exported Arms.' 17 February.

Reuters. (1999). 'US Adds Religious Freedom to Old Sanctions.' 23 December.

Reuters. (2016). 'U.S. Condemns South Sudan Opposition Leader's Call for Renewed War.' 28 September.

Reuters. (2016). 'U.S. Diplomats on South Sudan Conflict Over Machar's Fate.' 8 September.

Rice, Susan. (2007). 'Dithering on Darfur: U.S. Inaction in the Face of Genocide.' Foreign Relations Committee. United States Senate. Washington DC. 11 April.

Royal Ministry of Foreign Affairs. (1997). 'Evaluation of Norwegian Humanitarian Assistance to the Sudan.' Oslo. November.

Sen, Ashish Kumar. (2016). 'South Sudan: Paging Dr. Riek.' An interview with Dr Peter Pham. *Atlantic Council*. 20 April.

Senate Committee on Foreign Relations. (2015). Testimony of Special Envoy for Sudan and South Sudan Donald Booth. 'Independent South Sudan: A Failure of Leadership.' 10 December.

Shinn, David. (2011). 'U.S. Policy Toward the Horn of Africa.' *International Policy Digest.* 13 October.

Silverstein, Ken. (2005). 'Official Pariah Sudan Valuable to America's War on Terrorism.' *Los Angeles Times.* 29 April.

Silverstein, Ken. (2015). 'Why Is South Sudan a Hellhole? Blame George Clooney.' *Gawker.* 2 June.

Small Arms Survey. (2017). 'Spreading Fallout: The Collapse of the ARCSS and New Conflict along the Equatorias–DRC Border.' May.

South Sudan News Agency. (2013). 'Friends of South Sudan Warned of Serious Consequences if Serious Changes and Reform Are Not Made.' Washington DC. 8 July.

South Sudan News Agency. (2017). 'Egyptian Air Force Bombs South Sudanese Rebels in Upper Nile.' 3 February.

SPLA Chief of General Staffs. (2015). Letter signed by SPLA-IO Chief of Staff, Simon Gatwech, to President Omar Bashir. Pagak. 7 July.

SPLM/A Chairman and Commander-in-Chief. (2014). 'Establishment of General Staff Command for SPLA.' 21 December.

SPLM/A, Military Governor's Office. (2014). 'Resolutions by the Upper Nile Peace and Consultative Meeting,' Pagak, Upper Nile state. 28 November.

SPLM-IO. (2016). 'The Political Military Situation Following the Eruption of Violence in July 2016 and the Future of the Agreement.' Khartoum. 27 November.

SPLM/SPLA Consultative Conference. (2014). 'Resolutions.' Nasir. Upper Nile State. April.

Sudan Tribune. (2013). 'Riek Machar's End-Game: What Is It?' 29 December.

Sudan Tribune. (2016). 'African Union Tells South Sudan to Sack New Vice President Taban Deng.' 12 August.

Sudan Tribune. (2016). 'Former Minister Wants S. Sudan under UN Administration.' 3 August.

Sudan Tribune. (2016). 'S. Sudan President Rejects Consensus to Establish Cantonment Areas for SPLA-IO.' 25 June.

Sudan Tribune. (2016). 'South Sudan Armed Men Clash with Sudanese Rebels in Bahr el Ghazal.' Juba. 18 May.

Sudan Tribune. (2016). 'South Sudan Convenes First Cabinet Meeting after Forming Unity Government.' Juba. 6 May.

Sudan Tribune. (2016). 'South Sudan Defends Expulsion of Peace Monitor.' 28 April.

Sudan Tribune. (2016). 'South Sudan Presidency Defends Appointment of Advisors.' 7 June.

Sudan Tribune. (2016). 'South Sudan Welcomes U.S. Extension of Military Aid.' Juba. 8 October.

Sudan Tribune. (2016). 'South Sudan's FVP Machar Fires Taban Deng.' 23 July.

Sudan Tribune. (2016). 'UN Warns Over Replacement of Machar as First Vice President.' 27 July.

Sudan Tribune. (2017). 'Egypt Provides South Sudan with Arms and Ammunition: al-Bashir.' Khartoum. 22 February.

Sudan Tribune. (2017). 'U.S. Needs a New Track for Peace before It Discards Sudan's Sanctions: Expert.' 24 June.

The Irish Times. (2002). 'The Great Slave Scam.' 23 February.

The Political Opposition Forces. (2017). 'Communiqué.' 11 May.

The Sentry. (2017). thesentry.org.

The Washington Free Beacon. (2016). 'US, UN Stood By While South Sudan Troops Raped, Beat Aid Workers.' 15 August.

The Washington Post. (2013). 'South Sudan's Growing Conflict Reflects Rivalry between President and His Former Deputy.' 23 December.

The Washington Post. (2016). 'Obama Administration to Lift Some Sanctions against Sudan.' 13 January.

The Washington Times. (1997). 'Ex-President Opposes Policy of Aiding Khartoum's Foes.' 25 September.

Thomson Financial Publishing. (1997). 'The US Imposes New Sanctions on Sudan.' 4 November. www.tfp.com/news/USSudan.htm.

Time. (2012). 'Rocky Road from Air Force to Ambassador.' 14 August.

Transitional Constitution of South Sudan. (2011). Juba. 23 April.

Troika. (2015). Press release on South Sudan. London. 6 October.

Turse, Nick. (2013). 'The Pivot to Africa.' *TomDispatch.com.* 5 September.

Turse, Nick. (2015). 'The United States Is Supporting an Army That Is Recruiting Child Soldiers.' *The Nation.* 18 May.

United Nations. (2015). 'Final Report of the Panel of Experts on South Sudan Established Pursuant to Security Council Resolution 2206.' UN SC Doc. S/2016/70. para. 142. 22 January.

United Nations. (2016). Office of the Special Representative of the Secretary-General for Children and Armed Conflict. South Sudan. 20 April.

United Nations. (2016). 'WFP Condemns Looting of Food Warehouse in Juba, Still Assists Thousands Affected by Fighting.' World Food Programme. 14 July. www.wfp.org/news/news-release/wfp-condemns-looting-food-warehouse-juba-still-manages-assist-thousands-affected-f.

United Nations. (2017). 'Report of the Secretary-General on South Sudan (Covering the Period from 2 March to 1 June 2017).' 15 June.

United Nations. (2017). 'Speech of the Chair of the Commission on Human Rights in South Sudan to the Human Rights Council.' 14 March. www.ohchr.org/EN/NewsEvents/Pages/DisplayNews.aspx?NewsID=21374&LangID=E#sthash.CS7aHIRP.dpuf.

United Nations Mission in South Sudan. (2014). 'Human Rights Crisis in South Sudan, Report Coverage 15 December 2013 – 31 January 2014.' Human Rights Division. 21 February.

United Nations Security Council. (2016). 'United States of America Draft Resolution.' 23 December. www.securitycouncilreport.org/atf/cf/%7B65BFCF9B-6D27-4E9C-8CD3-CF6E4FF96FF9%7D/s_2016_1085.pdf.

United States Congress. (1999). S. Res. 109, 106th Congress. 1st Session. 1 July.

United States Congress. (1999). S.1453, 106th Congress. 1st Session. 19 November.

United States Department of State. (1997). *Sudan Country Reports on Human Rights Practices for 1996.* Bureau of Democracy, Human Rights and Labor. 30 January.

United States Department of State. (2003). www.UStreas.gov/ofac/legal/sudan.html.

United States Department of State. (2005). 'Roger P. Winter Appointed Special Representative for Sudan.' 26 July.

United States Department of State. (2007). 'Sudan Peace Act.' *Fact Sheet.* 21 October.

United States Department of State. (2011). 'Country Reports on Human Rights Practices for 2011.' www.state.govdocuments/organization/18790.pdf.

United States Department of State. (2014). Remarks by John Kerry, South Sudan Embassy. Juba. 2 May.

United States Government. (2002). *National Security Strategy Paper*. September.

United States Government. (2010). Office of Audits. 'Audit of Allegations Pertaining to Contract with DynCorp International for the Security Sector Transformation Project in South Sudan.' Report No. AUD/SI-10-23. Africa. August.

United States Government. (2017). ForeignAssistance.gov. South Sudan.

United States Institute of Peace. (1997). 'Religion, Nationalism and Peace in Sudan.' Washington DC. 17 December.

United States Institute of Peace. (1999). 'New Approach to Peace in Sudan.' Washington DC.

Verjee, Aly. (2016). 'The Future of South Sudan and the Peace Agreement.' Chatham House, Africa Programme Transcript. 26 October.

Verjee, Aly. (2017). Testimony before the Senate Foreign Relations Subcommittee on Africa and Global Health Policy. United States Institute of Peace. 26 July.

VOANEWS. (2016). 'UN Peacekeepers Accept Responsibility for Massacre at Malakal.' 24 June.

Voice of America. (2016). 'South Sudan Cease-Fire Panel Accuses President's Forces of Violations.' Juba. 12 May.

Walsh, Declan. (2002). 'Freeing Sudanese "Slaves" from "Arab Captors" Scam Exposed.' *The Independent*, 24 February. https://rense.com//general20/freeingsudanese.htm.

Wangdunkon Media. (2015). 'The Cool War between Governor Bakasoro and Dinka Council Elders.' 25 June.

Williamson, Richard. (2009). 'Sudan and the Implications for the Responsibility to Protect.' Stanley Foundation. October.

Williamson, Richard. (2010). Former US Special Envoy on Sudan. 'How Obama Betrayed Sudan.' *Foreign Policy Magazine*. Op-ed. November–December.

Winter, Roger. (2009). Testimony before the Subcommittee on Africa and Global Health, Committee of Foreign Affairs, House of Representatives. 111th Congress. Sudan: U.S. Policy and Implementation of the Comprehensive Peace Agreement. 29 July.

World News. (2016). 'South Sudanese Army "Getting Away with Murder" as Thousands Flee Abuses: Rights Group.' London. 24 May.

Young, John. (2007). 'Sudan People's Liberation Army: Disarmament in Jonglei and Its Implications.' Occasional Paper No. 137. Institute of Security Studies. Pretoria. April.

Young, John. (2012). *The Fate of Sudan: Origins and Consequences of a Flawed Peace Process*. Zed Books.

Young, John. (2015). 'A Fractious Rebellion: Inside the SPLM-IO.' *Small Arms Survey*. Graduate Institute of International Studies. Geneva.

Young, John. (2016). 'Popular Struggles and Elite Cooptation: The Nuer White Army in South Sudan's Civil War.' *Small Arms Survey*. Graduate Institute of International Studies. Geneva.

INDEX

Note: Following Sudanese naming convention, Sudanese names have been entered without inversion except for some of those with Westernised first names, e.g. Peter Gadet, John Garang, Paul Malong.

ZED

Zed is a platform for marginalised voices across the globe.

It is the world's largest publishing collective and a world leading example of alternative, non-hierarchical business practice.

It has no CEO, no MD and no bosses and is owned and managed by its workers who are all on equal pay.

It makes its content available in as many languages as possible.

It publishes content critical of oppressive power structures and regimes.

It publishes content that changes its readers' thinking.

It publishes content that other publishers won't and that the establishment finds threatening.

It has been subject to repeated acts of censorship by states and corporations.

It fights all forms of censorship.

It is financially and ideologically independent of any party, corporation, state or individual.

Its books are shared all over the world.

www.zedbooks.net
@ZedBooks